# CORVETTE SPECIAL EDITIONS

KEITH CORNETT

CarTech®

**CarTech®**

CarTech®, Inc.
838 Lake Street South
Forest Lake, MN 55025
Phone: 651-277-1200 or 800-551-4754
Fax: 651-277-1203
www.cartechbooks.com



Edit by Wes Eisenschenk
Layout by Hailey Samples
Cover Photography by A. J. Mueller Photography

ISBN 978-1-61325-393-9
Item No. CT622

Library of Congress Cataloging-in-Publication Data
Names: Cornett, Keith, author.
Title: Corvette special editions / Keith Cornett.
Description: Forest Lake, MN : CarTech Books, [2018] | Includes index.
Identifiers: LCCN 2017060498 | ISBN 9781613253939
Subjects: LCSH: Corvette automobile–History. | Automobiles–United States.
Classification: LCC TL215.C6 C55 2018 | DDC 629.222/2–dc23
LC record available at https://lccn.loc.gov/2017060498

Written, edited, and designed in the U.S.A.
Printed in China
10 9 8 7 6 5 4 3 2



DISTRIBUTION BY:

*Europe*
PGUK
63 Hatton Garden
London EC1N 8LE, England
Phone: 020 7061 1980 • Fax: 020 7242 3725
www.pguk.co.uk

*Australia*
Renniks Publications Ltd.
3/37-39 Green Street
Banksmeadow, NSW 2109, Australia
Phone: 2 9695 7055 • Fax: 2 9695 7355
www.renniks.com

*Canada*
Login Canada
300 Saulteaux Crescent
Winnipeg, MB, R3J 3T2 Canada
Phone: 800 665 1148 • Fax: 800 665 0103
www.lb.ca

# TABLE OF CONTENTS

# ACKNOWLEDGMENTS

After spending nearly a year researching and writing this book on Corvette special editions, I have a newfound respect for authors who have done it more than once. Having been through the process for my first time, I can attest that while the author himself/herself does the heavy lifting with the creation of the book, you do end up with a sizable support group of individuals and organizations who step in to help out with the process, from research and facts to providing photos of the Corvettes featured. I also have a deep heartfelt appreciation for those closest to me who offered strength and encouragement to keep the hammer down when it felt like the book would never be finished.

I would like to thank my wife, Sherry, especially, for being my biggest cheerleader throughout the year, as well as my kids, Phillip, Quinn, Darrell, and his wife Amira, and our family's newest edition, Athena.

Many contributors offered their personal images for the book, and I thank you all for your overwhelmingly positive responses to my multiple requests. I had several individuals and organizations that really went to bat for me that I would like to mention personally. A big thanks goes to CorvetteBlogger's Detroit Bureau Steve Burns, Bob Bubnis at the National Corvette Museum, Maureen Waller and John "Hutch" Hutchison at the Grand Sport Registry, Troy Worrell from Corvette Mike, Beth Waisner at ProTeam Corvette, Christine Giovingo at Mecum Auctions, Andrew Taylor from the Simeone Museum, Ken Lingenfelter and the Lingenfelter Collection, Ed Baumgarten and Mike Yager from Mid America Motorworks, Lance Miller at Corvettes at Carlisle, Michael Semon from Buyavette, and Wendy Miller from the Corvette team. Other individuals who really helped shape the subject matter include Martyn Schorr, Burt Greenwood, Howard Brown, Travis Raczynski, Nigel Scott Dobbie, Mike Furman, Gary Konner, Chris Chessnoe, and Tom Marcucci.

I'd like to thank Wes Eisenschenk and the staff at CarTech Books for providing me the opportunity to write about these Corvette special editions.

I hope you enjoy the book. Keep waving!!

# DEDICATION

This book on Corvette special editions is dedicated to my father, Phillip Cornett, who passed away at the young age of 44 years old in 1982. At the time of his passing, he left behind his beautiful wife Carole, two children, and a Tuxedo Black 1966 Corvette Sting Ray Convertible. I also dedicate this book to my son Phillip Cornett, who was born in 2000.

Like any son who looks up to his father, I hope that my life's body of work, which now includes this book about Corvettes, would make my father proud of what he started when he purchased the new Corvette convertible on June 29, 1966. As a father in my own right, I hope that my passion for the car serves to provide my son with inspiration and a sense of history for the day that he becomes the owner and caretaker of his grandfather's 1966 Sting Ray.

# INTRODUCTION

The Chevrolet Corvette is called America's Sports Car and for good reason. Not only is it the longest continually produced sports car in the history of the automobile but it also has become a fixture of American pop culture. As American as baseball and apple pie, as the old Chevy tagline went.

Chevrolet has produced more than 1.5 million Corvettes in its 65-year history, and the car shows no signs of slowing down. During the last three years, General Motors has committed nearly $900 million in investments in the Bowling Green assembly plant as it prepares the Corvette brand for the future.

Over the course of the 65 years that the Chevrolet Corvette has been in the spotlight, the brand has celebrated significant anniversaries, events, people, and technological improvements by offering a special-edition model for sale to the public. Some editions were created for exclusive overseas exports; there was even a special edition you could rent at the airport. Our criteria in identifying these officially produced special-edition Corvettes are generally (but not in all cases) one-year-only models or significant options that were marketed specifically as special or limited in production by Chevrolet. A total of 33 official special editions are presented within.

Most books tend to cover the various Corvette models chronologically and, in doing so, the subject matter becomes predictable as you turn from page to page. Here, our special-edition Corvettes are grouped and presented with these four main classifications: Anniversary Editions, Indy 500 Pace Cars, Commemoratives and Tributes, and, finally, a general Corvette Special Editions category to feature those models that belong in a category all their own.

As Corvette enthusiasts, we are always looking back into Corvette's history. Many of the modern-day special editions paid tribute to the historical models that preceded it. Prior to the offering of the first official special edition in 1978 are those special models or options that, while not officially offered as a special or limited edition, have since become their own special editions over the course of time. These models and options achieved this recognition and status through enthusiast appreciation and reverence, as well as the values that these unique and sought-after Corvettes generate at auctions and sales.

Finally, there are those special-edition Corvettes that were built outside of General Motors by third parties that used various aspects of the car to create their own specific models. Many different builders have come and gone over the years and, while it's impossible to show all, we take a look some of the more successful or notable third-party Corvette special editions produced.

CHAPTER 1

# ANNIVERSARY CORVETTES

The Chevrolet Corvette has been inspiring drivers around the world since the two-seat roadster first debuted in New York City during the 1953 General Motors Motorama show. As car manufacturing goes, it was developed rather quickly and went on sale to the public even faster. Its fiberglass body was initially seen as a way to speed prototype design work and then became a hallmark feature of the sports car.

Although many models have come and gone, the Corvette endures because those responsible for the car have always worked tirelessly to improve it. Conceived by GM designer Harley Earl and improved upon by Corvette's legendary first chief engineer, Zora Arkus-Duntov, the Corvette matured in the 1960s, was refined in the 1970s, and

***Chevrolet celebrated Corvette's milestones with these special and limited anniversary Corvettes. (Photo Courtesy Keith Cornett)***

was reborn as a performance icon in the 1980s, holding that status since. Today's Corvette team continues the tradition of pushing the envelope of style, performance, and utility while keeping the founding ideals of the car intact. Year after year, the Corvette gets better, people continue to buy it, and those who can't dream about the day they can.

Along this journey that now spans six decades, Chevrolet celebrated selected anniversaries of the 1953 Corvette beginning with the very first special edition in 1978: the 25th Anniversary Edition. Chevrolet has since offered a total of seven anniversary models, and they remain among the favorite and most-produced special editions of the Corvette's 65-year history.

*Car and Driver* ***tested the 1978 Corvettes, and the 220-hp L-82 with a 4-speed manual transmission was capable of 0–60 mph in 6.6 seconds and a top speed of 134 mph. The car would win a shoot-out to earn the title "Fastest Car in America." (Photo Courtesy Bill Day)***

## 1978 CORVETTE SILVER ANNIVERSARY

The Corvette marked its 25th anniversary in 1978, a huge milestone for the model that began modestly in 1953 on a temporary assembly line in a warehouse on Van Slyke Avenue in Flint, Michigan. So much had changed from the inaugural 1953 Corvette and the 24 successive models that followed. In those 25 years, three distinct generations were offered, along with multiple engine configurations and body styles. Somewhat ironic was the fact that the car that debuted as a roadster model before being offered as both a coupe and convertible would eventually be offered only as a T-top coupe.

| Base MSRP | $10,130.85 |
|---|---|
| Model Availability | T-Top Coupe |
| Engines | L48, L82 |
| Features | Custom paint, badging |
| Production Numbers | 15,283 |

***The 25th Anniversary Edition was the first Corvette to be planned as a special-edition model, and 15,283 Corvettes were eventually sold with the unique Charcoal Silver/Silver Metallic two-tone paint job. The model accounted for 33 percent of total 1978 Corvette production. (Photo Courtesy Bill Day)***

The old guard had changed as well. Gone were those legendary names that included Harley Earl, Zora Arkus-Duntov, Larry Shinoda, and Ed Cole as forced retirement from General Motors at age 65 or, in Shinoda's case, a move to Ford ended their contributions to America's sports car. In their place, a new generation of engineers and designers led by chief engineer Dave MacLellan was responsible for the Corvette by the time it would celebrate its silver anniversary.

The Corvette continued to evolve during its third generation, which began in 1968. The earlier years had brought even more powerful engines and unique packages with historic RPOs that included the L88, LT1, ZR1, and ZL1. After the oil embargos, the heydays of high horsepower fueled with cheap gas were replaced with the promise of a more refined driving experience, all while paying attention to meeting the latest EPA fuel mileage requirements.

The Corvette made it through the turmoil of the 1970s while still fulfilling its promise as many other

*The 1978 Corvette styling changes were centered on the new wrap-around rear glass that provided a significant amount of additional storage and greater rear quarter visibility. The surface area of the rear fastback was 1,425 square inches compared with 293 square inches on the former model. (Photo Courtesy Bill Day)*

*Most observers of the 1978 Silver Anniversary Edition will note the two-tone paint, but a closer look will show a graphics kit consisting of 17 individual pieces was also applied. The hood featured a stripe on each side of the power bulge, and pinstripes were applied to the top and bottom of each quarter panel. (Photo Courtesy Bill Day)*

*The 1978 Corvette was the first fastback model in 11 years. GM design chief Bill Mitchell wanted the body style originally on the 1968 model while Corvette chief engineer Zora Arkus-Duntov made a pitch for a fastback model with a functional hatchback in 1974. (Photo Courtesy Bill Day)*

muscle cars ceased to exist. And it's not like it was barely surviving. Corvettes were as popular as ever, and sales reached the pinnacle in 1977 with 49,213 Corvettes sold. More than a half million Corvettes had been sold by the time its silver anniversary arrived, and the sports car had developed a broad fan base and loyal customers.

*With the advent of the first special editions, it wasn't long before people were cloning standard versions. Check the trim tag for authenticity and confirm the 13/07 paint code for the two-tone paint. Some will paint a silver car's lower portion in charcoal to pass it off as a Silver Anniversary model to unsuspecting buyers. (Photo Courtesy Bill Day)*

*Chevrolet produced three separate models for 1978: the standard production model, the 25th Anniversary Edition, and the Replica Indianapolis 500 Pace Car. All three models received the Silver Anniversary badge on the Corvette's front nose. (Photo Courtesy Bill Day)*

### *Big Changes for 1978*

The C3 generation's shark design was now in its 10th year and was beginning to show its age. Chevrolet had something special planned for its 25th year, starting with the most significant redesign for the Corvette since 1968. The most prominent update was the addition of a fastback rear window.

The new aerodynamic rear window with its distinctive wraparound glass provided greater driver visibility while the cargo area behind the seats increased from 7.89 to 8.4 cubic feet. A retractable luggage cover helped conceal the contents and protected the interior from the sun. The larger rear window helped brighten the interior and aided those who said they felt claustrophobic in the tight confines of earlier C3s.

*The addition of optional Goodyear GT 255/60R15 tires resulted in a body that was slightly wider in the rear fender area than previous models, as the inner fenders were modified for clearance. Chevrolet utilized the same slotted wheels and crossed-flags center caps across the 1978 model year lineup. (Photo Courtesy Bill Day)*

As an added benefit, the design changes with the cargo area and the selection of a skinny, temporary spare tire allowed engineers to enlarge the size of the gas tank from 17 to 24 gallons, greatly increasing the cruising range of the Corvette.

Changes to the interior of the 1978 Corvette included a new one-piece dash pad with redesigned rectangular instrument cluster and a built-in lockable glove box. Door panels were of the "cut and sew" design, trimmed with vinyl and cut pile carpet. The door panels also received a map pocket. Instead of the traditional molded armrest, it was now a separate design affixed to the panel with screws. Carpeted panels ran alongside the center console. The alarm system was rewired to include the T-tops. Washer controls were moved to the instrument panel.

## The Original 1978 Indy 500 Pace Car

In the summer of 1977, Chevrolet hosted a ride and drive event for magazine journalists to preview the 1978 models, including the Silver Anniversary 1978 Corvette. Attending the preview was *Vette Vues* managing editor Jim Prather, whose reporting on the 1978 models in the September 1977 issue featured a preview of a limited-edition Indianapolis 500 Pace Car.

Original plans for the 1978 Indianapolis 500 Pace Car called for a 25th anniversary model with enhancements that included a special front and rear spoiler, a red pinstripe running down the beltline of the car, and special Goodyear tires with the word "CORVETTE" in white letters. The T-tops were made of a special reflective glass wrapped with a thin stainless-steel trim. The exterior graphic was a simple "1978 Indianapolis Pace Car" under a cross-flags emblem on the sides. At the time, the interior designs hadn't been finalized and so the car's windows were tinted black to prevent viewing.

Prather's reporting of the 1978 Indy 500 Pace Car, which was said at the time to be limited to just 1,000 units, sent Corvette enthusiasts to their local dealers, who accepted deposits on a Corvette that was unfinalized.

After that 1978 preview event, it was decided internally that the pace car should have its own design, and Jerry Palmer is credited with penning the two-tone black and silver livery with red pinstriping. The Indy 500 Pace Car would upstage the 1978 25th Anniversary Edition with a sales frenzy never experienced by Chevrolet dealers, as some customers paid nearly double the $13,653 MSRP.

### *Special Two-Tone Silver Anniversary Edition*

In September 1977, Chevrolet announced that it would commemorate the 25th year of Corvette production with a special silver anniversary two-tone paint option and with special 25th anniversary badges that would be on every 1978 Corvette. Later in the year, Chevrolet would also announce a limited-edition 1978 Indy 500 Pace Car Replica.

GM's design chief, Bill Mitchell, who led the department following the retirement of Harley Earl in 1958, was himself retiring in 1977. It was said that the 25th Anniversary Corvette would be one of the last to feel his influence.

Mitchell suggested an anniversary commemorative model in silver, which was his favorite color. Designer Jerry Palmer ran with Mitchell's idea and came up with a light silver upper over the charcoal gray lower, separated with a red stripe. That stripe would be changed to silver when production started. Along with the 1978 Indy 500 Pace Car Replicas, the 25th Silver Anniversary exterior would be the first two-tone paint scheme on a Corvette since 1961 and the era of side coves.

Three interior colors were offered with the Silver Anniversary option. Buyers could select black, oyster, or red.

The 1978 Corvette was offered with the L48 350 V-8 engine with 185 hp and a 4-speed manual transmission. Upgrades offered an L82 350-ci V-8 engine with 220 hp, and buyers could also upgrade to a redesigned 3-speed manual transmission at no additional cost.

### *Pricing and Production*

The 25th Anniversary paint scheme was listed as RPO B2Z and it cost $399. However, to get the special anniversary paint, you also had to order the D35 Sport Mirrors for $40 as well as the YJ8 aluminum wheels that added $340 to the MSRP of $9,351.85 for a total MSRP of $10,130.85.

The two-tone silver anniversary paint would have no production limits and Chevrolet would produce 15,283 Silver Anniversary Corvettes, representing 33 percent of the total production.

The most popular configuration for the 1978 models included the L48 350-ci V-8 mated to an automatic transmission. Today, collectors look for the L82-equipped V-8, which offered 220 hp and the 4-speed manual transmission.

## 1988 35TH ANNIVERSARY CORVETTE

Chevrolet's two-seat sports car turned 35 years old in 1988, and General Motors was ready to celebrate. More than 900,000 Corvettes had been built up to that date, and it had been 10 years since Chevrolet marked an anniversary with a special edition, the 1978 25th Anniversary Corvette.

When the new C4 generation was in the planning stages, the Corvette team planned to celebrate the 30th anniversary of the Corvette, which would have coincided with the new C4 Corvette's launch in 1983. But late development delays pushed the new model to be introduced as a 1984 model, quashing any 30th Anniversary Edition planned in conjunction with the introduction of the C4 model.

### *Continued Refinement of the C4*

Now in its fifth year of production as the fourth-generation body style, the C4 Corvette saw continued refinement throughout 1988. Each year since its introduction in 1984, the technologically advanced C4 Corvette had steadily increased in performance, handling, and sophistication.

| | |
|---|---|
| Base MSRP | $34,284 |
| Model Availability | Coupe |
| Engines | L98 |
| Features | Exterior paint, painted wheels, upholstery, badging |
| Production Numbers | 2,050 |

***The 35th Anniversary Edition is one of the most distinctive Corvettes ever produced with the White Out exterior and white-painted alloy wheels. The door handles and even the black rubber beltline around the cars were painted white. The Classic White exterior was broken up only by the black roof bow and the black rubber on the Goodyear tires. (Photo Courtesy Peter Johnson)***

*These two 1988 35th Anniversary Corvettes are on display at the American Muscle Car Museum in Melbourne, Florida. The 35th Anniversary model on the right has 44 original miles while the one on the left features the 4+3 transmission and has only 4 miles on the odometer. (Photo Courtesy Peter Johnson)*

*Chevrolet updated the Corvette's wheels for 1988, replacing the Cuisinart-style wheels with two new designs for the base model and those equipped with the Z51/Z52 packages. The 35th Anniversary Corvette had the cast-aluminum 17-inch Z51/Z52 wheels that were painted white. (Photo Courtesy Keith Cornett)*

In 1985, the cross-fire engine was replaced with a tuned port injection system as true fuel injection returned to the Corvette for the first time since 1965. In 1986, anti-lock brakes from Bosch gave drivers much more control by eliminating wheel lockup in extreme braking conditions. In 1987, a new sports handling package known as the Z52 addressed the harshness of the Z51's suspension with an improved ride through wider 9.5-inch wheels, a thicker front sway bar, and gas-charged shocks.

### Improvements for 1988

Improvements introduced in 1988 brought more horsepower and increased performance. The 5.7L V-8 with Tuned Port Injection (TPI) was outfitted with aluminum cylinder heads and large inlet ports for better breathing and high compressions. A new high-lift camshaft and less restrictive mufflers bumped the horsepower to 245 for the coupe.

The 1988 Corvettes received a new tire and wheel package with the selection of the Z51 and Z52 Handling packages. Goodyear Eagle GT tires were now Z-rated and could sustain driving speeds in excess of 149 mph. Larger 17x9.5–inch wheels were redesigned with a new 12-slot pattern and mated to the P275/40ZR-17 tires. The new rims became known as "Cuisinarts" because they resembled the blades from the food processor. The standard 16x8.5–inch rims were also updated with a new six-slot pattern with P55/50ZR-16 tires that were similarly Z-rated for high speed.

With the additional performance from the tires, Corvette engineers incorporated a zero-scrub front suspension to reduce uneven braking during hard stops while also offering better directional control. The five-link rear suspension was revised to reduce rear ride camber for improved handling and braking stability.

*Other accoutrements of the 35th Anniversary Corvette included a white version of the rear script logo and a special C4 emblem with a white background for the Chevrolet logo. (Photo Courtesy Peter Johnson)*

***The 35th anniversary logo featured a three-circle design with the original Chevrolet crossed-flags in the left circle, the C4 Corvette logo in the middle, and "35" in red on a white background to the right. The badges were mounted on the sides above the vents. (Photo Courtesy Ed Baumgarten / ©Mid America Motorworks)***

***Inside, the white and black theme continued with white leather seats, door panels, and white seat belts. The white leather steering wheel contrasted against the full black dash and console. Black carpet was used throughout the cabin, and the seat backs were black as well. (Photo Courtesy Keith Cornett)***

The brakes on the 1988 Corvette were also addressed with larger two-piston calipers added to the fronts and larger brake rotors added to both front and rear. A new integral handbrake was also introduced for the rear disc brakes, which replaced the small drum parking brakes on earlier C4 Corvettes. The parking brake lever was repositioned slightly in the cockpit to be less intrusive.

### *The Anniversary Edition Arrives*

The wait to celebrate an anniversary with a limited-edition vehicle was worth it, though, and Chevrolet would celebrate the Corvette's 35th anniversary in style. The 1988 35th Anniversary Corvette was introduced on April 1, 1988, at the New York Auto Show, recalling the debut of the Motorama Corvette at the Waldorf Astoria in 1953.

"The 35th Anniversary Edition Corvette is really no different than the 'Vette that began appealing to American speed and style fantasies 35 years ago, and even sports a look reminiscent of that first Corvette," said Chevrolet general manager Robert D. Burger in the official press release.

The 35th anniversary edition was officially known as RPO Z01, an Arctic White coupe with black roof bow, a dark blue acrylic roof panel, and white 17-inch wheels. The model was further enhanced with the RPO B57 "External Ornamentation Deluxe" and featured white door handles, white body side moldings, and a white Corvette emblem on the rear. Unique white

***A simple silver, black, and red version of the 35th anniversary logo was embroidered on the seat headrests. The stitched logo featured the three-circle design with only the C4 logo in the middle circle. (Photo Courtesy Ed Baumgarten / ©Mid America Motorworks)***

cross-flag emblems replaced the standard emblems on the hood, fuel door, and wheel center caps. Special 35th anniversary logos adorned each of the front quarter panels above the vents.

The interior also received the whiteout treatment with the B18 "Interior Ornamentation Deluxe" package. Contrasting with the black carpet and black dash was the bright white interior. White leather seats featured the 35th anniversary logo embroidered on the lower bottom right of the headrest. The door panels were also white with a black cutout for the door handle and lock. But perhaps the most distinctive interior feature was the two-spoke white leather-wrapped steering wheel with the white C4 logo on the horn button.

Each of the 2,050 Corvettes had a unique build sequence number engraved on a dash plaque displaying the 35th anniversary logo. The small plaque is located just below the shifter on the console.

### *Pricing and Production*

The Z01 35th Special Edition package was priced at $4,795 above the standard coupe's MSRP of $29,489 for a total sticker price of $34,284. It also included the dual six-way power sport seats, electronic air-conditioning control, Delco Bose sound, and heated side mirrors.

Chevrolet planned for a production run of 2,000 35th Anniversary Corvettes. They would make those and a few more with the build total reaching 2,050 Corvettes, 9 percent of production. A plaque with the engraved sequence number was presented on the console.

The 1988 Coupes that were optioned with the 3.07 Performance Axle (G92) received a 5-hp increase and were rated at 245 hp due to a less-restrictive exhaust. However, on the convertibles, the resonance was just too loud, and they continued to be rated at 240 hp. Of the 2,050 total Corvettes, only 180 were mated with the 4+3 manual transmission.

## The Ultimate Performance 35th Anniversary Edition

The 1988 anniversary models were ordered with the special Z01 RPO, and buyers could further equip their cars with a number of factory options such as the 4-speed manual transmission or the Z51 Performance Handling package. A handful of owners would go even further by including the twin-turbo RPO B2K option from Callaway Cars.

Of the 2,050 anniversary Corvettes built, only 7 were built with Callaway's RPO B2K, which offered a tire-shredding 382 hp and 565 ft-lbs of torque, an increase of 37 hp from the 345 hp offered in its first year (1987). The Callaway B2K package also added a Special Equipment Order (SEO Z5G) that included the long air dam, power steering cooler, J55 heavy-duty brakes, and free flow mufflers. Also new for the 1988 B2K package were the distinctive and lightweight 17-inch Dymag magnesium wheels.

The B2K option price was almost equal to the base price of the Corvette, bringing the window sticker price to $61,495.

***This special 1988 35th Anniversary Corvette features the Callaway Twin Turbo package. It's one of three RPO B2K Callaway 35th Anniversary Editions with the MM4 manual 4-speed transmission, and the one remaining Callaway Corvette that is still wearing the recalled 1988-only free-flow exhaust system. (Photo Courtesy Ed Baumgarten / ©Mid America Motorworks)***

*Interest in the 35th Anniversary Edition Corvettes was greatly boosted by the production of the 1 millionth Corvette on July 2, 1992. Three months later, Chevrolet would announce the availability of a 40th Anniversary package. (Photo Courtesy the Revs Institute, The Karl Ludvigsen Photograph Collection)*

## 1993 40TH ANNIVERSARY CORVETTE

By 1993, the Corvette had become the longest continually produced passenger car at Chevrolet and was one of the oldest automotive names in the industry. The Corvette name was synonymous with classic style, character, and personality. At 40 years old, Chevrolet's Corvette was not only a world-class sports car but also a pop culture icon as American as baseball and apple pie.

Interest in the Corvette was at a high, and the big news for Corvette that helped kick off the 40th anniversary year was the production of the 1 millionth Corvette, a 1992 Convertible, on July 2, 1992. Chevrolet issued a press release in September 1992 celebrating the two milestones: production of the 1 millionth Corvette and the availability of the 40th Anniversary package for 1993 Corvettes.

The 1993 Corvette's 40th Anniversary package was a very affordable appearance RPO that would be offered on all three Corvette models: coupe, convertible, and ZR-1.

| | |
|---|---|
| Base MSRP | $36,050 (coupe), $42,650 (convertible), $67,733 (ZR-1) |
| Model Availability | Coupe, Convertible, ZR-1 |
| Engines | LT-1, LT-5 |
| Features | Exclusive exterior and interior colors, badging |
| Production Numbers | 6,749 |

*A total of 21,590 Corvettes were built in 1993 with nearly 1 out of every 3 being a 40th Anniversary Edition. The package was credited with helping to generate the first increase in Corvette sales after four straight years of decline. It's the highest-volume special-edition Corvette that has ever been produced. (Photo Courtesy Manwar Yasin)*

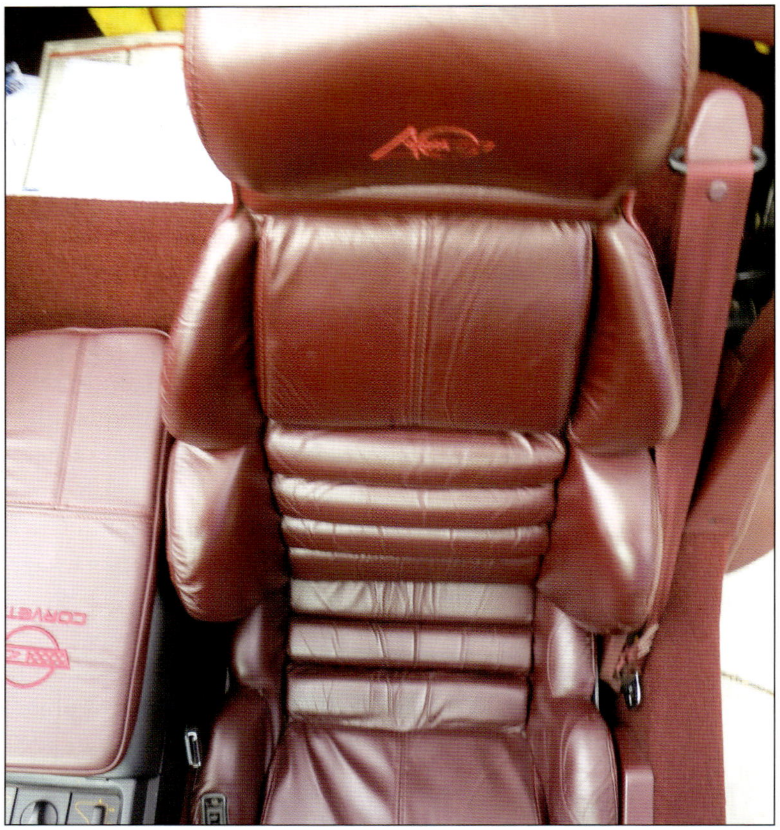

***All 1993 Corvettes with leather seats received the 40th anniversary logo embroidered on the headrests. (Photo Courtesy Ernie Pentland)***

***With each anniversary edition, Corvette has offered its very own logo for the year model. The 40th logo was integrated into the C4's current circle logo with the crossed-flags banner running in the middle. (Photo Courtesy Keith Cornett)***

### *The 40th Anniversary Edition Features*

The 40th Anniversary Edition Corvette featured an exclusive exterior and leather interior color called Ruby Red. Chevrolet created a special 40th anniversary logo featuring the number 40 along with the C4 crossed flags. These badges were affixed on the front quarter panels above the side vents. Bright C4 logo badges were placed on the hood and fuel door.

Inside the Corvettes, the Ruby Red leather interior included the sport seats, door panels, and carpet. The 40th anniversary logo was embroidered on the headrests. Convertible models included an exclusive Ruby Red cloth convertible top. The wheels received center wheel hub C4 crossed-flag emblems with Ruby Red inserts.

### *Pricing and Production*

The 40th Anniversary package was ordered with RPO Z25, which added an additional $1,455 to the base MSRP. Chevrolet would build a total of 6,749 40th anniversary models, and the popular package would account for 31 percent of all Corvettes. Although an official breakout by models is not available, based on certain option totals, we can estimate production to be 4,333 coupes, 2,171 convertibles, and 245 Corvette ZR-1s. The Z25 40th Anniversary package accounted for 55 percent of all ZR-1s produced.

***With the Corvette turning 40 years old, Chevrolet offered up a special one-year-only Ruby Red exterior. To ensure that anyone could get a 40th Anniversary Edition, Chevrolet made the package available across all three models with no production limits. The Z25 RPO would be priced at $1,455. (Photo Courtesy Ernie Pentland)***

### *More Powerful Corvettes*

The 1993 Corvette coupe and convertible models featured the powerful LT-1 V-8 capable of 300 hp and 340 ft-lbs of torque. The second-generation small-block was in its second year of production, and engineers worked to refine the engine. They gave it a quieter cam profile and swapped out the magnesium rocker covers with a composite cover with larger rubber gasket isolaters under the rocker cover bolts, which helped reduce engine noise. No horsepower was gained with these changes, but the LT-1 did see a modest increase in torque from 330 to 340 ft-lbs at 3,600 rpm.

The 1993 ZR-1 also received engine work, and for the first time since 1971, a Corvette engine would be rated at greater than 400 hp. Engineers increased the horsepower from 375 to 405 by making improvements in the LT-5's ability to breathe. This included cylinder head refinements as well as reshaping the intake valve head and valve seats for improved flow. Also new was the change to four-bolt main bearings, which required a redesign to the crankcase, front cover, oil pan, and oil pump.

### *Tires Play a Role*

Another important change to the performance and handling came in reducing the front wheel and tire sizes on the coupe and convertible models without the Z07 Performance package. The front wheels were reduced from 9.5x17 to 8.5x17, which reduced the tire sizes from P275/40ZR17 to P255/45ZR17. Rear tire size was increased from P275/40ZR17 to P285/40ZR17. The changes were designed to increase understeer, which is balanced by potential oversteer from the 300-hp LT-1, as well as decreasing the highway "groove-wandering" (a tire's tendency to follow highway rain grooves).

Corvettes equipped with the Z07 Performance package utilized the 9.5x17 wheels and P275/40ZR17 tires on both the front and rear. The new wheels were machined instead of painted gray, as they were in previous years.

Goodyear made changes in 1993 to the Eagle GS-C tires that had been standard on Corvettes since the 1984 model. The directional, asymmetric tires were now better equipped to handle the cornering stresses that occur on the inner and outer edges of the tire by increasing the contact area on the outer portion of the tread. This had the added benefit of reducing road noise. Owners had to be careful when ordering replacements, as the tires for each wheel were not interchangeable.

***Base Corvettes utilized smaller, 8.5x17-inch front wheels and the front tires were downsized to P255/45ZR17. The anniversary wheels featured a subtle Ruby Red center cap on the aluminum alloy wheels. Enthusiasts refer to these wheels as "sawblades" because of their directional design. (Photo Courtesy Ernie Pentland)***

### *Corvette's Anniversary Celebration*

Unlike the recent 1988 35th Anniversary Corvette that appeared as more of a one-year marketing ploy than a true celebration of the model, the coming 40th anniversary was treated as a historic milestone by General Motors.

Chevrolet planned several events to coincide with the 40th anniversary of the Corvette during the summer of 1993. On June 30, a 40th birthday party for the Corvette was celebrated by Chevrolet and GM employees outside the Chevrolet Central Office Building at the GM Technical Center in Warren, Michigan.

Elsewhere, 40th anniversary celebrations were planned in June for the Corvette Homecoming show at the Corvette assembly plant in Bowling Green, Kentucky, and the Bloomington Gold Corvette Show, which had just made the move to the Illinois State Fair Grounds in Springfield, Illinois.

***Both Corvette engines received updates for 1993. The LT1 wouldn't gain horsepower, but its torque increased from 330 to 340 ft-lbs. The ZR1's LT5 gained 30 hp with cylinder head improvements and other modifications. With a total output of 405 hp, the LT5 finally reached its initial design goal. (Photo Courtesy Ernie Pentland)***

## Sinkhole at the National Corvette Museum Swallows Convertible

In the early morning hours of February 12, 2014, a large sinkhole opened under the skydome at the National Corvette Museum. The collapse left a 40-foot-wide by 40-foot-deep hole, and eight Corvettes were swallowed as the floor underneath them gave way.

One of the "Great Eight" Corvettes that went into the hole was a 1993 40th Anniversary Corvette known as "Ruby." Karen Clark of Bay Village, Ohio, had purchased the anniversary Corvette and presented it to her husband, Hill, on his 50th birthday. The couple decided that they could never sell the car, and so they donated it to the National Corvette Museum, where they could see it any time.

Three weeks after the sinkhole took the Corvettes, workers were able to successfully extract the car, using a crane that was brought inside the skydome. When *Ruby* fell into the sinkhole, she came to rest at a 3/4 angle on her roof and passenger's side with the front facing downward. Workers looped the straps from the crane around the driver-side wheels and raised the car back to street level.

The 40th Anniversary Corvette was the second of eight Corvettes to be rescued. Due to the severe damage, the car will not be restored, and it is on display with the other Corvettes that were damaged during the "Corvette Cave In."

***A 1993 40th Anniversary Edition was one of eight Corvettes to fall into a sinkhole that opened under the National Corvette Museum. With security cameras capturing the moment the cars dropped into the 40-foot-deep cavern, news of the sinkhole and the eight Corvettes was covered by newspapers and television stations around the world. (Photo Courtesy of the National Corvette Museum)***

***The 1993 Ruby Red 40th Anniversary Coupe was pulled out of the sinkhole three weeks after the incident. Due to the amount of damage, the car will not be restored to its former glory. It's now back on display where it can be viewed along with the other seven sinkhole Corvettes. (Photo Courtesy of the National Corvette Museum)***

## 2003 50TH ANNIVERSARY CORVETTE

In 2003, Corvette was celebrating five decades of success, and it could be easy for any automotive brand to rest on its laurels after a 50-year run. But the Corvette kept charging forward, getting better year after year and living up to the expectations set by the original founders: Harley Earl, Zora Arkus-Duntov, Bill Mitchell, and Ed Cole.

It had been an exciting 50-year run for America's favorite sports car. Like any long journey, there were periods of highs and lows. From the stylish chrome-laden 1958s and the unbridled performance of the Chevy big-blocks in the 1960s and early 1970s to tightening EPA fuel economy restrictions and even tighter budgets in the 1970s. The 1980s and 1990s would see the Corvette's performance credentials rise once again, and by the new millennium the Corvette was as popular as ever. Regardless of the situation, whether good or bad, the Corvette team always rallied to deliver the best sports car possible, and the car's loyal customers were always there to support each new model, including the special editions.

By the 2003 model year, the Corvette lineup consisted of three distinct models: the coupe with its removable roof panel, a convertible, and a performance-oriented hardtop now in its third year bearing the legendary RPO of Z06. As was widely expected, a 50th Anniversary Edition was planned.

"Few vehicles have had the staying power of Corvette," said Rick Baldick, Corvette brand manager, in the official press release on the 50th Anniversary Edition. "We believe that much of that success comes from a willingness to embrace advancing technology while remaining true to Corvette's glorious history. As we celebrate our golden anniversary in 2003, we honor our past and cast a bright eye toward the future."

| | |
|---|---|
| Base MSRP | $48,895 (coupe), $56,155 (convertible) |
| Model Availability | Coupe, Convertible |
| Engines | LS1 |
| Features | Exclusive exterior and interior colors, badging |
| Production Numbers | 11,632 |

*Chevrolet marked one of the brand's biggest and most significant milestones in 2003 by celebrating the first Corvettes produced in 1953 with a special golden anniversary model. All 2003 Corvettes received special 50th anniversary badging, and a special Anniversary Red edition was offered as a coupe or a convertible. (Photo Courtesy Jeff Romm / Corvette Mike)*

*Like the two previous anniversary editions (1988 and 1993), the 2003 50th Anniversary Corvette featured a special 50th badge with the C5's Corvette crossed-flags logo integrated into the number. The chrome and gold badges were exclusive to the special edition and were found on the car's front quarter panels. (Photo Courtesy Keith Cornett)*

*All 2003 Corvettes received the special 50th anniversary crossed-flags badge on the nose and rear decks. The logo was also found on the tachometer and speedometer gauge faces on coupes and convertibles. (Photo Courtesy Keith Cornett)*

The 50th Anniversary Edition package was offered on coupe and convertible models only. It included special 50th Anniversary Red exterior paint with unique 50th anniversary badges and an exclusive Shale interior with embroidered seats and 50th anniversary–logo floor mats. Champaign-painted five-spoke wheels with special center caps were part of the package. Convertibles featured a Shale soft top.

All coupe and convertible models, including the 50th Anniversary Edition, were powered with the 346-ci LS1 V-8 engine as well as the new Magnetic Selective Ride Control option. Included options were a memory package, power telescoping and tilt-wheel steering column, Heads-Up Display (HUD), Twilight Sentinel, and electrochromic mirrors. The only optional equipment available for the anniversary edition was the 6-speed manual transmission (MN6), the performance axle on the automatic transmission (G92), dual roof package (C2L)/transparent roof panel (CC3), body side moldings (B84), and the 12-disc CD changer (U1S).

All 2003 Corvettes celebrated the 50th anniversary with special silver-colored emblems on the front and rear of the car (instead of the regular black emblems) and with a gold 50 inside a circle with "anniversary" spelled out along the top. Another logo specific to the 50th Anniversary Edition was found on the sides of the car and featured a gold 50 with the Corvette cross-flags logo on top of the "0" in 50.

The Shale interior on the 50th Anniversary Edition was a unique touch found only on the anniversary package and was made up of two separate-but-related colors. While all other C5 Corvettes had black instrument panels, the 50th Anniversary Edition featured a dark beige-gray color for the instrument panel (along with the console and upper door panels), and a contrasting lighter beige-gray was used for the seats and carpet.

***Each major element of the 2003 50th Anniversary Corvette had its own color. To dress up the wheels for a unique look, Chevrolet painted the standard wheels with a hue called Champagne. The color was very similar to the finish on the optional N73 magnesium wheels. The anniversary wheels included a 50th anniversary emblem on the center caps. (Photo Courtesy Keith Cornett)***

### Pricing and Production

The RPO ISC Preferred Option Group Number 2 was the checkbox that ordered the 50th Anniversary Edition package. The anniversary edition added $5,000 to the MSRP with a base coupe 50th Anniversary Edition starting at $48,895 and the convertible package priced at $55,370. In April 2003, the ISC Anniversary package was discounted to $3,500.

## Custom Colors Highlight the 50th Anniversary Edition

During the design stage, the 50th Anniversary Corvette was initially planned to be white with a red interior just like the original 300 Corvettes in 1953. However, Chevrolet designers did toy with the idea of a gold Corvette for the golden anniversary. In 1997, Chevrolet produced 15 1998 Corvettes painted Aztec Gold as a test. The color was too inconsistent and was dropped. That led the design team to Anniversary Red, a burgundy metallic color made with an Xirallic-based pigment containing aluminum-oxide flakes, which come alive in the sunlight. The Anniversary Red paint was applied over a gold basecoat, which gave it a deeper color than the Magnetic Red that had been used in 2002 and was applied over a silver basecoat.

***The Aztec Gold paint was so uneven on these 1998 Corvettes that workers in the Bowling Green assembly plant removed all the panels and laid them out on large padded shipping blankets on the plant's floor. Panels were mixed and matched based on similar appearance, and then the panels were reassembled to create the 15 test cars. (Photo Courtesy Ed Baumgarten / ©Mid America Motorworks)***

A unique interior color called Shale was used exclusively for the 2003 50th Anniversary Edition. It consisted of tan seats and a slightly darker tan console and dash. It was the first C5 Corvette to offer the dash in a color other than black. (Photo Courtesy Jeff Romm / Corvette Mike)

Designers of the 2003 50th Anniversary Edition convertible used the same unique Shale color from the interior to create an exclusive Shale-colored canvas soft top. A total of 7,547 50th Anniversary convertibles were produced. (Photo Courtesy Jeff Romm / Corvette Mike)

The 50th anniversary celebration for the 2003 Corvette didn't stop at the water's edge. Chevrolet made sure the 50th Anniversary Corvettes would be offered in Europe, and a total of 247 Corvettes were exported. (Photo Courtesy Jonny Bens)

Corvette drivers found a new switch on the console that allowed them to adjust the settings on the new F55 Magnetic Selective Ride Control. Tour mode provides a smoother ride while the Sport mode tightens up the suspension for performance driving. The $1,695 option was included on the 50th Anniversary package. (Photo Courtesy Jeff Romm / Corvette Mike)

Buyers loved the special edition and 11,632 50th Anniversary Corvettes were built, representing 32.8 percent of all Corvettes produced for the year and 43.3 percent of all coupes and convertibles. The totals by body style were 4,085 coupes and 7,547 convertibles. The 50th anniversary package was not available for the Z06.

Of the 11,632 Corvettes built with the 50th anniversary package, a total of 10,899 were built for US buyers, while the remaining 733 were exported. Canada received 450, Mexico got 36, and the remaining 247 were sold in Europe and other foreign markets.

### *Magnetic Selective Ride Control Makes Its Corvette Debut*

New for the anniversary model year was the innovative RPO F55 Magnetic Selective Ride Control, which was first introduced on the 2002 Cadillac STS. The MSRC shocks contained a special magneto-rheological fluid consisting of millions of tiny iron balls that would change consistency and viscosity as an electrical current was applied, thereby allowing the suspension damping to be adjusted nearly instantaneously. The system was controlled by a dual-processor computer chip capable of making more than 1,000 adjustments per second based on the speed of the car, steering wheel angle, wheel travel, lateral acceleration, and braking.

The F55 Ride Control also placed a switch on the center console that allowed the driver to select between Tour or Sport. Tour mode would make for a smoother, more comfortable ride whereas the Sport mode tightened up the suspension for more precise handling. The F55 suspension option was priced at $1,695 and was included on the 50th Anniversary Editions.

## Corvette Museum Celebrates the 50th Anniversary with Historic Motorama

To celebrate the 50th anniversary of the Chevrolet Corvette, the National Corvette Museum organized a unique "Historic Motorama," consisting of one Corvette from each model year. The Motorama would kick off its journey on June 21, 2003, in Flint, Michigan, where production of the first-year 1953 Corvettes took place.

After spending the weekend in Flint, on Monday the caravan moved south to Detroit, where several events took place around various GM facilities. On display were many special Corvettes from the GM Heritage Center and even a car show consisting of Corvettes owned by GM employees was held at the GM Tech Center.

From there, the Historic Motorama made its way to Joliet, Illinois, with a stop at Corvette Central in Sawyer, Michigan. After some time on the old Route 66, the caravan stopped in Effingham, Illinois, at Mid America Designs before finally pulling into St. Louis, where the cars were displayed under the Gateway Arch.

The next day, the Historic Motorama made its way to Evansville, Indiana, where the cars were displayed on the banks of the Ohio River as part of the Evansville Freedom Festival, complete with an air show by the Blue Angels. After a few hours, the caravan departed Evansville, where it received a police escort to the National Corvette Museum in Bowling Green, Kentucky. A large crowd greeted the cars as they arrived. After a group photo in front of the Bowling Green Assembly Plant, the plant suspended operations as the caravan paraded through the interior of the plant to the delight of the workers.

*As part of Corvette's 50th celebration, Chevrolet built a special one-of-one 2003 50th Anniversary Corvette in gold for the National Corvette Museum's "Going for the Gold" raffle. Special Gold paint, special graphics, Z06 brake ducts, and Z06 mesh grilles came from the factory on this standard coupe. The coupe is signed under the hood by the entire Bowling Green team that built the car and includes the signature of chief engineer Dave Hill. (Photo Courtesy Dave Salvatore / Kerbeck Corvette)*

## 2012 CENTENNIAL EDITION CORVETTE

Chevrolet is an automotive company born from racing. Many of the iconic images we see of founder Louis Chevrolet are those of him at the track, racing the cars he himself designed and built. Known as one of the great early race car drivers, Louis Chevrolet's racing career would take him to the famous Indianapolis 500 to compete four times from 1915 to 1920. His best finish would be seventh place in 1919.

Chevrolet had very little to do with the car company that was named after him, and the feeling was mutual with the company's execs, who did little to acknowledge the cofounder and company namesake through the years. But all that started to change as the company closed in on the 100th anniversary of its founding by Louis Chevrolet and William "Billy" Durant in 1911.

To celebrate the centennial anniversary of Chevrolet, the company's halo car carried the racing banner of its founding namesake, and the 2012 Corvette Centennial Edition celebrated that performance heritage. The Centennial Edition was available across the board on all Corvette models, including Grand Sport, Z06, and ZR1.

*Even Corvette Racing got in on the celebration of honoring Louis Chevrolet with his likeness behind the wheel displayed on the Corvette C6.R race cars in 2011. After all, both Corvette Racing and Louis Chevrolet shared a passion for automobile racing, both are champions, and both share the motto "Never Give Up." (Photo Courtesy Keith Cornett)*

| Base MSRP | $61,445 (coupe), $68,445 (convertible), $67,845 (Grand Sport coupe), $73,445 (Grand Sport convertible), $90,265 (Z06), $127,450 (ZR1) |
|---|---|
| Model Availability | Coupe, Convertible, Grand Sport, Z06, ZR1 |
| Engines | LS3, LS7, LS9 |
| Features | Exclusive exterior color, graphics, badging |
| Production Numbers | 2,201 |

### *Major Upgrades for the 2012 Corvette*

Corvette engineers worked to maximize the performance of the 2012 Corvette, and that performance started with Michelin's Pilot Sport Cup tires that were offered on select ZR1 and Z06

*The 2012 Centennial Edition's Carbon Flash Metallic Black exterior with Satin Black graphics created a unique black-on-black theme for Chevrolet's 100th anniversary. Even the interior was a full blackout with ebony leather on the instrument panel and doors complemented by microfiber suede on the steering wheel, seating surfaces, console, and shifter. (Photo Courtesy Jack McCarley)*

***The 2012 Corvette Grand Sport led production of the 2,201 Centennial Editions, and 71 percent of these were the Carbon Flash model. The Grand Sport coupe would account for 47 percent of all Centennial Editions. (Photo Courtesy Charles Smith)***

***Even though the Centennial Edition sold extremely well, it wasn't enough to lift Corvette sales, which recorded the lowest production totals in the modern era following the economic downturn that started in 2008. Sales of Corvettes in 2012 would reach the lowest in this period with only 11,647 produced. Other than 1997's shortened C5 inaugural launch, Corvette sales hadn't been this low since 1961. (Photo Courtesy Keith Cornett)***

packages. As an example of technology transfer from the Corvette race car to the street car, the tires were designed by Michelin engineer Lee Willard, who also designed the Michelin PS2 tires for the ZR1 and the racing tires used by Corvette Racing's C6.Rs in the American Le Mans Series.

The 2012 ZR1 transmission was tweaked in the fifth and sixth gears to give drivers an additional 2 mpg in the highway rating. That had the added benefit of lowering the gas-guzzler tax by $300 to $1,000. A special ZR1 Performance package (RPO PDE) added the new Michelin Pilot Sport Cup tires, Black Cup Style wheels, and the 6-speed close-ratio manual transmission.

For Z06 enthusiasts, the Ultimate Performance package included the Z07 package and added the sport cup tires, lightweight wheels, and the Performance Traction Management system found on the ZR1. The carbon fiber hood from the 2011 Carbon Edition was now a stand-alone option (RPO B92) for $2,495. The F55 Magnetic Selective Ride Control included the PTM system, black cup-style wheels, and Michelin PS2 tires.

Perhaps the most requested changes would come in the interior. New redesigned seats offered more support, and buyers who upgraded to 4LT interiors were able to get suede seat inserts that kept drivers firmly planted. A new steering wheel was offered, and the Bose stereo was redesigned to offer a new amp and nine speakers. Additional interior changes included some of the most popular options, such as navigation, Bluetooth, and heads-up display, moving down and becoming available in the 2LT trim level.

Lastly, buyers could personalize their 2012 Corvettes with a choice of brake caliper color in red, yellow, silver, or gray.

***The 2012 Centennial Edition Corvette Z06 number 100 sold at a Barrett-Jackson auction for $175,000. Proceeds from the sale benefited the Austin Hatcher Foundation for Pediatric Cancer. Chevrolet dealer and NASCAR team owner Rick Hendrick picked up the VIN 100 Corvette Z06 along with several others at the National Corvette Museum. (Photo Courtesy of the National Corvette Museum)***

### 2012 Corvette Centennial Edition Features

With the 2012 Centennial Edition Corvette, Chevrolet offered the celebratory model by declaring all black Corvettes across all four model lines a Centennial Edition. The Centennial Edition was marked with a special one-year black Carbon Flash metallic exterior with satin black graphics and unique Centennial satin black wheels with red brake calipers. The black aluminum wheels specific to the models were highlighted with a red stripe around the perimeter. All Centennial Edition Corvettes included the RPO F55 Magnetic Selective Ride Control.

A special 100-Years graphic showing Louis Chevrolet behind the steering wheel of his race car, complete with leather helmet and goggles, was displayed throughout: the B-pillars, center wheel caps, and the center of the steering wheel all featured the image. The graphics on the B-pillar were designed to blend with the black metallic exterior of the car. A small 100 replaced the fleur-de-lis symbol on the Corvette's crossed-flags logo.

Inside was an ebony leather-wrapped dash and doors with complementary red stitching. Suede accents used first on the 2011 Corvette Z06 Carbon were also found on the Centennial's seats, steering wheel, shifter, and armrests. The seats were embossed with a checkered flag design and the "100" found on the right lower side of the headrests.

### Pricing and Production

The Centennial Edition package price was $4,950 and was ordered with RPO ZLC. The special edition was available across all models. The only requirement was the upper level trim packages (3LT, 4LT, 3LZ, and 3ZR).

The 2012 Corvette Centennial Editions were in high demand with a total of 2,201 produced (18.9 percent). Centennial Editions accounted for nearly 1 in 5 Corvettes produced, and for the high-end Z06 and ZR1 models, the Centennial Edition was chosen by even more buyers. Just more than 50 percent of all ZR1s are Centennials, while nearly 41 percent of Z06s were decked out in Carbon Flash metallic.

*A special 100-Years graphic that signified Chevrolet's racing heritage featured company namesake Louis Chevrolet behind the steering wheel of one of his race cars. The graphic was placed on the B-pillars (or the rear fender for convertibles), the center caps of the wheels, and the center of the steering wheel. The redesigned seats were embossed with the centennial logo as well. (Photo Courtesy Keith Cornett)*

With the new additions and changes to the options packages, Chevrolet raised the prices of the trim packages significantly. The 2LT coupes and GS coupes would rise from 2011's price of $1,195 to $2,095. The 3LT coupes and Grand Sport coupes increased from $4,205 to $5,995, and 4LT coupes and GS coupes were raised from $7,705 to $9,495. The 2LT convertible and Grand Sport convertibles dropped from $3,190 to $2,095. The 3LT packages were up from 2011's package price of $6,200 to $7,995, and 4LT packages for the topless Corvettes increased from $9,700 to $11,495.

**2012 Corvette Centennial Edition Production Breakdown**

| Model | Quantity |
|---|---|
| Base Coupe | 172 |
| Base Convertible | 60 |
| Grand Sport Coupe | 1,040 |
| Grand Sport Convertible | 528 |
| Z06 | 195 |
| ZR1 | 206 |
| **Total** | **2,201** |

*The Centennial Edition's package price was $4,950, and the key component was the Carbon Flash metallic exterior. It was the first metallic black exterior offered for the Corvette, and it would be very popular, accounting for one in five Corvettes produced. (Photo Courtesy Kurt Ernst)*

*Chevrolet introduced new seats for the 2012 model year that did a better job at keeping drivers firmly planted with redesigned bolsters and utilizing suede seat inserts. The Centennial Edition's theme was carried over to the seats with red stitching and an exclusive 100-years logo embossed on the headrests. (Photo Courtesy Keith Cornett)*

# Centennial Edition Celebrates Life of Louis Chevrolet

Louis Chevrolet was born on December 25, 1878, in La Chaux-de-Fonds, Switzerland. Mechanically gifted at an early age, Chevrolet learned to repair bicycles and eventually got hooked by the racing bug. His interest in racing and repairing bicycles gradually migrated to automobiles, and he became quite adept at making cars go fast.

By 1901, Chevrolet was working in New York City as a chauffeur and mechanic. Over the next 10 years, he would become famous for his racing abilities and daredevil personality, but those who knew him say he was never reckless. Chevrolet once held, although briefly, the world speed record with a run of 119 mph on Daytona Beach.

Chevrolet met GM president William "Billy" Durant in 1907, and he was put to work as part of the Buick racing team, where he designed and drove the race cars to many victories. Following Durant's ousting from General Motors in 1910, the two would partner in 1911 to build passenger cars under the Chevrolet name. It wasn't much of a partnership, though. Chevrolet and Durant had differing opinions on what kind of car to produce. Chevrolet wanted to produce grand, luxurious cars; Durant wanted a cheaper car to compete with the Ford Model T. Things came to a head in 1913 after a heated disagreement when Chevrolet quit the company bearing his name.

In 1915, he made his inaugural start at the Indianapolis Motor Speedway, finishing in 20th place. Chevrolet returned with three cars in 1916, but none finished the 500-mile race. Following the conclusion of World War I, racing returned to Indianapolis in 1919 and so did Chevrolet, now joined by his brothers Arthur and Gaston. The following year, Louis would leave the race early while Gaston would go on to win the Indianapolis 500. Louis himself never won the Indianapolis 500, but three of his cars would find their way to victory circle.

Chevrolet started several ventures, some moderately successful and some outright failures. Following his breakup with Durant, Louis sold all his stock in the company and, in doing so, gave up the investment that would have made him wealthy. Destitute and in poor health during much of the 1930s, Chevrolet passed away on June 6, 1941, at the age of 62 of complications resulting from a leg amputation secondary to diabetes. He is buried along with his brothers in the Holy Cross and St. Joseph Cemetery in Indianapolis.

***Before his name was ever associated with a car company, Louis Chevrolet was one of the top race car drivers and builders of the era. His stint as a cofounder of Chevrolet was short-lived, and later in life he would say his accomplishments on the track were his finest memories. (Photo Courtesy General Motors Media Archives)***

***Chevrolet Motorcar Company and the Indianapolis 500 were both founded in 1911 and share close ties: Louis Chevrolet would race four times at the famous brickyard, and his cars would take the checkered flag three times. Louis Chevrolet is memorialized at the Indianapolis Motor Speedway Hall of Fame Museum with a bust that bears his motto "Never Give Up." (Photo Courtesy Keith Cornett)***

***Chevrolet was one of the original pioneers of speed, but he would never truly find success in business despite starting or cofounding several other automotive and airplane engine companies. Louis passed away on June 6, 1941, from complications following surgery. He is buried next to his brother Gaston at Holy Cross and St. Joseph Cemetery in Indianapolis. (Photo Courtesy Keith Cornett)***

## 2013 60TH ANNIVERSARY EDITION CORVETTE

The C6 Corvette era could best be described as the generation that cemented Corvette's reputation for offering supercar performance at a budget price. It could even be argued that the C6 was Chevrolet's exclamation point on the sport car's legacy.

The C6 Corvettes were among the most diverse and potent Corvettes ever built, with even the base models offering 430 hp. The brand was continually punching above its weight class, as the 505-hp Corvette Z06 and the 638-hp Corvette ZR1 outperformed exotic sports cars costing several times more. They would blast the competition at the Nürburgring in Germany and back home at *Car and Driver*'s Lightning Lap competition.

But at the dealerships, things were not all that rosy; Corvette sales dropped to half what they had been prior to the Great Recession and GM's bankruptcy in 2009. During the 2007 model year, more than 40,000 Corvettes were sold. Just five years later, sales of the 2012 models fell to just 11,647.

With the new C7 Corvette on the horizon, Chevrolet needed something to keep those final C6 Corvettes selling for just one more year. With both the 60th anniversary looming as well as the end of the C6, Chevrolet upped its game once again by offering the 2013 Corvette 427 Convertible Collector Edition and the 60th Anniversary package that would be available for all 2013 Corvette models.

***The 2013 Corvette ZR1 with the 60th Anniversary package became the 11th Corvette to pace the Indianapolis 500 on May 27, 2012. The Corvette's 6.2L LS9 with 638 hp had no problem leading the pack of Indy cars in the Greatest Spectacle in Racing. (Photo Courtesy Keith Cornett)***

### *60th Anniversary Package*

RPO Z25 was the 60th Anniversary package available for all 2013 Corvette models, including the new 427 Convertible. Highlights of the package included an Arctic White exterior with a Blue Diamond leather-wrapped interior with suede accents. Convertible models would also feature a blue top.

| | |
|---|---|
| Base MSRP | $61,145 (coupe), $68,145 (convertible), $67,545 (Grand Sport coupe), $73,145 (Grand Sport convertible), $87,475 (427 Edition), $86,510 (Z06), $123,650 (ZR1) |
| Model Availability | Coupe, Convertible, Grand Sport, 427 Edition, Z06, ZR1 |
| Engines | LS3, LS7, LS9 |
| Features | White exterior, custom interior color and convertible top, badging, graphics |
| Production Numbers | 2,059 |

***As the C6 Corvette's swan song for 2013, there was now a Corvette for everyone. The 60th Anniversary package was offered across six distinct models: coupe, convertible, Grand Sport (coupe and convertible), 427 Convertible, Z06, and ZR1. (Photo Courtesy Keith Cornett)***

The package also included a ZR1-style rear spoiler, special 60th anniversary badging, gray-painted brake calipers, and the 60th logo on the wheel center caps, steering wheel, and seat headrests. An optional graphics package (RPO Z30) added a new Pearl Silver Blue full-length racing stripe and, for convertibles, a tonal stripe stitched into the convertible top that extends the graphic theme over the roof.

All 2013 Corvettes featured the 60th anniversary badge on the front and rear as well as the waterfall panel on convertibles. The 60th logo was also on the instrument panel gauge cluster and the door sills. Only the 427 convertible with the heritage package featured a 60th anniversary badge that was unique to the special-edition model.

*The Blue Diamond leather-wrapped interior with suede inserts was the interior package on all 60th Anniversary Editions, but it did require the upper level trim groups (4LT/3LZ/3ZR). (Photo Courtesy Richard Straker)*

***The Tonal Convertible Top***

One of the key design elements of the Anniversary package was the optional stripe that was carried the full length of the car, including on the blue convertible top. The 60th anniversary's press release described "an optional graphics package [that] adds full-length racing stripes in Pearl Silver Blue, including a tonal stripe stitched into the convertible top, extending the graphic theme over the roof."

The convertible top was made of a

*As with most previous anniversary editions, Corvette's 2013 60th Anniversary Edition featured a one-year-only emblem. A 2013 60th anniversary crossed-flags emblem appeared on the front and rear of every 2013 Corvette. (Photo Courtesy Keith Cornett)*

*Corvette production was shortened to just nine months in 2013 because of the coming C7 Corvette. A total of 2,059 60th Anniversary Corvettes were offered in the shortened model year, 15.3 percent of all 2013 Corvettes built. (Photo Courtesy Richard Straker)*

*One of the unique design features of the 60th Anniversary Edition was offered exclusively for convertibles. The optional graphics package added full-length racing stripes in Pearl Silver Blue, and the stripe design was carried through the canvas soft top with tonal blue stripes blended into the convertible top and extending the graphics theme over the roof. (Photo Courtesy Gary Wollenhaupt)*

### THE MODEL BREAKDOWN OF THE 60TH ANNIVERSARY EDITION (Z25) AND ANNIVERSARY GRAPHICS (Z30)

| **Model** | **Z25** | **Z30** |
|---|---|---|
| Base Coupe | 41 | 34 |
| Base Convertible | 31 | 24 |
| Grand Sport Coupe | 400 | 355 |
| Grand Sport Convertible | 258 | 227 |
| 427 Convertible | 1,088 | 897 |
| Z06 | 103 | 85 |
| ZR1 | 138 | 131 |
| **Total** | **2,059** | **1,753** |

single piece of fabric, and the 60th anniversary convertible top was the first to feature this design. The tonal stripe was approximately the same width as the full body stripe and helped connect the stripe from front to rear when the top was up.

#### *Price and Production*

The 60th Anniversary package added $1,075 to the price and required the top-level trim packages to qualify. The coupe, convertible, Grand Sport, and 427 Convertibles all required the 4LT equipment group, while the Z06 required 3LZ, and the ZR1 required 3ZR. Additionally, the Z30 Anniversary Graphics package added $750.

A total of 2,059 60th Anniversary Corvettes were built. Of those, 1,753 also featured the Z30 Anniversary Graphics package.

Production of the 2013 model year was adjusted to accommodate a shutdown at the Corvette assembly plant as workers reconfigured the assembly process for the upcoming C7 Corvette. With a planned run of nine months, production started the first week of May 2012 and would officially come to an end on March 28, 2013.

The last 2013 Corvette (and last of the C6 generation) was a 427 Convertible 60th Anniversary Edition. The 505-hp LS7 engine was assembled by hand at GM's Performance Build Center in Wixom by Corvette chief engineer Tadge Juechter. The final C6 Corvette wasn't sold and instead resides in the GM private collection and is now on display at the GM Heritage Center in Sterling Heights, Michigan.

### THE 60TH ANNIVERSARY CORVETTE 427 EDITION

The Corvette team has always enjoyed a close relationship with enthusiasts and owners in the hobby, and they make themselves available at most of the major Corvette shows around the country. During these interactions, the team hears all sorts of requests and wish-list items directly from customers. Some of these ideas are implemented.

The 427 convertible was the answer for owners who repeatedly requested a Z06 convertible model. Because the C6 Z06 used an aluminum chassis, a convertible model wasn't possible due to body flex from the increased power of the 505-hp LS7 V-8. However, once Chevrolet started production of the C6 Corvette Grand Sport convertible, which had the wide-body design of the Z06 but was constructed on the base convertible's hydroformed steel frames, it became feasible to create a special one-year model to celebrate the end of the C6 Corvette by combining the Grand Sport's wide-body with the Z06's 505-hp LS7 V-8.

The 427 Convertible received more than just the Z06's powerplant to make it special. Many of the carbon fiber body panels, including the raised hood, Z06-style fenders, and floor panels, were also transplanted to the 427 convertible. The weight reduction gave the car an insanely low power-to-weight ratio of 1:6.64 (one horsepower per 6.64 pounds of vehicle mass). Chevrolet would call the 427 convertible the most capable convertible Corvette model ever produced.

***Chevrolet offered both anniversary and collector editions at various times in the past; the 2013 Corvette 427 Convertible represents the first time a collector edition and an anniversary edition were offered in the same year and both options available on the same car. (Photo Courtesy Richard Straker)***

***The special 60th anniversary badges appear only on the 427 Convertible with the 60th Anniversary package. All 2013 Corvettes have the special 60th anniversary crossed-flags badges, 60th anniversary sill plates, and the 60th graphics in the gauge cluster. (Photo Courtesy Keith Cornett)***

## 2018 CARBON 65 EDITION CORVETTE

When researching the various Corvette special editions for this book, it was easy to look back at past models and judge all aspects of the car, from the initial announcement and public reveal to final sales figures. How does history judge that special edition against all previous Corvette special editions in its category?

As this book was being written, Chevrolet introduced its new 2018 model year Corvettes in April 2017 at the National Corvette Museum's annual Bash event. The 2018 model lineup includes the latest special edition in Corvette's 65-year history, the 2018 Carbon 65.

As enthusiasts flocked to Bowling Green to celebrate another new model year, the Corvette brand was once again experiencing growing pains, even at the advanced age of 65 years old.

| | |
|---|---|
| Base MSRP | $90,240 (Grand Sport coupe), $94,240 (Grand Sport convertible), $103,440 (Z06 coupe), $107,440 (Z06 convertible) |
| Model Availability | Grand Sport, Z06 |
| Engines | LT1, LT4 |
| Features | Exterior graphics, carbon fiber components |
| Production Numbers | 650 |

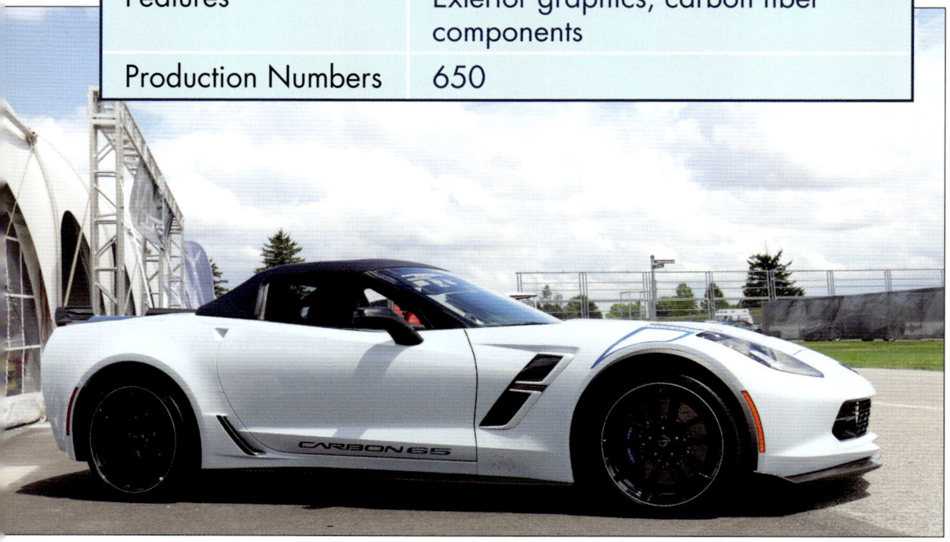

*The 2018 Carbon 65 is Chevrolet's sixth anniversary special edition offered to the public. Starting with the Silver Anniversary model in 1978, Chevrolet had produced anniversary editions to celebrate the 35th, 40th, 50th, 60th, and now the 65th. The first Corvette was completed on June 30, 1953, and except for 1983, has been in Chevrolet's model lineup every year since. (Photo Courtesy Keith Cornett)*

In the summer of 2017, rumors proliferated in the automotive magazines, forums, and blogs that Chevrolet was finally going to go to market with a mid-engine Corvette, known internally at General Motors as "ZERV," which is a play on Zora Arkus-Duntov's Chevrolet Engineering Research Vehicles known as "CERV." Spy photos in late 2016 and 2017 of a mid-engine C8 Corvette appeared to back up those claims. The next generation Corvette is expected to hit dealers sometime in the next three model years (2019–2021).

Chevrolet had also been testing a set of camouflaged C7 models that were rumored to be the return of the ZR1. The ZR1 prototypes had been spotted from Ohio to Colorado after being initially captured on GM's test track in Milford, Michigan. The ZR1 prototypes featured the wide-body design with larger front air intakes and a custom hood in both coupe and convertible body styles and two sizes of rear wing spoilers.

In late 2017, Chevrolet would reveal the 2019 Corvette ZR1 models at auto shows in Dubai and Los Angeles. Powered by the 755-hp LT5 engine, the cars are capable of a 212-mph top speed.

Rumors of a C8 mid-engine Corvette are serious enough that many dealers already are keeping a list of customer names for those wanting the latest and greatest Corvettes.

### *Major Updates at the Corvette Assembly Plant*

On the heels of speculation about new Corvettes under development came a massive upgrade over summer/fall 2017 of the Bowling Green assembly plant to modernize the systems it uses to paint and assemble vehicles. After starting 2018 production on June 5, the plant shut down on July 31 and remained closed through November to perform upgrades. Chevrolet resumed 2018 Corvette production on November 6, 2017; however the automaker announced that the 2018 model year would be shortened. Corvettes for the 2019 model year would start production at the end of January 2018.

The plant recently added a large new paint shop, which cost $439 million and nearly doubled the footprint of the factory. The new paint shop utilized specially designed robots and slow bake ovens for painting the unique composite panels that make up the Corvette's body. According to the plant's management, these assembly line changes were expected to increase both the quality of the exterior finish along with the total build quality during the assembly process.

It's also widely believed that the changes at the plant would allow multiple Corvette models (e.g., a front-engine Corvette and a mid-engine Corvette) on the same assembly line, utilizing flexible manufacturing techniques that General Motors has employed at other plants that assemble multiple models. Furthering speculation that future models would be built was that the plant announced the postponement of the VIP buyers tour and public tours starting in June 2017 and lasting up to 18 months, thereby eliminating opportunities for the public to view internal plant activities.

Sales of the 2018 Carbon 65 Edition were strong, with demand for the car outpacing the ability to produce it when the model first started production. Chevrolet built 356 of the 650 prior to the three-month assembly plant shutdown in the fall of 2017, and once the plant reopened, the final 294 were completed. (Photo Courtesy Rick Conti)

Since 2004, Chevrolet has led the way in carbon fiber body panels. The original B92 hood first made its appearance on the 2004 Z06, and it was the first carbon fiber painted hood used on a domestic vehicle. The hood returned in 2011 for the Carbon Edition and made its first appearance on C7 Corvettes in 2016 on the Corvette Z06 C7.R Edition. (Photo Courtesy Rick Conti)

### Minimal Changes for the 2018 Corvette

Amid looming changes to the future of the Corvette plant and the future Corvette model lineup (with no official comment from GM employees), the 2018 Corvette was introduced to the public.

The 2018 model year changes for the Corvette were minimal. A new color, Ceramic Matrix Gray Metallic, replaced Sterling Blue and, despite being called "gray," it was much closer to off-white with a tinge of blue (pastel, like the Boss 429s). In the sun, some metallic flake in the paint lights up. While it's not a true matte color in the traditional sense, that's the effect when viewed indoors or out of the direct sunlight.

For the Stingray, the base 18/19-inch wheel combo was retired and now all Corvettes ride on 19/20-inch wheels. And speaking of wheels, the Stingray and Z06 received additional wheel options. The Grand Sport could be ordered with the J57 Brembo carbon ceramic brakes

This limited-edition anniversary gift is wrapped in a brand-new exterior color called Ceramic Matrix Gray Metallic. Chevrolet first teased an off-white color back in 2010 on the Z06X Concept. The color is not exclusive to the Carbon 65 and could be ordered on all models. (Photo Courtesy Rick Conti)

Featured on the 2018 Carbon 65 was the exposed carbon fiber rear spoiler (RPO 5V5). The two-piece molded Stage 3 wickerbill spoiler was introduced in 2016 as an accessory option priced at $2,520. The spoiler is available through the **Genuine Corvette Accessories** catalog at Chevrolet dealer parts counters. (Photo Courtesy Keith Cornett)

If 25 years is celebrated with silver and 50 years with gold, the Corvette team said during introduction of the 65th Anniversary Corvette, 65 years should be celebrated with carbon fiber. (Photo Courtesy Keith Cornett)

The interior of the Carbon 65 Anniversary Edition is jet black suede wrapped with blue stitching while carbon fiber graces a new-for-2018 steering wheel and the high-gloss instrument trim panel. Competition Sports sets are standard along with the Carbon 65 Edition sill plates. (Photo Courtesy Keith Cornett)

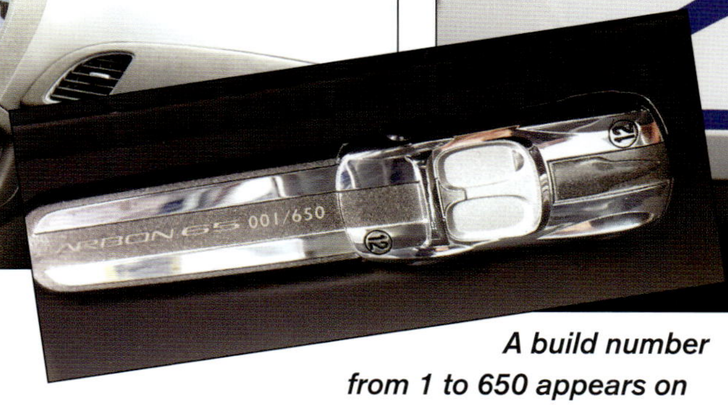


A build number from 1 to 650 appears on the Carbon 65's interior plaque, which is specific to the model. Z06 owners have the Z06-specific plaque while Grand Sport owners will have the George Wintersteen number 002 Corvette Grand Sport plaque. (Photo Courtesy Keith Cornett)

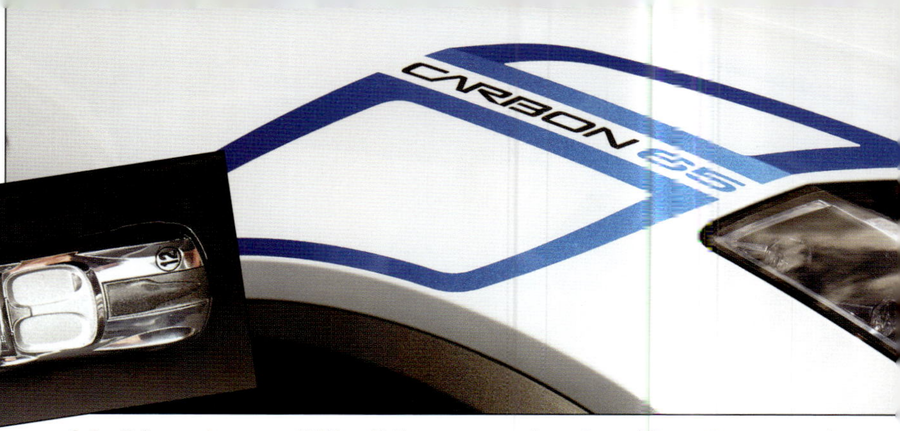


With all the exposed carbon fiber showcased on the car, 2018's Carbon 65 package is one of the more costly special editions with RPO Z30 listed for $15,000. The Grand Sport Carbon 65 Edition Coupe MSRP is $90,245 while a Carbon 65 Z06 Convertible starts at $107,445. (Photo Courtesy Keith Cornett)

without having to order the Z07 package. And finally, the limited-edition Carbon 65 package, which was expected not only to celebrate 65 years of the Corvette but also keep interest alive as the car once again went through growing pains, even at the advanced age of 65.

### *The 2018 Carbon 65 Marks Corvette's 65th Anniversary*

The 2018 Corvette Carbon 65 Edition was a special limited anniversary edition offered for the 2018 Z06 and Grand Sport models in both coupe and convertible configurations. The edition was limited to 650 units on a "built-to-order" sale. The only requirement is the 3LT/3LZ Trim Package.

The real star of 2018's anniversary edition was all-visible carbon fiber components inside and out. Starting from the top, the Carbon 65 received the C2Z carbon fiber visible roof and the B92 hood showing the visible carbon fiber weave over the power bulge. The Carbon 65 also featured a carbon fiber molded two-piece Stage 3 wickerbill spoiler. Also added to the list are the CFZ carbon fiber aerodynamic front splitter and rocker panels. Even the rear quarter panel air scoops were done in carbon fiber. Against the Ceramic Matrix Gray Metallic exterior, the visible carbon fiber really shines.

Inside the cabin was the 3LT/3LZ jet black suede interior available outside the limited design package from 2017. A new visible carbon fiber steering wheel and a gloss carbon fiber trim panel bring the Carbon 65's theme into the interior. A model-specific interior plaque listed the sequence number of the car. Other notable package additions were the return of blue-painted brake calipers exclusive to the Carbon 65, and inside, blue stitching on the leather interior.

Additional exterior appointments included blue-colored exterior graphics on the bottom of the door and front fenders proclaiming "Carbon 65." The Carbon 65 came with the black aluminum wheels with the machined grooves based on the model. (Cup wheels for the Grand Sport and Blade wheels for the Z06.) The wheel center caps show the Carbon 65 logo.

"Corvette is one of the most storied names in Chevrolet and sports car history, with a heritage few can match," said Paul Edwards, US vice president of Chevrolet Marketing, in the official press release. "The new Carbon 65 Edition honors that legacy, while offering customers another unique, special-edition model that personalizes the ownership experience."

### *Pricing and Production*

The 2018 Carbon 65 Package (RPO Z30) was priced at $15,000 plus the mandatory 3LT/3LZ Trim Package. That put the starting MSRP for the Grand Sport coupe at $90,240 on the low end; on the high end was the Z06 convertible with an MSRP starting at $107,440.

The Carbon 65 Edition was officially a sell out, as all 650 Corvettes were built, with the last of the series finished during the final weeks of 2018 model year production in January 2018. The 650 Carbon Editions were made up of 297 Grand Sports and 353 Z06s. Chevrolet would export 150 of the 650 Corvettes, with Europe receiving 127 followed by Canada (-9), Middle East (17), Mexico (12), and Japan (8).

## 2018 Carbon 65 Production Breakdown

| MODEL | TOTAL | Z07 | J57 BRAKES | 7-SPEED MANUAL | 8-SPEED AUTO |
|---|---|---|---|---|---|
| GS Coupe | 262 | 47 | 30 | 50 | 212 |
| GS Convertible | 35 | 5 | 2 | 8 | 27 |
| Z06 Coupe | 281 | 93 | 6 | 55 | 196 |
| Z06 Convertible | 72 | 17 | 5 | 15 | 57 |
| **Total** | **650** | **162** | **43** | **128** | **492** |

CHAPTER 2

# INDY 500 PACE CAR CORVETTES

It's only fitting that the Chevrolet Corvette has some of the strongest ties to the Indianapolis Motor Speedway. The speedway and Chevrolet were both founded in 1911, and Louis Chevrolet went on to drive in four Indy races. Louis, along with brother and former Indy 500 winner Gaston Chevrolet, are buried in an Indianapolis cemetery just 20 minutes from the track.

***The Chevrolet Corvette has become a regular fixture at the Indianapolis Motor Speedway by pacing the Greatest Spectacle in Racing a record 14 times. (Photo Courtesy Mecum Auctions)***

The first Indy 500 Corvette Pace Car was developed during the model's 25th anniversary and, together with the 1978 anniversary model, represented the first two special-edition Corvettes ever produced. But it was the public's insatiable demand for the black and silver 1978 Corvette Indy 500 Pace Car that showed Chevrolet just how much enthusiasm there could be for limited-edition and replica models.

Over the years, the Indianapolis 500 has provided Chevrolet the opportunity to build some iconic and even wild special editions to serve as the official pace car for the "Greatest Spectacle in Racing." Since 1978 and as recent as 2017, the Chevrolet Corvette has paced the Indianapolis 500 a record 14 times; 6 of those occasions have been marked with special-edition Pace Car Replicas that were offered for sale to the public.

## 1978 INDY 500 PACE CAR REPLICA

Chevrolet executives approached the Indianapolis 500 about using a Corvette as the pace car for the 1978 race to commemorate the model's 25th anniversary. Initially, the plan was to use the 1978 Silver Anniversary Edition, but once the car had been selected to be the pace car for the 1978 race, Corvette designer Jerry Palmer and his team came back with a striking design featuring a two-tone black over silver with red pinstriping. The story of the 1978 Corvette is one of the more fascinating in the model's long history.

Chevrolet initially planned a limited run of 1,000 Corvette Indy 500 Pace Cars, but as word got out and demand spread, and most likely after conversations with the automaker's legal team, Chevrolet agreed to produce one Pace Car Replica for each Chevrolet dealer in the United States and Canada. A total of 6,502 Corvette Pace Cars were built.

| Base MSRP | $13,653.21 |
|---|---|
| Model Availability | T-Top Coupe |
| Engines | L48, L82 |
| Features | Exclusive exterior and interior colors, graphics, unique VIN |
| Production Numbers | 6,502 |

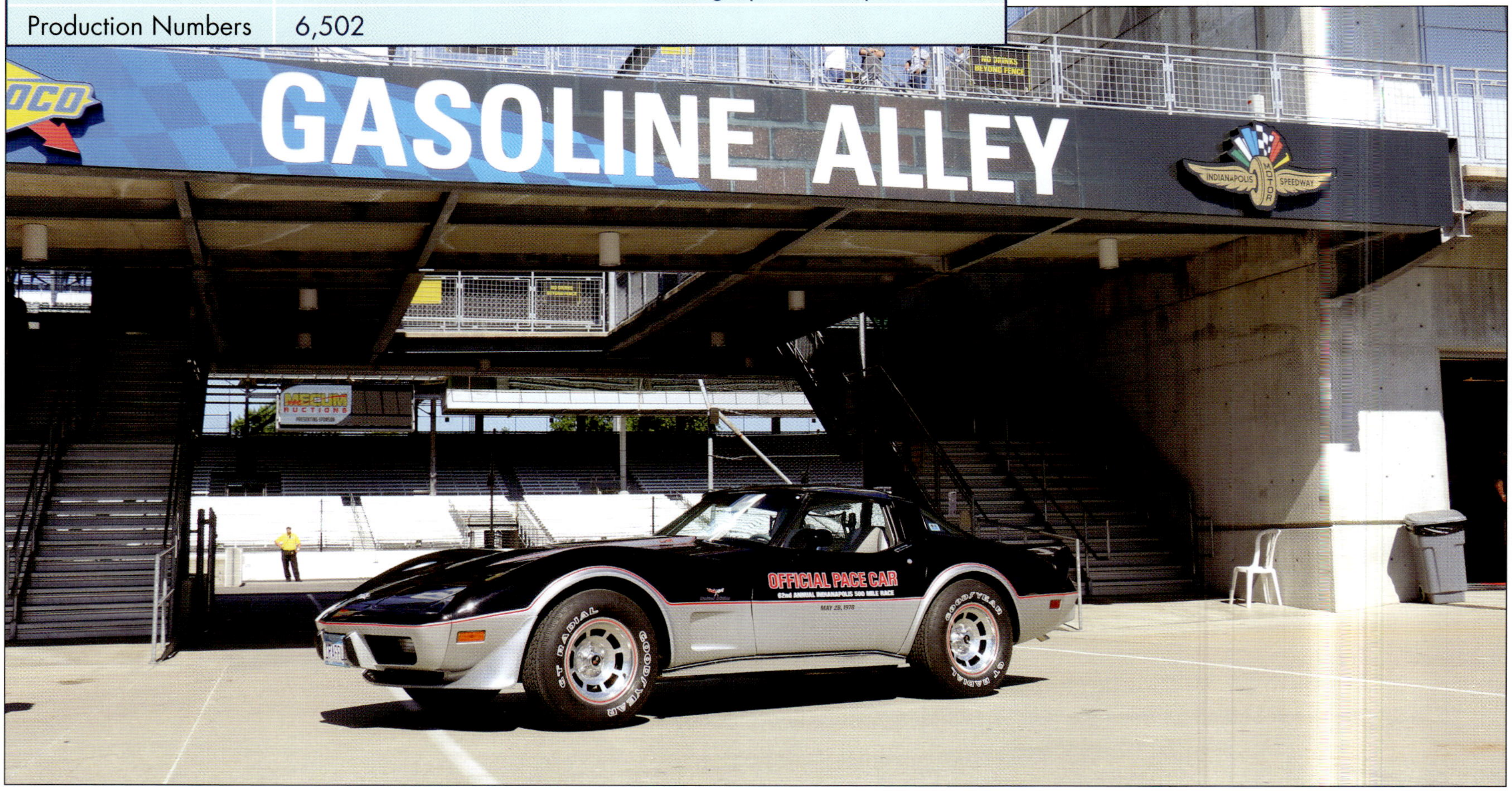


*The first Chevrolet paced the Indianapolis 500 in 1948. It would be another 30 years before the 1978 Corvette would perform the duties of the official pace car for the Greatest Spectacle in Racing. (Photo Courtesy Keith Cornett)*

**_Bold graphics proclaimed the car as the "Official Pace Car" of the "62nd Annual Indianapolis 500 Mile Race" on the upper black portion of the doors with the race date beneath. A graphic of the Indianapolis Motor Speedway's "wing and wheel" logo was on the rear fenders and the graphic "Limited Edition" appeared under the crossed-flags logos on the front fenders. (Photo Courtesy Keith Cornett)_**

Production of the Corvette Pace Car started in early March 1978 and wrapped up on May 19, 1978, nine days before the running of the 1978 Indianapolis 500. Dealers were already reporting strong demand when an article appeared in the *Wall Street Journal* on March 27, 1978, that touted the collectability of the limited-edition Corvette, causing speculators to bid up the price of the already premium sports car to new heights.

**_Chevrolet originally planned to run the 25th Anniversary Edition Corvette as the Indy 500 Pace Car. Corvette designer Jerry Palmer is credited with penning the now famous black and silver livery for the 1978 Pace Car. (Photo Courtesy John T. Perez / ClassicAndMuscleCar.com)_**

### *A Premium Price for a Limited-Edition Corvette*

While the regular 1978 Corvette's MSRP was set at $9,351.89, the 1978 Indy 500 Pace Car came in at $13,653.21. It was the first time a Corvette's MSRP crossed $10,000. But with speculation that collectors would be able to flip the cars for profit immediately or store them to sell later, many dealers charged a premium and found many eager buyers who were willing to spend $25,000 or more to secure their pace car.

After the race, interest in the cars waned quickly and those high prices that speculators were willing to pay dropped considerably. That led to many owners storing their cars until the market rebounded. Today, it's not uncommon to come across the sale of a low-mileage Indy 500 Pace Car that may even contain plastic factory wrapping still on the seats.

The Indy 500 Pace Car Replicas were the first Corvettes to have their own VIN sequence, with a "9" replacing the standard "4" in the eighth digit, making the cars increasingly difficult to clone.

**_Originally intended to debut in 1977, General Motors officially offered a choice of glass or painted fiberglass T-tops in 1978. The Indy 500 Pace Car came with glass T-tops, which appeared mirrored from the outside but, as could be seen from the inside, were tinted. (Photo Courtesy Jeff Romm / Corvette Mike)_**

## *Indy 500 Pace Car Design*

The most notable design feature was the black over silver exterior, which was divided by a red tape stripe. An additional silver stripe appeared on each side of the hood as well. The Pace Cars received polished aluminum alloy wheels that featured a thin red stripe along the edge of the wheel that accented nicely with the red body stripe.

The Corvettes had several exterior graphics identifying the car as an official pace car of the Indy 500. On the front quarter panels under the 1978 crossed-flags emblem, a graphic script read "Limited Edition," while the rear quarter panels sported the wings and tire icon of the Indianapolis Motor Speedway.

*The black and silver pace car (and its 25th anniversary sibling) were the first two-tone factory Corvettes since 1961. A red stripe wrapped all the way around the car at its beltline, and the polished alloy rims carried a red stripe on the outer edge. (Photo Courtesy Jeff Romm / Corvette Mike)*

Bright red graphics on each of the doors proclaimed "Official Pace Car" and under it read "62nd Annual Indianapolis 500 Mile Race" along with the date of May 28, 1978. Chevrolet chose to allow customers the opportunity to decide whether they wanted the door graphics, so they were shipped in a box with the car for the customer or dealer to apply.

Chevrolet also went to work on the interior, giving the Pace Car a bright silver interior, dash, and carpet. Redesigned seats destined for the 1979 model year were utilized, which gave the car even more exclusivity. A silver anniversary Corvette logo was featured on the steering wheel horn button while a dash plaque between the shifter and the power window buttons was inscribed with "25th Anniversary Corvette Limited Edition."

*The 1978 Corvette was redesigned for its 25th anniversary year, and all Corvettes, including the Indy 500 Pace Car, now featured a fastback window. The new look greatly enhanced the cargo area as well as visibility for the driver. A roll-up shade provided relief from the sun as well as hiding items in the rear cargo area. (Photo Courtesy Jeff Romm / Corvette Mike)*

*The Indianapolis 500 Pace Car Replicas were powered by the standard L48 V-8 rated at 185 hp, or buyers could option it with the same engine that the official pace car ran with on the track, the 220-hp L82 V-8. (Photo Courtesy John T. Perez / ClassicAndMuscleCar.com)*

## Wall Street Journal Article

Interest was already high in the 1978 Corvette, which featured a new fastback design and a special 25th anniversary model. Chevrolet showed long-lead journalists the complete 1978 lineup that also included a Corvette Pace Car for the Indianapolis 500. *Vette Vues* magazine broke the news in its September 1977 issue, confirming that the 1978 Corvette would be pacing the Indianapolis 500. General Motors and the Indianapolis Motor Speedway confirmed the news on October 17, 1977, with a press conference in Indianapolis to make it official. Chevrolet debated internally how many of the replicas should be produced and, after hearing from its legal team, officially announced in late December 1977 that one limited-edition Indy 500 Pace Car Replica would be offered to each dealer in the United States and Canada for resale.

Three months after Chevrolet set the allocation of the Indy 500 replicas at 6,500 units, the *Wall Street Journal* featured a front-page article titled "Few Want to Drive This Car, but Many Are Eager to Buy It" by Charles Camp (March 27, 1978). The article opened with the story of a customer suing his local Chevy dealer for refusing to sell him the Indy 500 Pace Car he was promised in September 1977, despite placing a $1,000 deposit on a car with an MSRP exceeding $13,600. The reason implied was that the dealer was backing out of the contract after learning he could sell it for more. Many dealers did sell their 1978 Corvette Pace Car Replicas for upward of $25,000.

"Corvette aficionados see the cars as instant collector's items—sort of automotive Rembrandts, flashy paint jobs and all. And many see something else in GM's decision to make only a handful of them: the chance to make a basketful of money," wrote Camp.

Camp surmised that since many Corvette "early-birds" got in early to put deposits down on the pace cars, it would lead to an explosive secondary market as they sold to those who missed their chance. Camp quoted Aaron (Bat) Masterson, the owner of a used-car lot and auto-leasing firm: "They'll be selling for $75,000 within 90 days . . . This is a one-time shot; either you're in now or you're not in at all."

Camp went on, "Then there is the 23-year-old Arizonan named Arman Verdone Jr. who cornered the market with 'at least 100' Pace Cars under contract for an average of $17,000 each. He thinks he'll clear $300,000 by selling them at an average of $20,000 each. His four-month campaign to get as many as he can may have also led dealers to believe in the premium pricing the cars were demanding."

***Like the silver anniversary models, the Pace Car interiors reflected the influence of retiring GM Design Chief Bill Mitchell with a black over silver exterior and featuring either full silver leather or silver leather/gray cloth interiors and matching gray carpeting. (Photo Courtesy Jeff Romm / Corvette Mike)***

***The Pace Cars included a front chin spoiler and rear ducktail spoiler that not only provided a sportier appearance but reduced front-end lift and helped plant the rear end to the road. The spoilers also had the effect of dropping the C3 Corvette's aerodynamic coefficient of drag (Cd) from 0.50 to 0.42. (Photo Courtesy John T. Perez / ClassicAndMuscleCar.com)***

## Wall Street Journal Article *continued*

Camp did offer restraint regarding the auto-buying hysteria with a reminder of what had happened when collectors bid up the "last American Convertible, the 1976 Cadillac Eldorado, to prices upward of $65,000."

Camp highlights another Corvette Pace Car speculator, a Kansas cattleman and real estate investor named Darrell Hills, who spent a week on the phone dialing Chevy dealers all around the country. Initially wanting just two cars, one for him and one for his son, his excitement got the best of him, and at the time of the article he had commitments for 70 cars in seven states. (He would end up with 125 total orders.)

GM vice president and Chevrolet general manager Robert Lund said the interest in the 1978 Indy 500 Corvette Pace Car "is tremendous," but said he refused to get involved in helping people obtain the cars or resolving disputes between dealers and customers. "Once a car becomes the dealer's property," he said, "he can do anything he wants with it. He can even push it in the ocean."

***Exclusive options and colors separate the Pace Car from other 1978 Corvettes. The silver interior was offered only on the Pace Cars. Redesigned seats were scheduled to debut on the 1979 model but were rushed so they could be featured in the 1978 Indy 500 Pace Car. (Photo Courtesy John T. Perez / ClassicAndMuscle-Car.com)***

## The 62nd Indianapolis 500

***May 28, 1978***

Jim Rathmann was chosen to drive the official pace car for the fifth time. Rathmann was a former Indy driver who had raced in 14 Indy 500s and won the race in 1960. Rathmann would be known as the Florida Chevrolet dealer who came up with the idea to lease new Corvettes to the astronauts stationed at Cape Canaveral. Images of the Mercury 7 astronauts were featured in *Life* magazine, cementing the relationship between Corvettes and the early space program.

Al Unser Sr. won the race for his third time. Unser had a comfortable lead when he pitted with 20 laps to go. A front wing on his Lola race car was bent during a tire change and slowed him considerably. Second-place Tom Sneva nearly caught him, but Unser Sr. won by an 8-second margin.

***Former Indy 500 winner (1960) Jim Rathmann takes to the famous 2.5-mile Indianapolis Motor Speedway with the 1978 Corvette Indy 500 Pace Car. This was Chevrolet's first trip to the Brickyard; eventually, the Corvette would pace more races than any other model. (Photo Credit: IMS Photo)***

## 1986 INDY 500 CONVERTIBLE PACE CAR REPLICA

It is said that when Harley Earl first conceived of the Corvette he saw the pure fun these little roadsters could offer and set out to design a car to compete with the European sports cars, such as Jaguar's XK120, the Triumph TR2, and Austin Healys, which were growing in popularity in America. The all-American two-seater Corvette sports car was born as a convertible model only in 1953, and the drop-top model existed in the Corvette lineup through 1975, when the last one was produced.

The last few years leading up to that moment had been difficult. After the introduction of the C3 1968 convertibles, which saw 18,630 produced, sales dropped significantly after 1969 and declined to the low point in 1975 with only 4,629 convertibles produced.

***With the reintroduction of the convertible model in 1986, Chevrolet offered three colors of soft-tops. Black was the number-one choice with 3,685 produced, followed by white with 2,685, and saddle with 948. The yellow Corvettes, such as the official pace car, had either a black or white soft top. (Photo Courtesy Jeff Romm / Corvette Mike)***

### *The Demise of the Corvette Convertible*

Not only were federal regulations on fuel economy squeezing the once-mighty performance numbers from American automobiles, the government was actively looking to pass legislation to end production of open-air cars in the name of safety. That legislation never passed, but by that time manufacturers had seen the writing on the wall. Customers weren't buying convertibles like they once had, and the government saw the open-air models as unsafe. The final 1975 Corvette convertible was completed in July 1975, and the convertible Corvette model was officially dead.

During the 11 years that the Corvette was sold only as a coupe, the public's buying habits changed once again. The economy was good, and people were optimistic; soon convertibles would be back in vogue. The 1980s were all about enjoying yourself, and in no other car could you do that better than in a Corvette convertible.

| Base MSRP | $32,032 |
|---|---|
| Model Availability | Convertible |
| Engines | L98 |
| Features | Graphics, interior badge |
| Production Numbers | 6,502 |

***All 7,315 convertibles in 1986 were declared official pace cars, but the Corvettes that served at the track were exclusively yellow. Chevrolet produced 732 yellow convertibles in 1986, and 56 convertibles and 2 coupes were sent to the Speedway for festival and race duties. (Photo Courtesy Jeff Romm / Corvette Mike)***

### *Engineering the Corvette Convertible*

Chevrolet's engineers always contended that the C4 Corvette's design incorporated the convertible model from the beginning; some renderings from designer Jerry Palmer that were used to promote the early C4s featured a convertible C4 model.

Other than the packaging challenges that always present themselves when designing a convertible, the Corvette team was focused on preserving the stiffness of the car and decreasing the usual body flex caused by the lack of a roof structure. Engineers from the American Sunroof Company worked with the Corvette assembly plant in Bowling Green to beef up the convertible's frame, adding several crossmembers, braces, and structural reinforcements to various components on the frame. The result was a convertible body that weighed just 50 pounds more than the coupe's, but was much stiffer than the coupe version.

*The 1986 Corvette offered the first convertible model since 1975. And what a difference 11 years made to the price. The 1975 Corvette Convertible's MSRP was $6,550.10 compared to the new base 1986 Corvette Convertible that came in at $32,032. (Photo Courtesy Jeff Romm / Corvette Mike)*

*With many states requiring registered autos to have license plates on both front and back, the C4 Corvettes were designed with a front license plate holder integrated into the molded bumper. (Photo Courtesy Jeff Romm / Corvette Mike)*

### *Security and Safety Highlighted New Standard Options*

A startling fact for Chevrolet was that the rate of thefts for 1984 and 1985 Corvettes was 7 percent based on figures compiled by the Automobile Club of Michigan. In 1986, a new security feature called Vehicle Anti-Theft System (VATS) was implemented on all Corvettes as a standard option. The system consisted of a tiny chip with a specific electrical resistance embedded on the key and a hidden decoder in the key cylinder that unlocked the system to start the engine. Without the correct key, the VATS shut down the starter and fuel pump for 2 minutes before resetting. The new "pass-key" system dropped theft rate of 1986 Corvettes to just 1 percent, and by 1988 the number was near 0 percent.

Further enhancements to the 1986 models included the ABS braking system based on the Bosch ABS II as standard equipment. Rotational sensors monitored each wheel and a computer controller prevented the brakes from locking up in extreme braking conditions, allowing the driver to retain control of the vehicle.

In 1986, engineers switched the cast-iron cylinder heads to a lightweight aluminum version. That move, along with other weight-saving measures, dropped 125 pounds from the curb weight of the car, making it the first Corvette in 20 years to weigh in at less than 3,000 pounds.

Aesthetically, the exterior was nearly unchanged from when the C4 was introduced in 1983. One change distinguishing the 1986 models from the 1984 and 1985 was a new center-mounted rear brake light mandated by federal regulations. The convertibles were mounted in the rear fascia while the coupe models were mounted above the rear window.

### *Corvette Returns to the Brickyard*

To celebrate the convertible model's return to the Corvette lineup, a bright yellow Corvette convertible was used to pace the 1986 Indianapolis 500.

This was the Corvette's second round for serving as the official pace car, the first being the Corvette's silver anniversary in 1978. In that inaugural year, Chevrolet initially planned to build 1,000 Pace Car Replicas, and that number increased to 6,500 to meet demand from dealers and the public, some willing to spend double the MSRP of $13,653 to buy the car.

Perhaps to avoid that same experience in producing a limited-edition 1986 Indy 500 Pace Car, Chevrolet proclaimed all 1986 Corvette convertibles as Pace Car Editions. Every convertible received the dealer- or individual-installed Official Pace Car Indianapolis 500 graphics regardless of color.

### *Price and Production*

The 1986 Corvette convertible was the first Corvette to break through the $30,000 price barrier with a healthy MSRP of $32,032. That was $5,005 more than the coupe model's MSRP of $27,027.

Corvette prices increased nearly $9,500 in the five model years separating the 1982 Collector Edition ($22,537.59) and the 1986 Corvette con-

*The engine powering the 1986 Corvettes was the L98 350-ci V-8. The engine was rated at 230 hp and 330 ft-lbs of torque. Due to greater aerodynamic drag over the convertible top, the top speed was rated as 144 mph. The car recorded a nimble .85 g on the skid pad. (Photo Courtesy Jeff Romm / Corvette Mike)*

***The 100 Corvette Pace Cars and Festival Cars sent to the Indianapolis Motor Speedway were used throughout May 1986 by IMS executives, track officials, and media. The official pace car driver for 1986, General Chuck Yeager, was assigned to car number 61. (Photo Courtesy Bruce Bryan)***

***A graphics kit for the 1986 Corvette Pace Car was supplied to all buyers of the convertible models and consisted of two "Official Pace Car" door decals, two "70th Indianapolis 500, May 25, 1986" lower-door decals, and two Indianapolis 500 fender badges. (Photo Courtesy Jeff Romm / Corvette Mike)***

***The 1986 Corvette Convertible Pace Car is one of the most understated special editions in Corvette's 65 years. Other than the optionally installed exterior graphics, the Corvette Convertibles had a small dash plaque with the Indy 500 logo. The colorful badge is located on the center instrument panel to the right of the heat/AC controls. (Photo Courtesy Jeff Romm / Corvette Mike)***

vertible ($32,032). In comparison, the 1976 Corvette cost a mere $7,604.85.

Production of the convertible models started in January 1986. Chevrolet originally projected sales of the convertible to be between 5,000 and 6,000. At the end of 1986 production, sales exceeded those projections with a total of 7,315 convertibles produced. Convertibles made up 20.8 percent of Corvette production, which totaled 35,109 for the year.

Although all 1986 Corvette convertibles are considered Indy 500 Pace Car Replicas, only 732 were painted in Corvette Yellow, the same color as the actual pace cars that served in the 1986 race.

## The 70th Indianapolis 500

***May 25, 1986***

Retired general Chuck Yeager was chosen to drive the official pace car during the Indy 500. He was the first man to break the sound barrier and the first to fly at twice the speed of sound. Yeager's story, along with that of the original Mercury 7 astronauts, was told in the popular 1983 movie *The Right Stuff*.

The Indianapolis 500 was scheduled for Sunday, May 25, as the date on the door livery reads, but the start was delayed because of rain. It was run the following Saturday, May 31.

Bobby Rahal would take the win, finishing just ahead of Kevin Cogan and Rick Mears.

***Retired general Chuck Yeager had the right stuff to drive Corvette's Indy 500 Pace Car Convertible in 1986. General Yeager served as the official pace car driver in two Indy 500s, the 1986 race in the Corvette and 1988 in an Oldsmobile Cutlass Supreme. He is 1 of only 15 people to drive the pace car in two or more races. (Photo Credit: IMS Photo)***

## 1995 INDY 500 PACE CAR REPLICA

The fourth-generation Corvette marked its 11th anniversary with the 1995 model year. By now, plans were already in place for the C5 Corvette's debut in 1997, so overt changes were minimal while the team focused on refining the performance and quality of the cars.

The LT1 engine powering the 1995 Corvette was in its fourth year of production and was rated at 300 hp at 5,000 rpm and 340 ft-lbs of torque that propelled the Corvette to a 0–60 mph time of 5.1 seconds. Engineers worked to make the engine quieter and improve the performance of ethanol fuels in the fuel-injection system. Refinements in the 4-speed automatic transmission produced smoother shifting.

All 1995 Corvettes received the heavy-duty ZR-1 brakes and the new Bosch ABS/traction control system (ABS/ASR-5). All models received DeCarbon gas-charged shocks, which were less stiff than the previous shocks and provided an improved ride. Optional extended mobility tires, better known as run-flats, were offered for the low upgrade price of just $70.

The 1995 models did get a minor exterior change with new gill-type air vents on the front quarter panels. Additional refinements addressed the build quality of the cars. Rattles and squeaks were addressed with the use of adhesive tape, the leather seats received a stronger "French seam," and the CD player was reinforced to prevent skipping.

The big news for the 1995 Corvette: It was selected to be the official pace car at the 79th Indianapolis 500, the 3rd time for the sports car and the 10th time for Chevrolet. Also for the 3rd time, Chevrolet offered a replica Indy 500 Pace Car for sale.

### *1995 Indy 500 Pace Car Features*

The 1995 Indy 500 Pace Car made its public debut at the Indianapolis Auto Show just after Christmas 1994. Chevrolet announced that a limited-edition Corvette Pace Car would be reproduced for the public. Only 527 would be built, making these the second-lowest-production special edition, second only to the 50 Malcolm Konner Corvettes in 1986.

***Powering the 1995 Corvette Indy 500 Pace Car was GM's Gen II small-block V-8. The 350-ci LT1 was introduced in 1992 and was rated at 300 hp at 5,000 rpm and 350 ft-lbs of torque at 4,000 rpm. Official performance figures included 0–60 mph in 5.1 seconds on top of a 17/24 mpg fuel economy estimate. (Photo Courtesy Jeff Romm / Corvette Mike)***

| Base MSRP | $46,481 |
|---|---|
| Model Availability | Convertible |
| Engines | LT1 |
| Features | Custom exterior and interior colors, graphics, wheels |
| Production Numbers | 527 |

***For only the third time in its history, Corvette paced the Indianapolis 500 with a nearly stock LT1-powered Convertible. Chevrolet celebrated the event with its third special-edition Pace Car Replica. RPO Z4Z was priced at $2,816 and was limited to 527 convertibles. The Pace Car retailed for $46,481. (Photo Courtesy Jeff Romm / Corvette Mike)***

***The 1995 distinctive Purple Metallic and Arctic White Indy 500 design was one of the boldest Corvette designs to date. Bowling Green had last painted a two-tone Corvette in 1987. The Pace Car's flowing ribbon design extended along the doors and rear deck while understated race details ran along the door under the beltline. (Photo Courtesy Jeff Romm / Corvette Mike)***

The 1995 Indy 500 Pace Cars featured the Dark Purple Metallic over Arctic White paint with the flowing ribbon-styled graphics along the side of the car. All Pace Cars were convertibles that came with a white convertible top and silver ZR-1 wheels. Also standard to the Pace Car package was the automatic transmission, but the MN6 6-speed manual transmission could be selected with no difference in price.

The cockpit featured black leather sport bucket seats with purple inserts and the Indy 500 logos embroidered on the headrests. Electronic air-conditioning and the Delco/Bose audio system were standard.

### Price and Production

The base price of the 1995 Corvette Indy 500 Pace Car (RPO Z4Z) was listed $2,816 above the convertible model's MSRP of $43,665 for a base price of $46,481. Almost all options were available for the Pace Car, and a fully loaded model could cost more than $51,500.

The Pace Cars were built during March and April 1995. The first 50 Corvette Pace Cars had a black-only interior while all the later cars had the black/purple seats.

Of the 527 Corvettes produced, 504 were built for US customers and 23 were listed as exports. The Pace Car was not assigned its own VIN sequence, and instead the special edition was mixed with all other 1995 convertibles. Chevrolet allocated one Corvette Pace Car Replica to each of the top Corvette dealers.

***The purple two-tone theme was carried into the cockpit of the Indy 500 replicas with two-tone purple and black leather seats. An embroidered headrest featured the logo for the 79th Indianapolis 500. (Photo Courtesy Jeff Romm / Corvette Mike)***

### Life as an Official Pace Car

Chevrolet sent 87 Corvettes to the Indianapolis 500 to serve as track cars for officials and drivers. Of those, three were designated as official pace cars. Two of the three official pace cars came with the automatic transmission, but the pace car that was used was a 6-speed manual. The third pace car was driven by Chevrolet general manager Jim Perkins, his third time leading the pack at Indy.

In addition to their safety-mandated roll bars and strobe lights, the three official Corvette Pace Cars had their exhausts opened up, which gave the 300-hp LT1 more power, as well as making them louder. The suspension was stiffened by modifying the stock springs, and the cars were lowered an inch.

***The 1995 Indy 500 Pace Car's graphics were applied at the assembly plant prior to shipment to the dealer. The window shield decal and the event logo on the lower door were packaged separately to be installed by the dealer at the buyer's discretion. (Photo Courtesy Jeff Romm / Corvette Mike)***

***To prepare the official Corvette Pace Car for track duty, Chevrolet added the USAC-mandated roll bar on the convertible. This was covered from the rear with a special body-color hoop tonneau integrated with the safety strobe lights. (Photo Courtesy Keith Cornett)***

## The 79th Indianapolis 500

***May 28, 1995***

Chevrolet general manager Jim Perkins served as the official pace car driver for his third time. Perkins was a strong supporter of the Corvette program during his tenure and was instrumental in keeping it alive. He was inducted into the National Corvette Museum's Hall of Fame in 1999.

The 1995 Indianapolis 500 had its share of drama, including Roger Penske's failure to make the race for the first time since 1969.

With 10 laps to go and the field going to green, Scott Goodyear jumped the restart and passed the Corvette Pace Car as it was pulling into the pits. Goodyear was assessed a stop-and-go penalty but refused to pit, claiming the light was green. He got the black flag on lap 195, and Jacques Villeneuve won the Indianapolis 500. Following the race, the replay showed the light was yellow when Goodyear passed the pace car.

***Chevrolet general manager Jim Perkins drove the pace car in three Indy 500s (1990, 1993, 1995) before retiring in 1995. During a time when budgets were tight, he was a tireless supporter of the Corvette program. He was inducted into the Corvette Hall of Fame in 1999. (Photo Credit: IMS Photo)***

***The 1995 Corvette Indy 500 Pace Car was the eighth special-edition Corvette produced since the first Indy 500 Pace Car and the 25th Anniversary Edition were offered in 1978. Other than the 50 Malcom Konner 1986 dealer specials, the 1995 Corvette Pace Cars had the lowest production of any special edition at the time with 527 produced. (Photo Courtesy Jeff Romm / Corvette Mike)***

***Of the 527 Indy Pace Cars built, 87 of the first 145 were sent to the Indianapolis Motor Speedway where 3 served as official pace cars and the rest as festival/track cars, used by IMS officials and other VIPs. After the race, the cars were sold through Chevrolet's dealer network. (Photo Courtesy Keith Cornett)***

## 1998 INDY 500 PACE CAR REPLICA

Following the rollout of the C5 coupe in 1997, Chevrolet reintroduced a convertible model to the lineup in 1998. The 1998 convertible was very well received and won the prestigious 1998 North American Car of the Year award as well as being named 1998's *Motor Trend* Car of the Year.

The new C5 Corvette coupes were a hit and, despite a shortened production run during the inaugural year, were quick sellers. Chevrolet had designed the C5 Corvette to be a convertible first, making sure the car was structurally rigid to support the performance characteristics of the Corvette with an open-top car. The secondary concern was the packaging for the convertible top and associated hardware. In the end, the convertible model weighed just 1 pound more than the coupe. It wasn't as rigid as the coupe body, but it was close. The new convertible came in 114 pounds lighter than the 1996 convertible but was four times more torsionally sound than the previous generation.

One aspect of the new model was brought about through extensive consumer research and design testing: Buyers wanted a convertible and storage space. Chevrolet delivered with a 1998 convertible featuring an actual rear trunk; it was the first time since 1962 that an exterior trunk was on the sports car. It wasn't small either. The C5's capacity came in at 13.9 cubic feet.

Another design feature that came from the early Corvettes was the waterfall panel flowing between the two seats. The design showed off the Corvette crossed-flags logo that was also redesigned specifically for the C5 Corvettes.

### *Active Handling Comes to the Corvette*

The introduction of the Active Handling Chassis Control System was one of the exciting new options for the 1998 Corvette. Using a yaw sensor, steering angle sensor, and a lateral accelerometer, and working in conjunction with the antilock braking system (ABS), the new design enhanced the Corvette's suspension with additional accident-avoidance capabilities.

The system also included a Competitive Driving mode for autocross or other track-only events. With the Corvette running and stopped, this competition mode was activated by holding down the active handling off switch for 5 seconds. Once in competition mode, ABS and active handling remained active while traction control was turned off.

| | |
|---|---|
| Base MSRP | $49,464 |
| Model Availability | Convertible |
| Engines | LS1 |
| Features | Custom exterior and interior colors, graphics, wheels |
| Production Numbers | 1,163 |

*There's bold styling and then there's "in-your-face," as Chevrolet described the 1998 Pace Car's Radar Blue exterior with bright yellow wheels. If that's not enough, a graphics package featuring a flowing checkered-flag motif ran down the sides while twin graduated stripes were installed on the hood's power bulge. (Photo Courtesy Keith Cornett)*

***The 1998 convertibles were filled with technological enhancements and upgrades from hydroformed steel frames to the new active handling system. But many customers were excited that the C5 convertible featured the first exterior trunk on a Corvette since 1962. (Photo Courtesy Keith Cornett)***

***The 1998 Corvette Pace Cars all featured Chevrolet's new Active Handling Chassis Control System (RPO JL4), which was introduced halfway through the 1998 model year. The system selectively used the four individual brakes to correct oversteer or understeer in wet or extreme handling conditions. (Photo Courtesy Bruce Bryan)***

### *1998 Corvette Indy 500 Pace Car Features*

The Corvette convertible was selected to pace the 82nd running of the Indianapolis 500. This was the fourth time for Corvette to pace the 500 and would also be the fourth time for Chevrolet to offer a replica pace car edition for sale. The official announcement was made in November 1997 at the Specialty Equipment Marketing Association (SEMA) automotive trade show in Las Vegas by Mary Hulman George of the Indianapolis Motor Speedway and Chevrolet general manager John Middlebrook.

Perhaps no one design in the Corvette's long history elicits as many strong opinions from Corvette enthusiasts as the 1998 Indy 500 Pace Car. The paint scheme featured a Radar Blue exterior with Bright Yellow painted wheels and graphics. The factory-applied yellow graphics package featured a checkered flag motif that stretched from the Corvette's front quarter panel vent to the rear of the car and over its tail. In the official press release, Chevrolet called it an "in-your-face" and "attention-getting" design!

Inside, the Bright Yellow sport seats contrasted with the black interior. Yellow stitching adorned the sport seats as well as the black leather steering wheel, shift knob, and shift boot.

Like all 1998 Corvettes, the Pace Car was powered by the 5.7L LS1 346-ci V-8 engine that produced 345 hp and 350 ft-lbs of torque.

The Indy 500 Pace Car was ordered with RPO Z4Z. Its standard options included a black convertible top, the Delco AM/FM radio/CD player with Bose speaker system, electronic dual-zone heating and air-conditioning, dual-power leather adjustable bucket sport seats with memory package, and floor mats. Included in the package was the active handling system, a $500 option.

The 4-speed automatic transmission came standard with the performance axle, but buyers could choose the optional 6-speed manual transmission for $815 more.

***The official Indy 500 Pace Cars featured hoop tonneaus molded on the decklid, which helped to blend in the mandated roll bars and safety harness for the convertible's occupants. Inside the tonneaus were rear-facing safety strobe lights and the fire suppression system. (Photo Courtesy Keith Cornett)***

### *Production and Price*

Total production for the 1998 Indy 500 Pace Car was 1,163. That figure included the 1,158 production cars and the 5 pilot cars built in November 1997. Of the total, 1,111 were offered in the United States, 15 went to Canada, and the final 37 were exports. A further breakdown shows there were 616 MX0 automatic transmission Pace Cars versus 547 MN6 6-speed manual transmission Pace Cars built.

The Pace Car wasn't cheap either. The convertible MSRP was $44,425 and the Z4Z Pace Car RPO added $5,039 for the automatic version or $5,804 for the manual transmission version.

One of the more subtle details on the Pace Car can be found on the very bold yellow painted five-spoke wheels. Most see the bright yellow wheels and miss the thin outline of aluminum on the outside lip of the 17- and 18-inch wheels. The center cap's lug nut covers are yellow and accented by a carbon fiber pattern ring that surrounds a polished silver center with the outline of the C5 crossed-flags logo. (Photo Courtesy Keith Cornett)

*Retail production of the 1998 Corvettes began on January 5, 1998. Of the first 45 Pace Cars produced, 37 were for export outside of the United States and Canada. The 15th and final Pace Car for Canada was completed on January 14. The rest were for domestic use, and production of the final Pace Car was completed on February 27, 1998. (Photo Courtesy Keith Cornett)*

The design team of John Cafaro and Randy Wittine was said to have pulled out all the stops to make sure the Pace Car would stand out during motorsport's biggest event. Most would say they were successful. Cafaro once commented that "as a street car it's a lot to digest," but enthusiasts loved it, and Chevrolet built 1,163 Pace Car Replicas. (Photo Courtesy Keith Cornett)

Like Graceland for Elvis fans, the Indy 500 and the Indianapolis Motor Speedway is a must-visit destination for Pace Cars owners. It's not uncommon to see Corvettes such as this 1998 Indy 500 Pace Car parked outside the Indianapolis Motor Speedway Museum. (Photo Courtesy Keith Cornett)

### *"The Greatest Spectacle in Racing"*

The 1998 Corvette Pace Car used officially in the race was slightly modified from the replica models. The LS1 V-8 was increased from 345 to 370 hp thanks to a freer-flowing intake manifold and a low-restriction exhaust system that netted the additional 25 hp. The ride height was lowered to improve handling, and a roll bar was integrated behind each seat, which also contained rear-facing strobe lights.

A total of 105 Corvette Pace Car Replicas were used at the 82nd Indianapolis 500. Following tradition, the winning driver of the race, Eddie Cheever Jr., was awarded one of the track pace cars (Track Car 33).

It was rumored that Track Car 71 was driven during the parade lap by Wil Cooksey, Corvette plant manager at Bowling Green, Kentucky. Riding shotgun with him was none other than Dave Hill, Corvette chief engineer.

## The 82nd Indianapolis 500

***May 24, 1998***

Professional golfer and Chevrolet spokesperson Greg "the Shark" Norman was selected to drive the official pace car and participated in making the practice runs at the track. But he had to pull out at the last minute because of shoulder surgery. Parnelli Jones, winner of the 1963 Indy 500, replaced Norman in the 11th hour.

The start of the race was marred by a morning rain that delayed the green flag by 35 minutes. As the track was drying, a dog got loose on turn four and officials gave chase halfway around the famous oval until it was caught in turn two.

Eddie Cheever won his first and only Indianapolis 500, edging Buddy Lazier by 3 seconds.

***Although he participated in practice and the official PR photos, Greg Norman was unable to fulfill the official pace car duties after having surgery on his shoulder. Former Indy 500 winner Parnelli Jones (1963) took over at the last minute. Parnelli was the first driver to qualify at greater than 150 mph (1962) and was named Rookie of the Year in 1961, sharing the honor with Bobby Marshman. (Photo Credit: IMS Photo)***

## 2007 INDY 500 PACE CAR REPLICA

The mid-2000s were filled with new Corvettes as Chevrolet marked the beginning of the sixth generation of Corvette with coupe and convertible models launched in 2005 and the 505-hp Corvette Z06 joining them in 2006. Now that the primary models had been launched, designers turned to refining and personalization of the Corvettes for the 2007 model year. They still had a couple of surprises in store for enthusiasts in the form of two special-edition Corvettes for 2007.

| | |
|---|---|
| Base MSRP | $66,995 |
| Model Availability | Convertible |
| Engines | LS2 |
| Features | Graphics, engine cover, interior trim, embroidered seats |
| Production Numbers | 1,163 |

***The 2007 Corvette Indy 500 Pace Car was the first replica produced for resale since the 1998 race even though Chevrolet had paced the prestigious race four other times since the last replica was offered. The wait was worth it, though, as the 2007 Pace Car design on top of the Atomic Orange is one of the favorites of Pace Car enthusiasts. (Photo Courtesy Frank Smychynsky)***

The Atomic Orange exterior of the 2007 Indy 500 Pace Car was carried to the interior and under the hood, as well. The 2007 Pace Cars received a special Atomic Orange center console trim cover and button surrounds on the dash while the standard black engine covers were swapped for Atomic Orange versions. (Photo Courtesy Keith Cornett)

The 2007 Corvette Indy 500 Pace Car's gold flowing ribbons exit the vent and wash along the side of the car while the door features the Indy 500 shield identifying the race's date and time. (Photo Courtesy Frank Smychynsky)

## New-for-2007 Corvettes

The interiors were addressed as new options for 2007, including two-tone leather seats with the 2LT and 3LT trim packages. The seats were offered in Red, Cashmere or Titanium and featured embroidered crossed-flags logos and contrasting stitching. The contrasting interior color was also carried through the door panels, instrument panel, and center console.

Buttons on the steering wheel controlled the optional Bose audio system, and the glove compartment gained extra capacity due to the reduction of the air bag. For convertible owners, the power soft top was included as standard equipment with the 3LT package. Magnetic Selective Ride Control (RPO F55) now included the heavy-duty brakes with cross-drilled rotors that previously were offered only on the Z51 Performance Package.

The 2007 model year introduced a new catalog of GM-approved accessories that were ordered and installed by dealers. These accessories included a hood blanket, racing stripes, body side moldings, stainless-steel mesh inserts for the front grille and side covers, premium floor mats, and a protective cover for the rear fascia.

## Corvette to Pace the Indianapolis 500 for Record Ninth Time

The Chevrolet Corvette was selected in 2007 to pace the Indianapolis 500. This was the ninth time that Corvette served as the official pace car, and it was also the first time in nine years (since 1998) that Chevrolet offered an Indy 500 Pace Car Replica to the public.

The 2007 Indy 500 Pace Car Replicas were all convertibles wearing Atomic Orange with gold ribbon graphics flowing from the front quarter panel vents and along the sides of the hood. Also found on those fenders were the wing and wheel Indy 500 logos, while the official event graphic was featured prominently on the doors. The Chevrolet bowtie logo made a rare appearance on a Corvette with the graphic placed in gold on the hood.

While previous Indy 500 pace cars required extensive modification to perform their on-track duties, the performance-bred Corvette required only the mandated safety equipment and strobe lights. The 400-hp LS2 V-8 provided plenty of motivation to stay ahead of the pack around the Brickyard. (Photo Courtesy Frank Smychynsky)

All the Pace Cars had black convertible tops and the Z06 rear spoiler and were outfitted with new aluminum split-spoke wheels in Sterling Silver. The door handles were finished in Atomic Orange.

The interior featured a unique Atomic Orange center console trim plate as well as pods surrounding the gauge cluster. The ebony leather seats were embroidered with a full-color logo depicting the 2007 Indy 500 logo. Under the hood, the engine was dressed in Atomic Orange fuel rail covers.

Powered by the LS2 400-hp V-8 with 400 ft-lbs of torque, the Indy 500 Pace Car came with a 6-speed manual transmission and the Z51 Performance Package as standard options, along with the Bose navigation system with OnStar.

## Pricing and Production

The official MSRP for the 2007 Indy 500 Pace Car convertible was $66,995 with the standard options. Upgrading to the paddle-shift 6-speed

***Chevrolet produced the 500 Corvette Indy 500 Replicas after the race had been run. With a premium price of $66,994, the car was notoriously hard to sell when most enthusiasts knew about the 2008 Corvette's 30-hp increase with the new LS3 engine. (Photo Courtesy Keith Cornett)***

automatic added $1,250, bringing the MSRP to $68,245. Buyers could opt for Museum Delivery ($490) at the National Corvette Museum.

With only 500 Indy Pace Cars produced, the limited edition accounted for 1.2 percent of all 2007 Corvette production and 4.6 percent of all convertibles. Pace Car production started on March 1, 2007, with the first 57 Corvettes built in two days. Chevrolet sent these 57 Indy 500 Pace Car Replicas to Indianapolis Motor Speedway as the official track and festival committee vehicles. The remaining 443 Corvette Pace Cars started assembly on June 4, 2007, and ended on June 21, 2007.

The Corvettes were allocated a minimum of one to each of the top-selling dealers with the criteria that they must have sold at least 24 or more Corvettes during the previous year. Some dealers received multiple allocations.

### *Official Festival Indy 500 Pace Cars*

Chevrolet sent the first batch of 500 Indy 500 Pace Car Replicas to Indianapolis Motor Speedway as the official track and festival committee vehicles. VIPs and others drove the cars to the official events that led up to the running of the Indianapolis 500. While performing their duties as official festival pace cars, most got to perform parade laps around the Indianapolis Motor Speedway.

The 57 Corvettes sent to the track for the 2007 Indy 500 were all 6-speed automatics. Once at the track, they received special Chevrolet windshield banners and were assigned their official track car numbers. The first seven cars were called "track cars" and these included the official pace car, the backup pace cars, and several cars for the Indy 500 leadership. The remaining 50 Corvettes were used as festival cars. Each replica officially used at the track received an Indy 500 Festival Parade 50th Anniversary decal on the rear fascia and a hologram sticker on the inside of the windshield with the car's official festival number.

## THE 91ST INDIANAPOLIS 500

***May 27, 2007***

Actor, race car team co-owner, and race car driver Patrick Dempsey served as the official driver of the Corvette Pace Car. Although best known as Dr. Derek Shepard (aka McDreamy) on the ABC television show *Grey's Anatomy*, Dempsey was co-owner of Vision Racing. Several years later, he would co-drive in major racing events, including the 24 Hours of Le Mans and the Rolex 24 at Daytona. Dempsey once declared his willingness to walk away from acting so he could pursue racing on a full-time basis.

The 91st Indianapolis 500 started at 1:11 p.m. and ran until a heavy rain fell, halting the field at 113 laps. The rain fell for nearly three hours, and once the track was dried the field restarted at 6:00 p.m. After 160 laps and with the skies threatening once again, Dario Franchitti held the lead when Marco Andretti's car flipped after contact with Dan Wheldon, which also caught up Buddy Rice. A heavy storm rolled in again before the track could be cleared and officials called the race with 166 laps run. Franchitti was declared the winner.

***Although Indy 500 Pace Car driver Patrick Dempsey is best known for his acting, he is also regarded as a dedicated racing enthusiast. Dempsey led the field of 33 drivers during the world's largest single-day spectator sporting event. (Photo Credit: IMS Photo)***

***Chevrolet committed to build 500 Corvette Indy 500 Pace Car Replicas with most of the series built after the race had been run. Chevrolet built a fixed number of Pace Cars ahead of sales, and once interest in the cars waned, many dealers offered substantial discounts to move the cars off the lot. (Photo Courtesy Keith Cornett)***

Once the race concluded, the festival Corvettes were sent to a select number of dealers, where they were sold as pre-owned with the remaining balance of the 5-year/100,000-mile warranty; however, the cars were still untitled. These cars usually come with unique documentation and other details that show they were officially part of the Greatest Spectacle in Racing.

## 2008 INDY 500 PACE CAR REPLICA

Chevrolet anticipated 2008 to be a great year for Corvettes and, by the numbers, the model year was a success, despite tumbling sales in the late half of the 2008 calendar year amid the economic uncertainty that turned into the Great Recession. In 2007, the model surpassed 40,000 in sales; the 2008 model saw 35,310 sold, a respectable number by all accounts. Chevrolet had laid out an ambitious update for the 2008 Corvettes as well as including an engine update and several special editions.

The C6 Corvette received an engine upgrade in 2008, and the new 430-hp 6.0L LS3 was now the most-powerful base engine (on paper) in Corvette's long history. The 30th Anniversary Indy 500 Corvette Pace Car had no problem leading the pack of Indy cars during the race. (Photo Courtesy Michael Semon of Buyavette.net)

| Base MSRP | $59,090 (coupe), $68,160 (convertible) |
|---|---|
| Model Availability | Coupe, Convertible |
| Engines | LS3 |
| Features | Graphics, embroidered seats, signature edition |
| Production Numbers | 500 |

### *Power Upgrades for the 2008 Corvette*

For the 2008 model year, Chevrolet once again went to work on the venerable pushrod small-block V-8 and introduced an upgrade to the previous 400-hp 6.0L LS2. The new 6.2L LS3, capable of 430 hp and 424 ft-lbs of torque at 5,900 rpm, became the new base engine for both the coupe and convertible Corvette. The LS3 was designed to operate at a lower compression ratio that allows the use of E85 ethanol fuel (a priority for General Motors was to make all its vehicles capable of running on E85). Yet the new V-8 with a 6-speed paddle-shift automatic was capable of 0–60 in 4.3 seconds with a top speed of 190 mph.

At the other end of the car, Chevrolet introduced the optional Dual Mode Exhaust System (RPO NPP), a version for the coupe and convertible that was similar to but had noticeable differences from the Z06 system. The dual-mode exhaust featured a 2.5-inch-diameter exhaust and used vacuum-actuated butterfly valves that stayed closed during normal driving and opened for maximum performance once the RPM and throttle position reached a predetermined level. With the NPP exhaust power rose from 430 hp to 436 hp. Not only did owners like the increase in performance, the aggressive sound from the exhaust system was music to their ears!

In 1978, Chevrolet celebrated its first time pacing the Indianapolis 500 by offering the 1978 Indy 500 Pace Car Replica. Chevrolet paced the Indianapolis 500 30 years later for a record 10th time. To celebrate that milestone, it offered the 2008 30th Anniversary Indy 500 Pace Car Replica for sale to the public. (Photo Courtesy Michael Semon of Buyavette.net)

*Chevrolet showed off its new-for-2008 two-tone Titanium/Black seats for the 2008 Indy 500 Pace Car. Featured prominently on the headrests was a full-color wing and wheel Indianapolis 500 logo. (Photo Courtesy Michael Semon of Buyavette.net)*

Corvette designers also went to work on the interior of the car, offering a custom leather-wrapped interior. The two-tone leather-wrapped package covered the upper and lower instrument panel, door pads, and seats in two new colors, Linen and Sienna. All Corvettes also came standard with OnStar and XM Satellite Radio, along with auto-dimming rear-view mirrors and an audio-input jack for hooking up iPods and other audio devices for playback through the car's stereo.

Finally, Chevrolet offered not one but three very different special editions during 2008. In addition to the 2008 Indy 500 Pace Car Replicas, Chevrolet also offered the 2008 427 Edition Corvette Z06 (better known as the Wil Cooksey Z06) and the special ZHZ Edition Corvettes that served as rental cars for Hertz. All three special editions planned for 2008 sold out.

### 2008 Indy 500 Pace Car Replica Features

The 2008 Indy 500 Pace Cars were shown on December 27, 2007, at a special unveiling ceremony during the Indianapolis Auto Show. Executives from General Motors and Chevrolet were joined by elected officials and representatives from the Indianapolis Motor Speedway. Chevrolet made sure a large contingent of Corvette fans were present to witness the historic unveiling. One of the special guests in attendance was the 1978 Indy 500 Pace Car number 0001 that was brought down from the GM Heritage Center.

For the first time in history, two different models served as the official pace car for the same race. Two Corvette Pace Cars, one representing the future and the other a tribute to the past, were selected to pace the 92nd running of the Indianapolis 500. It was also announced that two-time Indy 500 winner Emerson Fittipaldi would serve as the official pace car driver.

A customized Z06 E85 Concept allowed General Motors to promote its progress in alternative fuel solutions while the second Corvette paid homage to the first Corvette to ever pace the Indy 500, the 1978 Corvette Pace Car. A 30th Anniversary Commemorative Edition, complete with black and silver graphics, was available as both a coupe and a convertible and was limited to a production run of 500 Corvettes.

*The Chevrolet Corvette paced the 2008 Indianapolis 500 for a record 10th time. The Corvette had been on a roll since 2000, having been chosen as the official pace car in six of eight Indy 500 races. (Photo Courtesy Michael Semon of Buyavette.net)*

*Two different convertible top colors, gray and black, were offered on the 2008 Pace Car. The [illegible]4 Indy 500 Corvette convertibles built after the running of the 92nd Indianapolis 500 on May 25, 2008, had a black top. (Photo Courtesy Michael Semon of Buyavette.net)*

The 2008 Indianapolis 500 marked Corvette's 10th appearance at the Greatest Spectacle in Racing, and it was a record 5th consecutive race with the Corvette serving pace car duties. It was also the 2nd year in a row that Chevrolet offered a limited-edition pace car to the public.

### 2008 30th Anniversary Commemorative Edition Pace Car

While the Gold Rush Green E85 concept Z06 was intriguing as a one-off concept that promoted the ability of the high-performance Corvette to use alternative fuels, such as ethanol, it was the 30th Anniversary model that had Corvette enthusiasts excited. The 2008 Indy Pace Car Replica was one of the most serious-looking Pace Car designs incorporated since the original scheme 30 years before. For the first time, buyers could select between the coupe and the convertible as well as order either a 6-speed manual or paddle-shift automatic. The Pace Cars included the Z51 suspension and NPP

### BREAKDOWN OF 2008 INDY 500 PACE CAR REPLICAS

| Model | Auto | Manual | Total |
|---|---|---|---|
| Coupe | 77 | 157 | **234** |
| Convertible | 71 | 195 | **266** |

*Emerson Fittipaldi visited the National Corvette Museum and then headed over to the Bowling Green assembly plant, where he signed the console lids and numbered each of the Indy 500 Pace Cars. Chevrolet offered two signature series Corvettes in 2008. The other was the 2008 427 Edition signed by longtime Corvette assembly plant manager Wil Cooksey. (Photo Courtesy Michael Semon of Buyavette.net)*

Performance Exhaust.

In addition to the black and silver Pace Car livery, the replicas featured new forged chrome five-spoke aluminum wheels, a Corvette Z06 rear spoiler, and Indy 500 logo fender badges. Inside, the Indianapolis 500 logo was embroidered on the two-tone Titanium/Black leather seats. Convertibles received either a gray or black convertible top.

Each of the Indy 500 Pace Cars was personally signed by Emerson Fittipaldi. His signature and the sequence number of the car reside on the inside of the center console armrest.

#### Pricing and Production

RPO Z4Z cost a little more than $13,000 for the coupe; the convertible

*The Corvettes that served as the actual pace car for their race still come out to the Indianapolis Motor Speedway for select events. Here, the two official 2008 Corvette Pace Cars are getting ready to lead a Corvette Club for laps around the famous 2.5-mile oval. (Photo Courtesy Bruce Bryan)*

## THE 92ND INDIANAPOLIS 500

***May 25, 2008***

Two-time Indy 500 winner and Formula One Champion Emerson Fittipaldi was named to drive the Corvette Pace Car. He piloted the E85 Concept Z06 for the first half of the race and the 30th Anniversary Commemorative Edition car for the second half. The call to start your engines for the 92nd Indianapolis 500 came just after 1:00 p.m. on Sunday, May 25, 2008.

The first half was marred with several cautions from single car accidents. Polesitter Scott Dixon traded the lead with teammate Dan Wheldon throughout the first half until a charge by Tony Kanaan just before the halfway mark. Kanaan took the lead and set a record for leading a lap in seven consecutive Indy 500 races. Unfortunately, he got too high and lost control.

In the second half, it came down to a race between Scott Dixon, Marco Andretti, and Vitor Meira. An incident between Ryan Briscoe and Danika Patrick on pit lane knocked them both out of the race, and they were both fined $100,000 for the incident. Dixon went on to win with Vitor Meira just 1.7 seconds behind. The New Zealander was the 19th pole winner to win the Indianapolis 500.

*With General Motors going all in on its line of flex-fuel vehicles, the carmaker turned to Brazilian racer Emerson Fittipaldi to drive the first Indy 500 Corvette Pace Car powered by E85, an ethanol-based alternative fuel. For the second half of the race, he drove the 30th Anniversary Corvette Pace Car. (Photo Credit: IMS Photo)*

was priced at $13,825 more than the base convertible. MSRP for the coupe started at $59,090 and for the convertible $68,160. The run was limited to 500 cars, and the limited edition eventually sold out.

Production of the Indy 500 Pace Car Replicas started March 4 and ended June 6, a week after the race was completed. Knowing that some cars would be delivered after the race, those convertibles received black tops instead of the standard gray tops that came with cars prior to the race. In all, 44 convertibles received the black convertible top.

Of the total 500 Pace Car Replicas built, 449 stayed in the United States, and the rest were exported. Export totals included 25 to Europe, 21 to Canada, and 5 for the Middle East.

*For the first time, Chevrolet offered a limited-edition Pace Car available either as a coupe or convertible model. The convertible outsold the coupe in quantity and in the number equipped with a manual transmission. (Photo Courtesy Michael Semon of Buyavette.net)*

## THE 2008 CORVETTE Z06 E85 CONCEPT AND EMERSON FITTIPALDI

In the mid-2000s, Chevrolet was pushing its alternative fuel–capable vehicles, including those that ran E85 ethanol fuels, a renewable alternative fuel produced from crops, mainly corn. E85 is a blend of 85 percent ethanol and 15 percent gasoline, and its benefits include reduced emissions of greenhouse gasses and a reduced dependence on petroleum. In 2008, General Motors was the undisputed leader in E85 production with more than 2.5 million E85-capable models sold. The Corvette Z06 E85 Concept was the perfect way for the automaker to show that its alternative fuel technology could be adapted to even the most demanding platforms.

Emerson Fittipaldi was chosen as the official pace car driver not only for his two victories at the Indianapolis 500 (in 1989 and 1993), but also because the Brazilian native was an ambassador of ethanol. The two-time Indy champion has also promoted the idea of racing with ethanol-based fuels as a showcase for environmentally conscious racing technology. Brazil, the fifth largest country, has nearly weaned itself from importing oil, as ethanol has become an important source of energy production.

During the Pace Car's official unveiling ceremony, Chevrolet's general manager Ed Peper said, "As an ethanol refiner in his native Brazil, Emerson Fittipaldi is the fitting Chevrolet champion to help support GM's efforts with E85 and celebrate 30 years of the Corvette pacing the Indianapolis 500."

*The 2008 Corvette Z06 E85 Concept is finished in a unique color-shifting exterior called Gold Rush Green, which changes from various hues of gold and green depending on the viewing angle of the car and the available light. The Z06 Pace Car shares the 30th Anniversary Pace Car's subtle checkered-flag motif along the sides of the car. (Photo Courtesy Keith Cornett)*

*The 2008 Indy 500 Pace Car featured bold green striping on the sides and hood as a nod to Emerson Fittipaldi's support of green energy, particularly ethanol, in his native Brazil. In addition to his personal signature on the center console lid, his name and signature appeared on the Pace Car's rear quarter panels. (Photo Courtesy Michael Semon of Buyavette.net)*

CHAPTER 3

# COMMEMORATIVE AND TRIBUTE CORVETTES

Chevrolet's first foray into producing special-edition Corvettes started in 1978 with anniversary and pace car edition. Later, more model years were added to these two popular categories. Soon after, the GM team began using the Corvette to pay tribute to people and events associated with the model.

Over the years, but very sparingly, Chevrolet has acknowledged the contributions of several people by commemorating their accomplishments with a special-edition Corvette. The later commemoratives were not only limited in production, they also featured several signature editions by the people honored. Chevrolet also commemorated various achievements by its factory racing team. Most notable are several C6 commemorative Corvettes that pay tribute to Corvette's success at the 24 Hours of Le Mans.

***Chevrolet utilized special- and limited-edition Corvettes to honor and pay tribute to those who helped make it an American Icon. This 2009 GT1 Championship Edition celebrated the achievements of the Corvette Racing team. (Photo Courtesy Charley Robertson)***

## 1986 MALCOLM KONNER COMMEMORATIVE EDITION

The 1986 Corvette marked the return of the convertible model, the first since 1975. The C4 model was in its third year and sales were very robust with 35,109 units sold.

Ask Corvette enthusiasts to name the two special editions built in 1986 and maybe, just maybe, you'll hear "Indy 500 Pace Car." That's an easy guess as Chevrolet designated every convertible in 1986 as an Indy 500 Pace Car Replica, despite the fact that hardly any 1986 convertibles are found today wearing the optional Indy 500 Pace Car door graphics. But if someone answers "Malcolm Konner Edition," you'll know you're talking with a Corvette trivia master.

### *Malcolm Konner Chevrolet*

Malcolm Konner Chevrolet was one of the premier Corvette dealerships from the 1950s through the early 1990s when the dealership was sold. Malcolm Konner opened his first dealership at the age of 21 selling DeSotos, Plymouths, and GMC trucks in Caldwell, New Jersey. In 1955, the Chevrolet dealer in town went out of business and Konner purchased the dealership, naming it Malcolm Konner Chevrolet. The dealership also offered British sports cars (Triumph, MG, and Jaguar) in a separate showroom on Route 17 in Paramus, New Jersey, alongside the Corvettes. Eventually, the British cars were dropped and the showroom became the exclusive home to Corvette.

The dealership specialized in Corvettes, and vintage ads show the catchphrase "New Jersey's headquarters for Corvettes." Malcolm Konner Chevrolet developed a reputation as the place to buy a Corvette, and it was the number-one dealership in Corvette sales for many years running.

| Base MSRP | $27,527 |
|---|---|
| Model Availability | Coupe |
| Engines | L98 |
| Features | Special two-tone exterior, interior badge |
| Production Numbers | 50 |

### *1959 Corvette Road Rally*

In 1959, when the Corvette was just six years old, Malcolm Konner rounded up a group of his Corvette customers and chartered a plane to St. Louis, Missouri. After a group tour of the Corvette assembly plant, Konner's customers took delivery of their new Corvettes and then undertook a road rally back to New Jersey as a group. Talk about seeing the USA in a new Chevrolet!

Malcolm Konner enjoyed a special relationship with Chevrolet and many of the key figures on the team, including his personal friendships with Corvette chief engineer Zora Arkus-Duntov and his wife, Elfi, as well as Corvette designer Larry Shinoda. The Duntovs stayed with Malcolm and his wife, Florence, whenever they were in town.

As the dealership grew, it also became a resource for Chevrolet, providing engineers with real-world feedback used to troubleshoot issues that arose. It wasn't unusual to see a factory engineer or two in Malcolm Konner's service department.

Malcolm Konner Chevrolet also became known for its annual Corvette show held the first week in June. Duntov was a regular at the show, and Chevrolet always sent a special display of one-of-a-kind Corvettes, such as the Mako Shark concepts, the Corvette Indy concept or one of the five Corvette Grand Sport race cars.

Sadly, Konner passed away in 1983 while on a Chevrolet trip to Italy. His sons, R. J. and Gary, took over the dealership and were looking for a way to memorialize their father. After many calls, Chevrolet agreed to build a special run of 50 Corvettes known as the Malcolm Konner Commemorative Edition.

### *Malcolm Konner Commemorative Edition Features*

For obvious reasons, Chevrolet couldn't create an elaborate special edition with a unique color for a run of just 50 Corvettes, so they utilized two current colors, Silver Beige and Black, and offered them as an exclu-

***For 1986, Chevrolet paid tribute to the late Malcolm Konner with 50 Malcolm Konner Commemorative Editions. Konner was a long-time Chevrolet dealer whose dealership in Paramus, New Jersey, sold more Corvettes than any other in the world. (Photo credit: © Bill Erdman)***

*The 1986 Malcolm Konner Commemorative Edition was the first special-edition Corvette to be named after a person and the first vehicle from any GM division to honor a specific dealer. (Photo Courtesy Mecum Auctions)*

*Following Mr. Konner's death in 1983, his two sons leveraged their contacts with the Corvette team and Chevrolet to create a commemorative edition to honor their father. They finally succeeded in getting the approval from Chevrolet general manager Bob Berger, who liked the idea of honoring the dealer who had sold more Corvettes than any other. (Photo Courtesy Mecum Auctions)*

sive two-tone exterior with Silver-Beige upper and Black lower.

A special graphic was applied inside the C4 Corvette badges on the front nose and the rear fuel door that read "Malcolm Konner" in script at the top while "Commemorative Edition" was printed in block letters.

All the Konner editions received a graphite interior, and a small brass plaque on the center console read "Malcolm Konner Commemorative Edition."

The commemorative editions were powered by the standard L98 350-ci V-8, providing 230 hp and 330 ft-lbs of torque. Two transmissions were offered: a 4-speed automatic and the Doug Nash 4+3 manual transmission. Of the 50 Corvettes in the series, 30 were built with the automatics while 20 came with the manual gearbox. Divided equally between the two transmissions were 20 Malcolm Konner Editions with RPO Z51 suspensions. Finally, 1 of the 50 became the first Callaway twin turbo engine conversion.

### Pricing and Production

The package was ordered with RPO 4001ZA and was priced with an additional cost of $500. The Malcolm Konner Corvettes didn't have a unique VIN sequence, but all 50 were built within a span of 300 Corvettes with the VIN start and end range being 1G1YY0781G5108043

*A group of buyers came to Bowling Green, toured the Corvette assembly plant, and then picked up their new commemorative editions. The factory tour, on-site delivery, and road rally back to the New Jersey dealership was a re-creation of a similar trip Malcolm Konner made with customers in 1959. (Photo Courtesy General Motors Media Archive)*

*The Malcolm Konner Commemorative Edition was an easy design to pull off. Each car received a custom two-tone paint job, special exterior badges, and an interior dash plaque. The total special edition added just $500 to the MSRP. (Photo credit: © Bill Erdman)*

to 1G1YY0781G5108343. Malcolm Konner Chevrolet also offered its own dealer-installed option that included a set of silver-beige BBS wheels and a custom-installed radar detector.

Sales of the Malcolm Konner Commemorative Editions were handled exclusively by Malcolm Konner Chevrolet, and to make the experience of buying one of the limited-edition Corvettes even more exclusive, Malcolm's sons R. J. and Gary re-created their father's 1959 road rally from the Corvette assembly plant.

### *Road Rally Re-created*

Eighteen of Konner's customers who purchased a Malcolm Konner Edition were flown to Bowling Green, Kentucky, on a chartered airplane, where they toured the Corvette assembly plant. Following the tour and a photo session in front of the plant, the new owners picked up their Corvettes and then participated in a charted 900-mile, three-day road rally back to Paramus, New Jersey. They were met with a gala reception, and trophies and other prizes were awarded to those who participated.

## 2004 LE MANS 24 HOUR COMMEMORATIVE EDITION

The Chevrolet Corvette got its mojo back during the C5 era, winning accolades and awards from the press while the racing team was earning checkered flags on the track. The 2004 model year was the final year of the fifth-generation Corvettes and, like its predecessors, Chevrolet used the occasion to celebrate, and there was a lot to celebrate!

### *A Track Record of Success*

During the eight-year run of the C5 Corvette, short by Corvette standards, accolades included the sports car being named North American Car of the Year (1998) and *Motor Trend*'s Car of the Year (1998). It earned two consecutive J. D. Power awards for quality and was named to *Car and Driver's* annual "10 Best List" in 1998, 1999, 2002, 2003, and 2004.

Chevrolet also won the hearts and minds of Corvette enthusiasts as evidenced by one of the strongest sales runs in Corvette's modern history, with Chevy selling a yearly average of more than 31,000 Corvettes during the eight-year run for a total production of 248,715.

It was common knowledge by 2004 that a new Corvette was on the way, and Chevrolet knew that the way to keep interest in the final year of a Corvette generation was to offer a special edition. For 2004, Chevrolet brought forth the commemorative edition Corvettes honoring the Corvette Racing team and the accomplishments of the Corvette C5-R at the 24 Hours of Le Mans.

### *Le Mans Commemorative Edition Features*

The 2004 Corvette commemorative editions were offered on all three models in 2004: the coupe, the convertible, and the Z06. All came with the brilliant Le Mans Blue exterior and all were adorned with special 24:00 Heures Du Mans 2 GTS Wins badges.

"At Chevrolet and especially with the Corvette, racing is part of our DNA," said Rick Baldick, Corvette marketing director, in the official press release. "The 2004 Commemorative Edition provides us the opportunity to connect our customers even more closely with this unprecedented era of Corvette Racing."

| | |
|---|---|
| Base MSRP | $48,053 (coupe), $55,235 (convertible), $56,720 (Z06) |
| Model Availability | Coupe, Convertible, Z06 |
| Engines | LS1, LS6 |
| Features | Blue exterior, badging, carbon fiber hood, and graphics on Z06 |
| Production Numbers | 6,899 |

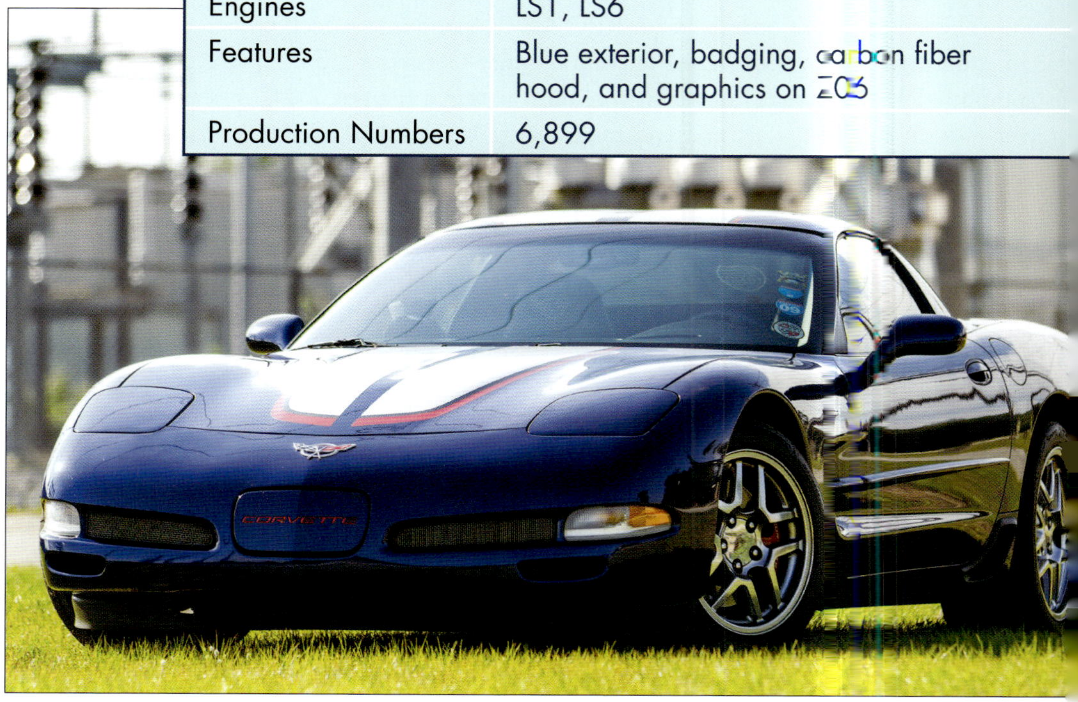

*To honor Corvette Racing's C5-R success, the 2004 Commemorative Edition package could be ordered on all three Corvette models (coupe, convertible, and Z06) and featured the previous year's 50th anniversary Shale interior with a contrasting Le Mans Blue exterior. The Z06 went one step further with a special Le Mans–inspired stripe over the top and the inclusion of a lightweight carbon fiber hood. (Photo Courtesy Howard Brown Photographic)*

*Chevrolet reached back into its storied history to name the performance version of the C5 Corvette after the legendary Z06 RPO code that first appeared as a special options and handling package on the 1963 Corvette. (Photo Courtesy Howard Brown Photographic)*

### Commemorative Edition Coupes and Convertibles

The coupe and convertible models featured a special Shale interior and polished aluminum wheels with commemorative edition center caps. The convertible's top was Shale to match the interior. The C5 Corvette logo was embroidered on the headrests while the word "Commemorative" was imprinted on the seatbacks. Priced at an additional $3,700, the commemorative edition package was ordered with the 1SC equipment group and included Heads-Up Display (HUD), power-telescopic steering column, auto-dimming mirrors, memory package, and twilight sentinel.

### The Z06 Commemorative Edition

The Corvette Z06 Commemorative Edition was even bolder; therefore, its package price was $4,335. The C5-R Le Mans stripe scheme featuring

*Owners of special-edition Corvettes often bond at the national Corvette shows and cruise-ins. During the 2014 National Caravan to the National Corvette Museum, owners of the 2004 Centennial Edition got together for a group photo. (Photo Courtesy Howard Brown Photographic)*

*The convertible model outsold both the coupe and the much snazzier Z06. (Photo Courtesy Meg Hallam)*

*The Shale interior found on the 2003 Corvette 50th Anniversary Edition was also featured on 2004 commemorative edition coupes and convertibles. Z06 commemorative buyers had their choice of black or Shale. (Photo Courtesy Keith Cornett)*

silver graphics edged with red striping ran on the hood, roof, and rear deck. Polished aluminum Z06 wheels with commemorative edition center caps were included along with the special "24:00 Heures Du Mans 2 GTS Wins" badges. The Z06 interior was ebony with the C5 logo embroidered on the headrests.

### Corvette's First Carbon Fiber Hood

One of the unique aspects of the 2004 Corvette Z06 was the first-time use of carbon fiber on the production sports car, an example of technology transferring from the racing program to the street cars. The strong, lightweight carbon fiber material resulted in a panel that weighed just 20.5 pounds while also removing 10.6 pounds off the front of the car. In a special production process, the carbon fibers of the panels were aligned in a single direction; this allowed the exterior to be painted, marking the first use of this material for a painted exterior panel on a vehicle produced in North America.

### Nürburgring Tuned Suspension

The most significant contribution to the 2004 Corvette Z06 came after extensive testing of the car on the Nürburgring, a 12.9-mile public track in Germany that's widely used by manufacturers for benchmark testing. During its testing run, the 2004 Corvette Z06 reported a very respectable lap time of 7 minutes and 56 seconds.

The chassis upgrades from the Nürburgring tests were designed to increase vehicle control and reduce the time it took for the Z06 to settle in on transient maneuvers, allowing the car to feel more poised. Corvette product manager Harlan Charles described it as "more tied down, more glued to the road." Changes for the suspension included revising the dampings in the Sachs gas-pressure shock absorbers and adding stiffer bushings to the upper control arms while adding softer bushings to the rear anti-roll bar.

### Price and Production

To order a commemorative edition, buyers selected their model and then added the appropriate equipment group to the order. The coupe and convertible package price of $3,700 brought the starting MSRP to $48,235 for a coupe and $55,235 for a convertible. The Z06 Commemorative Edition package was priced higher at $4,335, and its MSRP started at $56,720.

Chevrolet committed to building 2,000 Commemorative Edition Z06s, and official production shows 2,025. Coupe and convertible production combined was 4,874.

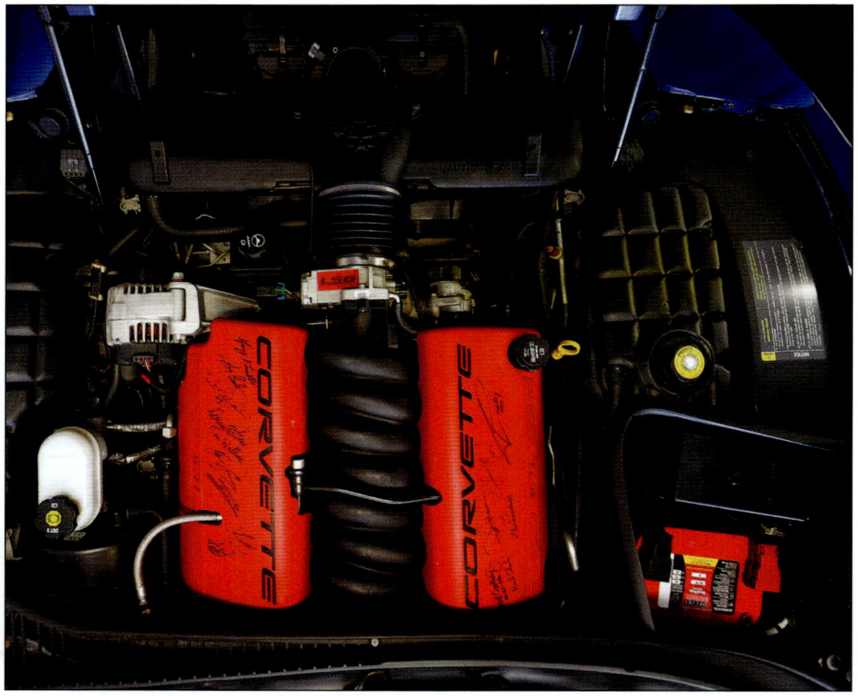


*Chevrolet first introduced the C5 Z06's LS6 V-8 in 2001 with a 385-hp declaration; it grew to 405 hp for 2002–2004 Z06 models. Chevrolet made it easy to recognize the LS6 by offering it with an exclusive red engine dress compared to the black fuel rail covers on the standard coupes and convertibles. (Photo Courtesy Howard Brown Photographic)*

*One of the earliest examples of technology transfer from the racing program to the street car was evident on the 2004 Corvette Z06 Commemorative Edition: a carbon fiber hood. Race cars make extensive use of the sturdy, lightweight material, and the Z06 was able to shave a little more than 10 pounds off with the carbon fiber hood. (Photo Courtesy Keith Cornett)*

*The 2004 Corvette Z06 was one of the few production vehicles to have broken the 8-minute barrier for lap times at the 170-turn, 12.9-mile Nürburgring circuit in Germany. The 2004 Z06 was the first Corvette to make the modern-day benchmarking list with a lap time of 7:56, and that was starting the lap from a dead stop, not like the flying laps that are done today. (Photo Courtesy Howard Brown Photographic)*

*Because the 2004 Z06 wasn't exported to Europe, Chevrolet offered the Z18 Commemorative Edition coupes that included the Z06 Commemorative Edition's carbon fiber hood and hood graphics, along with red brake calipers. The interior featured the commemorative edition seats. A total of 46 Commemorative Edition coupes were exported to Europe. (Photo Courtesy Jonny Bens)*

## Breakdown of Commemorative Edition Z06s

| **Model** | **Quantity** |
|---|---|
| Z06 | 2,025 |
| Coupe | 2,215 |
| Convertible | 2,659 |
| **Total** | **6,899** |

## Corvette Racing at Le Mans

Corvette Racing's first visit to the summer classic known as the 24 Hours of Le Mans came in 2000, and the team's inaugural run earned them 3rd- and 4th-place finishes in class. The Corvette team became an instant favorite with the French fans after crewmembers donned berets and fake mustaches for an unofficial team photo and allowed kids to sit in the cockpits of the race cars to have their pictures taken.

The two Corvette C5-Rs were invited back in 2001, and this time there would be no denying the win. The C5-Rs finished 1st and 2nd in the GTS class with Ron Fellows, Johnny O'Connell, and Scott Pruett taking the checkered flag ahead of teammates Andy Pilgrim, Kelly Collins, and Franck Fréon. The Corvettes returned in 2002 and proved that their previous year's 1-2 finish wasn't a fluke by going out and doing it again. This time it was Fellows and O'Connell teamed with Englishman Oliver Gavin while Pilgrim, Collins, and Fréon finished 2nd. The streak of wins took the year off in 2003, as the C5-Rs finished 2nd and 3rd in the GTS class. The final year of the C5-R, 2004, saw another 1-2 finish with Oliver Gavin, Olivier Beretta, and Jan Magnussen taking the checkered flag.

The C5-R's wins weren't limited to the 24 Hours of Le Mans. In 2002, the Corvette earned 9 wins in 10 American Le Mans Series races and won the 2002 GTS Manufacturer and Team Championship awards.

In their final year, the Corvette C5-Rs went undefeated in the 2004 American Le Mans Series, with the number-3 Corvette C5-R edging the number-4 C5-R in five races to four.

*With the commemorative edition designed to celebrate the success of Corvette Racing at Le Mans, it was appropriate that the racing team paid back the designers by finishing 1-2 in class at the 24 Hours of Le Mans in the summer of 2004. The team had three wins at Le Mans in its first five years. (Photo Courtesy Keith Cornett)*

## 2007 RON FELLOWS ALMS GT1 CHAMPIONSHIP CORVETTE Z06

Chevrolet spent the first two years of C6 production launching the latest-generation models: The standard 400-hp coupe and convertibles came in 2005 followed by the 505-hp Corvette Z06 in 2006. Once initial launches were completed, the Corvette team focused on making these cars even more refined and offering additional ways to personalize. The 2007 model year marked the beginning of annual special editions.

To this point, Chevrolet had mostly limited the production of special-edition Corvettes to anniversary years, collector editions at the end of a generation, or the Indy 500 Pace Cars. The others were a 1996 Grand Sport and a couple of commemoratives, one for Chevrolet Dealer Malcom Konner (1986) and another for the 2004 24 Hours of Le Mans. Previous special editions spanned years between production, but from 2007 through 2018, Chevrolet produced one and sometimes two special editions each year. And with Corvette owners and collectors enthusiastically buying these specials, Chevrolet shows no sign of stopping this trend.

| Base MSRP | $77,500 |
|---|---|
| Model Availability | Z06 |
| Engines | LS7 |
| Features | Exclusive white exterior, graphics, interior badge, signature series |
| Production Numbers | 399 |

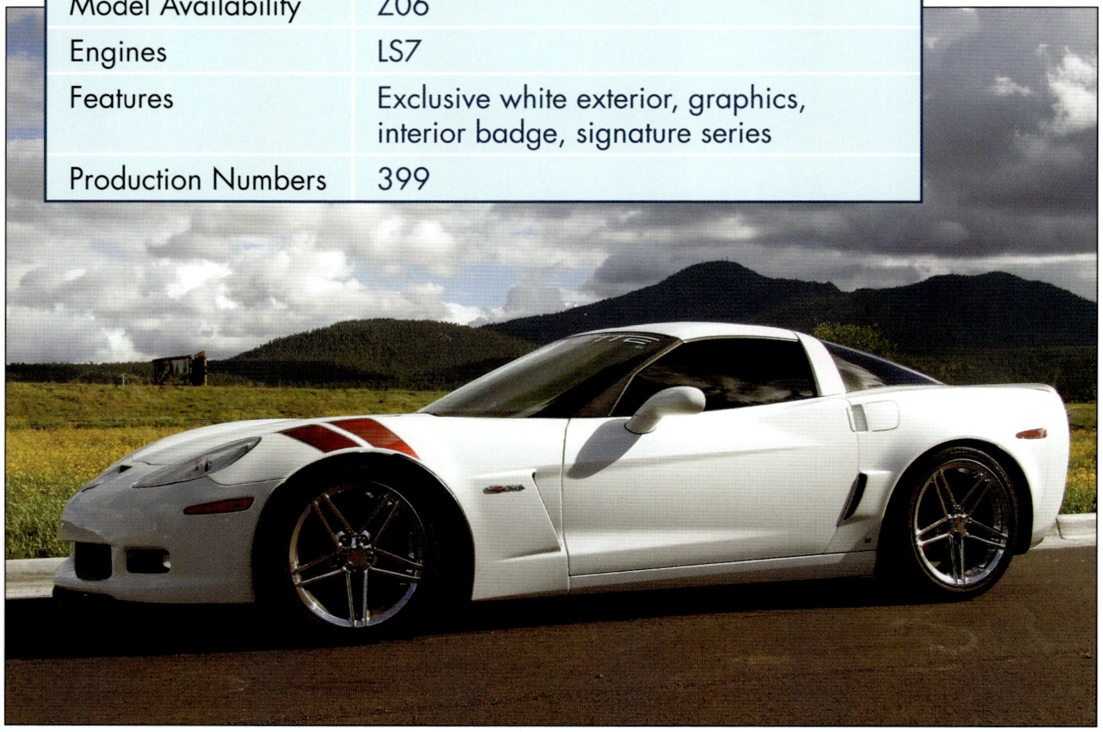

***The 2007 Corvette Z06 Ron Fellows ALMS GT1 Championship Edition is a really long name for a Corvette, so most enthusiasts and owners simply refer to the car as the "Ron Fellows Z06." The limited-edition Corvette was only the second to commemorate an individual (the 1986 Malcolm Konner Edition was the first). (Photo Courtesy David Flateau)***

### *The First Signature Edition Corvette*

Marking a first in Corvette's 54-year history, the 2007 model year featured the first signature special edition. That honor was bestowed upon Corvette Racing driver Ron Fellows, whose storied racing career with the factory-backed Corvette team in the American Le Mans Series (ALMS) culminated with six consecutive ALMS GT1 manufacturers' championships.

"Ron Fellows is also a part of Chevrolet's racing heritage, and he has been instrumental in the remarkable success of the Corvette Racing team in the American Le Mans Series. The special signature-series Z06 model that bears his name will forever link him to one of the greatest eras in factory racing, which has produced six consecutive ALMS GT1 manufacturers' championships, and counting," GM public relations stated.

### *Ron Fellows ALMS GT1 Championship Edition Z06 Features*

The Ron Fellows Z06 limited edition was offered exclusively in Arctic White, the first Z06 since the 2001 Z06 to wear the color. Exterior appointments included a full-width spoiler, chrome wheels, and red brake calipers, along with a unique Corvette windshield banner.

The most distinguishable feature on this signature model was the hash marks on the fenders, a nod to the identifying graphics found on the Corvette GT1 race car. The hash marks were done in Monterey Red Metallic with Machine Silver borders. Inside the hash marks was a Canadian Maple Leaf graphic (another nod, this time to Fellows's Canadian heritage) and Ron Fellows's name along with the years of Corvette's ALMS GT1 championships.

Inside the cockpit, red leather trimmed the sides and bolsters of black leather seats with embroidered Z06 logos on the headrests. The red theme was carried from the lower door panels to the bottom of the dash and instrument panel. The armrest was covered in red leather and featured an embossed Corvette crossed-flags logo. Another distinguishing feature was a tech-patterned interior trim panel surrounding the center console.

### *Limited to 399*

The Ron Fellows ALMS GT1 Championship Corvette Z06 was limited to 399 cars and was one of the lowest-quantity special editions produced at the time.

Fellows visited the Bowling Green assembly plant in January 2007 and, while there, hand-signed and numbered the underside of each center armrest cover. Original owners also received the Official Ron Fellows Limited Edition Letter of Authenticity from General Motors, verifying the unique provenance of this special edition.

*The 2007 Ron Fellows ALMS GT1 Championship Z06 became the first signature edition in Corvette history; Ron Fellows's autograph and the build number can be found on the inside of the console lid. Fellows visited the Bowling Green assembly plant in January 2007 and signed all 399 console lids in a single day. (Photo Courtesy David Flateau)*

*As Ron Fellows hails from Windsor, Ontario, the Arctic White exterior with Monterey Red hash marks color scheme pays homage to his Canadian heritage. The hash marks graphics contain the outline of the Canadian Maple Leaf. (Photo Courtesy Keith Cornett)*

*Ron Fellows is most associated with driving the number-3 Corvette C5-R and C6.Rs. The number 3 is featured in the production of the Ron Fellows Z06. The official RPO for ordering the limited edition was Z33. Chevrolet produced 399 Ron Fellows Z06s with 300 for the United States, 33 for Canada, and 66 for export to Europe, Asia, and the Middle East. (Photo Courtesy Michael Semon of Buyavette.net)*

*Dressing up the performance-oriented cockpit is a tech-patterned trim plate that surrounds the entertainment center, climate control panels, and manual shifter. (Photo Courtesy Michael Semon of Buyavette.net)*

The Arctic White Z06 was introduced to the world on February 1, 2007, at the Chicago Auto Show. It was joined by another special edition also slated for production in the spring, the 2007 Corvette Indy 500 Pace Car convertible.

Chevrolet donated the last Ron Fellows Corvette Z06, number 399 in the series, to a nonprofit group called Autism Speaks. The White Z06 was auctioned at the 2007 Monterey Sports & Classic Car Auction hosted by RM Auctions. The last Ron Fellows Z06 blasted through the presale estimates of $80,000 to $100,000 and sold for $121,000.

### *Pricing and Production*

The MSRP of the 2007 Ron Fellows ALMS GT1 Championship Corvette Z06 was $77,500 and was ordered under RPO code Z33. Only two options were available, navigation and OnStar, which maxed out the MSRP to $79,945.

Production of the Ron Fellows Corvettes began with the first three cars completed on January 23, 2007. The final 396 units were built in March and April 2007. Of the total, 300 stayed in the United States, 33 went to Canada, and the remaining 66 were offered to other export markets.

The 2007 Ron Fellows ALMS GT1 Championship Corvette Z06 remains one of the most popular special editions of the C6 generation, loved by collectors and enthusiasts alike.

## A Fateful Phone Call

In the summer of 2006, Corvette marketing manager Gary Claudio called his friend Ron Fellows and surprised him with the news that Chevrolet was going to honor him with a special-edition Corvette the following year. At the time, Fellows had been in discussions with Corvette Racing and Chevrolet about his planned retirement from being one of four full-time drivers and switching to more of a part-time endurance driver and ambassador role with the racing team.

"I just got goosebumps," said Fellows when asked how he was told about the special edition in his honor. "He wouldn't share any more and said the rest was going to be a surprise," he continued. "It was at the Chicago Auto Show where they did the official unveiling, and it won some kind of prize, which was cool. Later, in June of that year, I was out to dinner and GM chairman Bob Lutz came up and said to me, 'Congratulations on that car. I am happy to tell you that we sold out, and they sold quick!'"

Fellows said it meant a lot that his friend Gary Claudio called him with the news, and that to see the special edition in Arctic White with the red interior and red hash marks was very exciting. Fellows still owns the VIN 001 2007 Ron Fellows ALMS GT1 Champion Corvette Z06.

***The interior of the Ron Fellows C6 Z06 is all business. The two-tone red and black theme abounds with red-leather-trimmed seats and door panels, and a red leather center console lid with embroidered crossed-flags logo. A new embroidery style for the 2007 Z06's headrests now showed a full-color Z06 logo instead of the outline-style logo of the previous year. (Photo Courtesy Michael Semon of Buyavette.net)***

***For Corvette enthusiasts, identifying a Ron Fellows Corvette Z06 was very easy, at least until 2010. The Ron Fellows Z06 was the only Arctic White Corvette Z06 offered between 2006 and 2009. In 2010, Chevrolet offered Arctic White for the Z06 as well as for the new Grand Sport model, which utilized the wide-body design. (Photo Courtesy Michael Semon for Buyavette.net)***

*The Corvette Z06's naturally aspirated 505-hp 7.0L LS7 engine was a direct result of lessons learned from the racing Corvettes of the C5-R era. Corvette Racing's C6.R GT1 engine was the LS7.R manufactured by Katech Performance. (Photo Courtesy Michael Semon of Buyavette.net)*

*With its production limited to 399, the Z06's MSRP was set at $77,500, or $79,945 with navigation and OnStar. Race enthusiasts loved the car because it celebrated one of Corvette Racing's most popular drivers. Collectors loved the Ron Fellows Z06 due to its low numbers, unique color, and distinction as the first signature edition in Corvette's history. (Photo Courtesy David Flateau)*

## Corvette Racing's Ron Fellows

Ron Fellows's impressive skill as a driver for the Corvette Racing team earned him the respect of Corvette fans everywhere. His 27 wins, 3 ALMS championships, and 2 wins at the 24 Hours of Le Mans, along with his unprecedented 4 consecutive Most Popular Driver awards from ALMS fans are testament to his success. Fellows's last season as a driver for Corvette Racing was in 2008; he transitioned into an ambassadorial role, in which he remains one of the most recognizable, respected, and popular personalities to ever represent Corvette's racing heritage.

Today, Fellows picks up the occasional driving gig with NASCAR and helps develop the Ron Fellows Performance Driving School at Spring Mountain Motor Resort and Country Club, which serves as Chevrolet's official Corvette owners school. Fellows is also part of the ownership group of the Canadian Tire Motorsport Park (formerly known as Mosport). Fellows was inducted into the Corvette Hall of Fame in 2011.

*If racing has a consummate good guy, it is Ron Fellows. His easygoing personality is infectious, but when he is behind the wheel he is as focused and serious as they come. Known for his stellar career in the ALMS and at Le Mans, Fellows also has four wins in NASCAR's Camping World Truck Series, two wins in Xfinity, and three Top-5 finishes in the Monster Energy NASCAR Cup Series. (Photo Courtesy Keith Cornett)*

## 2007 VICTORY EDITION (EUROPEAN EXCLUSIVE)

Just like in America, Europe is full of automotive enthusiasts who live and breathe Corvettes. Most European countries have a Corvette club, and enthusiasts enjoy getting out their American sports cars and attending car shows or parking in the corral at Le Mans or one of the other tracks.

The popularity of Corvette Racing in Europe is very strong, which says a lot considering the factory Corvettes race on the continent only once each year. The team's popularity has been buoyed by the fact that the majority of the drivers during Corvette Racing's history hailed from various European countries and serve as unofficial ambassadors for the Corvette brand in their home countries.

In the first few days of February 2007, Chevrolet announced no less than three special-edition models that would go on sale in the coming months. The 2007 Corvette Indy 500 Pace Car and the 2007 Ron Fellows Corvette Z06 were announced on February 1, 2007. Two days later, Chevrolet completed GM's trifecta of news about limited-production Corvettes with ties to racing with the announcement of the 2007 Corvette Victory Edition Coupe produced exclusively for the European market.

The 2007 Corvette Victory Editions are tied to Corvette's success in racing, particularly at the prestigious 24 Hours of Le Mans held annually in France, in which Corvette earned five class wins between 2001 and 2006.

| | |
|---|---|
| Base MSRP | £51,285 |
| Model Availability | Coupe |
| Engines | LS2 |
| Features | Exterior colors, exclusive wheels, interior badge, seat colors |
| Production Numbers | 250 |

*The 2007 Corvette Victory Edition was the first special-edition Corvette package created exclusively for Europe. A limited-edition run of just 250 coupes was offered. (Photo Courtesy Jean-Marc Lepain)*

### *Victory Edition Features*

Chevrolet offered just 250 Victory Edition Corvettes for sale in Europe. The C6 coupes were powered by the standard LS2 6.0L V-8 producing 297kW (404 hp) and 546 Nm of torque and mated to a 6-speed manual. The electronically controlled 6-speed automatic transmission with paddle shift was available as an option.

The Victory Edition Corvettes were available in Black and Velocity Yellow, two colors that pay homage to the legacy of Corvette Racing. The model was further enhanced with 18/19-inch Competition Grey aluminum wheels along with a body-color full-width rear spoiler.

The interior of the Victory Edition included two-tone leather seats with the Corvette crossed-flags logo embroidered on them. The Black Victory Editions received an Ebony and Red interior while the Velocity Yellow Victor Editions were Ebony and Titanium Grey. Other package details included Competition Grey door sill plates and a carbon-patterned interior trim package.

The Victory Editions were loaded with the European Luxury package, which outfitted the Corvettes with heated seats, memory package with presets for two drivers for the six-way power driver's seat, exterior mirrors, and powered telescopic steering wheel. They also included a Heads-Up Display (HUD) with g-force meter auto-dimming inside rearview mirror, and a premium Bose seven-speaker sound

New two-tone seats with crossed-flags embroidery along with red seat belts, a red center console cover, and red door panels added more than a splash of color to the Ebony interior of the 2007 Corvette coupe. (Photo Courtesy Jean-Marc Lepain)

Chevrolet marketed the 2007 Victory Edition Corvette to celebrate Corvette Racing's unprecedented 50 victories combined in the American Le Mans Series and the 24 Hours of Le Mans since 1999. (Photo Courtesy Jean-Marc Lepain)

European Corvettes can be distinguished from their American counterparts by a number of required equipment that includes the pop-up headlight washers, side markers, and the rear brake lenses with amber-colored lower lenses. (Photo Courtesy Jean-Marc Lepain)

The interior colors were keyed to the Victory Edition's exterior with the Velocity Yellow cars receiving a two-tone black and Titanium Grey interior while the black Victory Editions were outfitted with a two-tone black and red. A carbon fiber–styled interior trim package and Competition Grey door sills completed the look. (Photo Courtesy Jean-Marc Lepain)

Each Victory Edition Corvette was identified by its own unique sequence number on a small plaque. The plaque lists the build number out of 250 total and its success at Le Mans by highlighting the "5 times Le Mans GT1 Champion 2001–2006." (Photo Courtesy Jean-Marc Lepain)

system. Finishing off the list of options was the DVD navigation system with touch screen and voice guidance.

### Unique Owner Options

Each of the Victory Editions received an interior badge featuring the car's unique ID number in the build sequence. Chevrolet's 2007 Victory Edition roll-out included a one-day track experience with professional drivers. The track dates were held at various locations throughout Europe and offered Victory Corvette owners a demonstration of their Corvette's on-track capabilities.

*The purchase of the 2007 Corvette Victory Edition also included a one-day track event for owners to learn more about the capabilities of their new Corvettes. Chevrolet brought this concept back to the United States with the rollout of the 2009 Corvette ZR1. (Photo Courtesy Jonny Bens)*

### Forebearer to Future Offerings

Looking at the 2007 Corvette Victory Edition, you can see that it would eventually evolve and split into the two special editions for 2009: the Competition Sport and the GT1 Championship Editions. The Competition Sports were Z51 manual 6-speeds with Competition Gray wheels. The GT1 Corvettes also saluted the racing team's success with numbered black and yellow Corvettes.

Another first for the Victory Edition was the inclusion of the free one-day Corvette Drivers' Training Event. These driver-training events gave many Corvette owners their first taste of the true performance capabilities of their cars. Chevrolet rolled out a similar program for North American buyers of the 2009 Corvette ZR1 by offering a two-day voucher for the course at Bob Bondurant's School of High Performance Driving or Spring Mountain Motorsports Ranch.

### Pricing and Production

A total of 1,327 Corvettes were exported to Europe in 2007 and the 250 Victory Editions were 18.8 percent of all exports to the continent. Prices started at £51,285 for the manual version and £53,685 for the auto version.

## 2008 Z06 427 LIMITED EDITION (WIL COOKSEY)

Following the success of the 2007 special editions, which saw an Indy 500 Pace Car model paired with a limited-edition Z06, Chevrolet offered up the same combination with both the 30th Anniversary Edition of the 2008 Indy 500 Pace Car along with the 2008 427 Limited Edition Corvette Z06.

The 427 remains one of the most iconic car culture status symbols of the 1960s. In fact, there is probably no Corvette more coveted and collected than a Corvette with a 427 big-block engine.

Introduced at the February 2008 Cleveland Auto Show, the 2008 427 Limited Edition celebrates the legendary Corvette 427 engines from the 1960s by drawing a parallel to the C6 Corvette Z06's newly legendary LS7 427-ci small-block. Despite the focus on the engine displacement, the 427 Limited Edition was a trim package only, and no performance modifications were made.

But then none were really needed. The latest 427 uses racing-derived technology developed from its partnership with the Corvette Racing team.

| Base MSRP | $84,195 |
|---|---|
| Model Availability | Z06 |
| Engines | LS7 |
| Features | Exclusive red exterior, graphics, badging, signature series |
| Production Numbers | 505 |

*Following on the success of the 2007 Ron Fellows Signature Edition Z06, Chevrolet introduced the 2008 427 Limited Edition Corvette Z06 with an exclusive color, graphics, and hood badging for the 505-hp sports car. (Photo Courtesy Howard Brown Photographic)*

***The reveal of the 2008 427 Limited Edition Z06 was held at the most unlikely of venues, the February 22 opening of the Cleveland Auto Show. The Wil Cooksey debut came exactly one month after the debut of the supercharged 2009 Corvette ZR1 at the Detroit Auto Show. (Photo Courtesy Howard Brown Photographic)***

The LS7 utilizes titanium connecting rods and intake valves to help boost horsepower and RPM. The 505-hp V-8 propelled the car 0–60 mph in 3.7 seconds and a quarter-mile time of 11.7 seconds at 125 mph. The Z06 was clocked with a top speed of 198 mph on the German autobahn.

### *Better Known as the Wil Cooksey Edition*

Each of the 427 Limited Editions was signed by Wil Cooksey, the longtime manager of the Bowling Green assembly plant who retired in the spring of 2008 after leading the Corvette factory for 15 years. Cooksey's signature and build number are on the inside lid of the center armrest. Original buyers also received a certificate of authenticity. While its official name is the 427 Limited Edition, just about everyone refers to it as the Wil Cooksey edition or simply the Cooksey edition.

***Because Wil Cooksey was still the manager of the Corvette assembly plant when production started, he was able to sign the console lids in his office. After signing the day's batch of lids, he personally delivered them to the station for installation. The sequence number for each 427 Limited Edition was listed both on a numbered dash plaque and on the inside of the console lids. (Photo Courtesy Howard Brown Photographic)***

Chevrolet offered the 427 Limited Edition in Crystal Red Metallic, a Xirallic-based color that had not been previously available on the Z06. A black hood stinger graphic and 427 badges along the side of the hood bulge are reminiscent of the 1967 427 Sting Rays.

Other exterior features included a unique set of spyder-style chrome wheels exclusive to the 427 LE, a body-colored spoiler instead of the standard black spoiler, and body-color door handles.

All 427 Limited Editions came with the 3LZ Preferred Equipment package, and the interior features a Dark Titanium leather-wrapped cockpit and special Crystal Red center trim plate. The seat inserts were dark gray with black surrounding them. Other appointments included red 427 logos embroidered on the seats and floor mats, as well as Z06 door sill plates.

### *Pricing and Production*

The MSRP on the 427 Limited Edition was $84,195, which came in about $3,000 more than a similarly equipped Z06. The only option available

***Chevrolet equipped the 427 Limited Edition Z06s with an exclusive spyder-style wheel in a bright chrome finish. The 427's spyder wheel design was among the first of the C6 models to deviate from the standard five-spoke design that had dominated Corvette design since the C4 ZR-1. (Photo Courtesy Keith Cornett)***

***The 2008 Corvette 427 Limited Edition Z06 pays homage to the fabled 427 engines of the past. With the 427 signifying the cubic-inch displacement of Chevrolet's big-block offered on Corvettes between 1966 and 1969, that same 427 now resides on the hood that covers the Z06's 7.0L small-block V-8. (Photo Courtesy Keith Cornett)***

to buyers was the $1,750 Bose navigation system. The RPO to order the 427 Limited Edition was Z44.

Production of the 427 Limited Edition Corvette Z06 was limited to just 505 Corvettes, the same number as the LS7's 505 hp. Of those, 427 stayed in the United States and the other 78 Z06s were offered to export markets.

General Motors teamed up with Barrett-Jackson in 2010 to pare down its collection amid its reorganization. The final North American model, number 427, was auctioned for charity and sold for $200,000. All proceeds from the sale went to the American Red Cross relief fund for Haiti.

*Corvette featured its darker shade of red on the Z06 for the first time. Crystal Red Metallic was the second most popular color in 2008, trailing black, and it went on to be one of the more popular colors during its run. The special tint featured a Xirallic-based pigment containing aluminum-oxide flakes that came alive in the sunlight. (Photo Courtesy Howard Brown Photographic)*

*Chevrolet played a numbers game with the production of the 427 Limited Edition. The company built 505 of the Crystal Red Z06s, a nod to the 427's 7.0L LS7 with 505 hp. Of that total, 427 were offered in the United States and 78 were exported. (Photo Courtesy Howard Brown Photographic)*

*All 427 Limited Editions were loaded with the 3LZ Preferred Equipment package that featured the new special Dark Titanium interior with seats and floor mats embroidered with 427. The center console brought the darker red into the cabin with a Crystal Red trim plate that had a red carbon fiber–styled pattern. (Photo Courtesy Keith Cornett)*

## Wil Cooksey, Bowling Green Assembly Plant Manager

"If I could get the opportunity to work at the Corvette plant, and just try to do the best I can . . . maybe one day I could be influential." —Wilmer Cooksey Jr.

Wilmer (Wil) Cooksey served as the manager of the Bowling Green assembly plant from February 1993 to March 2008. In that position, he was the longest-serving manager of the Corvette factory, his leadership spanning three generations of Corvettes.

Cooksey was born in Fort Worth, Texas, in 1942. In 1965, he received his bachelor of science degree in electrical engineering from Tennessee State University. A master's degree in industrial engineering from the University of Toledo was granted in 1972 followed by postgraduate doctorate work in mechanical engineering at Michigan State University.

Before his career with General Motors, Cooksey served in the US Army. A distinguished graduate of the Officer's Training School, he served as an executive officer with the rank of second lieutenant in the US Army Artillery. He served a year in Vietnam and was awarded the Bronze Star.

Cooksey began his career at General Motors as an assistant professor at the General Motors Institute (GMI) in Flint. In 1976, he transferred to the Corvette assembly plant in St. Louis, Missouri, where he held several positions before moving to a superintendent position at Doraville in Atlanta, Georgia. From there, he served as production manager at Fairfax (Kansas) before being named plant manager at Bowling Green.

With a larger-than-life personality, Cooksey was well respected and admired by the plant's rank and file workers as well as by members of the Corvette team in Detroit. Early on, he focused on quality, and his attention to detail ingratiated him with customers, many of whom he considers close friends. Wil Cooksey was inducted into the Corvette Hall of Fame in 2013.

***In His Own Words***

Before Wil Cooksey's retirement in the spring of 2008, Chevrolet desired his input and effort to implement one more special edition into the regular production schedule.

He had previously talked with Corvette product manager Harlan Charles about some ideas to motivate customers to buy special editions. Cooksey said he always liked the 1967 tri-power Sting Rays with the stinger hood and thought the Z06s hood had similar features that could be accented.

He recounts the day the Corvette team pitched the 2008 427 Limited Edition:

> "They showed me the pictures in my office of a 1967 big-block and they had what they proposed, but at that time they hadn't talked about the autograph. They were just trying to get me to build the car, and I told them how disruptive it is when you are actually trying to set up a manufacturing line and then guys like him (people from headquarters) come in and start mixing up the operators and start giving you build issues possibly. But when they showed me the whole car and told me, 'We can do it in Crystal Red,' which I had a lot of customers who wanted Crystal Red! So, we're going to do Crystal Red, and the whole stinger treatment with the 427 on it . . . 'Hey, that sounds pretty good.' It was then they said they were going to do some things on the inside. And that's when they told me, 'Yeah, we want you to autograph all of them.' I said (laughing), 'Hey, I think we can work this out.'"

One of Cooksey's fears was that he would retire before production started, but he got his wish. Some of his last days were spent in his office autographing all the center consoles. He would deliver the batch to the assembly line, where they were installed in their numbers-matching 427 Edition.

Cooksey said that it was hard not to think of the autograph as a sign that he stood behind the work of the finished vehicle like a guarantee. He never expected the honor of being able to sign those Corvettes, but that signature led people to call it the Wil Cooksey Edition.

Cooksey was offered any of the builds from the batch and, although it was a toss-up between owning the VIN 001 version or the VIN 427, in the end he went with the first 427 Limited Edition built.

***Chevrolet had big shoes to fill with the retirement of Wilmer (Wil) Cooksey as the Corvette assembly plant manager in 2008. His attention to increasing quality and his outgoing personality earned him the respect and admiration of Corvette enthusiasts and those who built the cars under his watch. (Photo Courtesy the National Corvette Museum)***

## 2008 CORVETTE COMPETITION (EUROPEAN EXCLUSIVE)

| Base MSRP | N/A |
|---|---|
| Model Availability | Europe |
| Engines | LS3 |
| Features | Z51 Performance Package, Z06 rear spoiler, Competition Grey wheels |
| Production Numbers | N/A |

With Corvette Racing's popularity reaching new heights in Europe, General Motors unleashed another special-edition Corvette built exclusively for the European continent. Chevrolet announced the new 2008 Corvette Competition in the spring of 2008, following Corvette Racing's GT1 victory at the 56th 12 Hours of Sebring. Like the Corvette C6.R, the Corvette Competition is purpose-built to win both hearts and races for enthusiasts living "across the pond," according to Chevrolet.

*Feedback about the track experience offered with the purchase of the 2007 Victory Edition Corvettes was so positive that Chevrolet decided to somewhat replicate the practice back home. It offered a free two-day driving school with the purchase of the 2009 Corvette ZR1 and a discounted two-day driving school for all C7 Corvette buyers. (Photo Courtesy Nigel Scott Dobbie)*

### *The 2008 Corvette Competition*

Celebrating Corvette's racing heritage, the Competition makes the most of the LS3's 437 horses through maximizing Corvette's superior power-to-weight ratio by keeping extras to a minimum.

The Corvette Competition isn't just a trim package like 2007's Victory Edition. The Competition comes standard with an upgraded Z51 Performance package, a Z06 rear spoiler, and Competition Grey wheels. The Competition Corvette was made available in black only, and production was limited.

### *Performance Features Come Standard*

Included as standard options on the 2008 Corvette Competition were these performance-enhancing features:

- A precise 6-speed gearbox with a direct-operating gear lever
- Standard Z51 Performance package with upgraded torsion bars, brakes, and Eagle F1 Run Flat tires
- Brake cooling ducts for the cross-drilled brake rotors
- Active handling system with a competitive mode for advanced drivers
- Z06 rear spoiler for improved downforce and high-speed stability

Chevrolet added a few nice design touches to the edition, including front and rear sport mesh grilles, carbon fiber trim for the center console, black leather seats, and Competition Grey aluminum wheels.

This was the second special edition built exclusively for Europe. The 2007 Victory Edition had given European Corvette buyers their very own special edition that celebrated the Corvette's success in the GT1 class at the 24 Hours of Le Mans.

### *Price and Production*

For 2008, Corvette sales to Europe were among the highest for the C6 generation with European exports, totaling 1,300. Pricing was not announced, and quantities sold were unreported. The Corvette Competition was a package built on black C6 Corvettes with several options installed by Chevrolet Europe and did not have an official RPO number.

## 2009 GT1 CHAMPIONSHIP EDITION

After 10 years of Corvette Racing's dominance in the American Le Mans Series GT1 class, the factory-backed race team transitioned to a GT2-spec C6.R race car following the 2009 24 Hours of Le Mans. Homologated on the new 2009 ZR1, the GT2-spec race cars required the use of many production-based components, including the ZR1's aluminum frame, chassis, and steering system. The move to the GT2 class also meant that Corvette would be racing against its competition in the marketplace: Porsche, Ferrari, and BMW.

By the end of Corvette's GT1 era, Corvette Racing had earned 74 victories, including an overall win at the Rolex 24 at Daytona, 8 consecutive GT1 Manufacturers Championships, and 5 GT1 class victories at the 24 Hours of Le Mans. With that track record of success, Chevrolet and Corvette Racing celebrated the end of the GT1 era with a limited commemorative appearance package known as the 2009 GT1 Championship Edition.

| Base MSRP | $65,410 (coupe), $71,915 (convertible), $86,486 (Z06) |
|---|---|
| Model Availability | Coupe, Convertible, Z06 |
| Engines | LS3, LS7 |
| Features | Exterior colors, graphics, embroidery |
| Production Numbers | 125 |

*As Corvette Racing extended its dominance on the track, Chevrolet saw benefits in the showroom with the close connection fans had to factory race cars. The GT1 Championship Edition was both a celebration of the team's success and a reward for its most passionate fans. (Photo Courtesy Dawn Jobe / DJ Carbon Flash Photography)*

### The 2009 GT1 Championship Edition

Tom Hill, quality engineering manager at the Corvette assembly plant, announced to National Corvette Restorers Society (NCRS) members attending the Winter Regional Meet in Kissimmee, Florida, in January 2009 that a new limited-edition package called the GT1 Edition would be produced in the spring. Like the 2009 Competition Sport Package, the GT1 Edition centered around Corvette Racing livery with team mascot Jake prominently displayed.

Chevrolet had big plans for the limited edition and worked in concert with the racing team to create a unique appearance package that would be matched by the team's racing livery. Other than the required race numbers and sponsorship stickers, the appearance to the GT1 Championship Edition street cars was nearly spot on to the new GT2 C6.R race cars.

The GT1 Championship Edition was made available in coupe, convertible, or Z06 models in either 45U Velocity Yellow or 41U Black. To bolster collectability, the series had its own specific VIN sequences: 300001 for the Velocity Yellows, which represent the number-3 Corvette C6.R, and 40001 for black, which represents the number-4 C6.R. Each model and color was originally limited to 200 for each body style and 100 in each color, resulting in the planned total of 600 units.

### Race-Inspired Livery

The GT1 Championship Edition featured C6.R livery–inspired graphics that showcased the mascot Jake ghost-painted on the hood bulge, the years of the championships, and drivers's nationality flags. Making the Corvettes unique were the ZR1 full-width body-color spoiler and chrome wheels. The coupes and convertibles included the Z51 Performance package, NPP performance exhaust, and MX0 6-speed paddle-shift automatics.

*The 2009 GT1 Championship Edition was the ultimate tribute vehicle for fans of Corvette Racing. The yellow and black street versions represented their support and pride for the racing team's accomplishments. Owners also took pride knowing that the technology transfer from racing program to street car was more than just yellow or black graphics. (Photo Courtesy Dawn Jobe / DJ Carbon Flash Photography)*

*The GT1 Championship Edition shows the national flags of all the drivers who have driven for Corvette Racing. The flags from eight countries are shown: Switzerland, Italy, Canada, England, United States, Denmark, Monaco, and France. (Photo Courtesy Keith Cornett)*

The GT1 Corvette Coupe was also optioned with the C2L dual roof package. All three GT1 models received the optional U3U navigation system as well.

Inside the GT1 Corvettes was a custom leather-wrapped Ebony interior with exclusive Velocity Yellow accent stitching, and GT1 embroidery on the leather seats, instrument panel, and center console armrest. Under the hood was a special engine cover with a carbon pattern and yellow Corvette lettering. A windshield banner was also included and was installed by either the dealer or the owner.

### GT1 Street Versions Make Their Debut at the Track

The Corvette GT1 Championship cars were shown in public for the first time at the Mobil 1 12 Hours of Sebring in March 2009. Chevrolet displayed the first six cars of the series. Chief engineer Tadge Juechter remarked at the introduction that the Corvettes had been completed within the previous week and shipped down from Bowling Green.

At the track, Corvette Racing's six drivers picked up the key fobs to each of the six Corvettes following an ALMS drivers meeting and drove them down to Corvette Racing's paddock, where they were parked in front of the two C6.R garages. A little later, the six Corvette Racing drivers drove them to the Corvette Corral to be viewed by the enthusiasts gathered at the hospitality tent.

### Pricing and Production

Pricing for the GT1 Championship Edition started at $65,410 for the 4LT Coupe; $71,915 for the 4LT Convertible; and $86,486 for the 3LZ Corvette Z06.

Although there was plenty of interest in the GT1 Corvettes, and the fan base from Corvette Racing was among those most enthusiastic, the timing couldn't have been worse in terms of selling the premium sports cars. With the country in the midst of the Great Recession, Corvette deliveries had cratered in months leading to the spring of 2009, with sales dropping 56 percent when comparing March 2009 to March 2008. General Motors filed for Chapter 11 Reorganization in June 2009, and there was even talk that the Corvette program could be canceled.

In the middle of all this uncertainty, Chevrolet built just 125 GT1 Championship models. The reduced production made the car an instant collectible model based on the low production numbers for each of the six variants.

*The set of six GT1 Championship Editions was completed at the last minute before being shipped to central Florida for a public debut at the 2009 12 Hours of Sebring. Standing in the middle with the black shirt is Corvette Racing's program manager, Doug Fehan, who is seeing the tribute cars for the first time. (Photo Courtesy Keith Cornett)*

*Collectors love exclusivity, and Corvette Racing fans love their GT1 editions. Only 125 GT1 Corvettes were built, and they don't come up for sale often on the open market. (Photo Courtesy Travis Raczynski)*

*The Corvette team featured Corvette Racing's Jake logo (the skull with the crossed-flags eyes) on no less than three different Corvette models in 2009: the GT1 Championship Edition, the Competition Sport package, and the new 2009 Corvette ZR1, where Jake appears in the engine bay on the cold air intake. (Photo Courtesy Travis Raczynski)*

***To ensure the collectability of the car, the GT1 Editions were given two sequence numbers based on the color of the vehicle, a first for a Corvette special-edition model. (Photo Courtesy Dawn Jobe / DJ Carbon Flash Photography)***

## 2009 GT1 Championship Edition Production Breakdown

| Model | Color | Quantity |
|---|---|---|
| Coupe | Yellow | 29 |
| Coupe | Black | 24 |
| Convertible | Yellow | 10 |
| Convertible | Black | 07 |
| Z06 | Yellow | 38 |
| Z06 | Black | 17 |
| **Total:** | | **125** |

## Corvette Racing Livery Matches Production Corvette

One of the anticipations for each new racing season is when the Corvette Racing team rolls out the new livery. For 2009, Corvette Racing and General Motors closed the marketing loop by running the two C6.Rs with the new GT1 Championship livery. Like the forthcoming limited-edition GT1 Championship coupes, convertibles, and Z06s, the new livery featured the number-3 C6.R in familiar Velocity Yellow with black striping while the number-4 C6.R was reversed in black with yellow accents.

Over the years we've been treated to some great designs, including 2008's Jake Scrape livery and the Bad Boy Jake livery at Monterey in 2007. The 2009 GT1 Championship livery was a hit, as a C6.R in black is just about the most menacing-looking car on the track. The fact that you could buy a street version of these Corvettes made the livery special as well. Only one other time has General Motors offered an ALMS C6.R replica, which was the 2007 Arctic White Ron Fellows Edition Z06.

***The graphics on the sides of the Corvette proclaim the success in racing. The driver's side of the GT1 lists the eight years that Corvette Racing won the ALMS Drivers Championships. On the passenger's side, the graphic lists the five years that Corvette won the 24 Hours of Le Mans. (Photo Courtesy Charley Robertson)***

## History of Corvette Racing's Jake Mascot

Corvette Racing's mascot, Jake, made his third appearance on a 2009 Corvette model by appearing on the Competition Sport. The iconic logo had been introduced earlier in the year with an under-the-hood placement on the 638-hp Corvette ZR1. Jake was also a major design feature on the other 2009 special edition, which celebrated Corvette Racing's eight GT1 Championships.

At the 2004 24 Hours of Le Mans, the Corvette team was using "Take No Prisoners" as their unofficial motto, and a black skull representing that attitude was painted on the pit garage floor. Corvette Racing and the C5-R finished first and second in class at the 2004 24 Hours of Le Mans.

Enter Kick Design, a New York–based brand agency engaged by General Motors to create a licensing style guide to help celebrate the 50th anniversary (2003) the year before. During their research, they learned that Corvette had won the legendary 24-hour race at Le Mans, beating the likes of Lamborghini, Aston Martin, and Ferrari. Eddie Jabbour of Kick Design attended the 24 Hours of Le Mans in 2004 and saw "Take No Prisoners" written on the wall. Following the race and after a few beers, Jake (named by the crew after Jake from *The Blues Brothers*) was officially born when Eddie drew the skull with Corvette's C6-generation crossed-flags logo serving as the eyes on a cocktail napkin.

Jake officially made his debut at the 2005 24 Hours of Le Mans by appearing on the B-pillars of the Chevrolet Corvette C6.R race cars. Team members also painted his likeness on the floor of Corvette Racing's pit stalls.

Corvette Racing pulled off another 1–2 victory in 2005, and Jake's place on the team, and in Corvette history, was forever cemented.

***This cocktail napkin is the origin of Corvette Racing's Jake mascot that has been featured on Corvette race cars since 2005. The team was already using a skull when a branding executive sketched in the Corvette's crossed-flags logo as the eyes. (Photo Courtesy Eddie Jabbour)***

## 2016 CORVETTE Z06 C7.R EDITION

The C7 Corvette Z06 and Corvette Racing's C7.R share a development history that started with the C5 Corvette generation and the very first C5-R Corvette. Today, these latest iterations have been refined through the transfer of technology from street car to race car and back to street car, with each generation building upon lessons learned during racing and applying them to the Corvettes that sold to the public. It's safe to say that neither the Z06 nor the C7.R would exist without the other and, due to their intertwined development history, both Corvettes were introduced together in January 2014 at the North American International Auto Show in Detroit.

| Base MSRP | $111,400 (coupe), $116,495 (convertible) |
|---|---|
| Model Availability | Z06 |
| Engines | LT4 |
| Features | Exterior colors, carbon fiber hood, graphics, interior badging, seats, and embroidery |
| Production Numbers | 650 |

***The Z06 C7.R Edition not only paid homage to the factory C7.R Corvette race cars, it represented the tip of the technological spear for Chevrolet. Everything that has been learned in the course of racing the Corvette was applied to the street cars. (Photo Courtesy Keith Cornett)***

As the Corvette C7.R is homologated from the C7 Corvette Z06, the two cars share the same hydro-formed aluminum frame built in Bowling Green, Kentucky. Other design similarities include most elements of bodywork and aerodynamics.

*Corvette Racing fans lined up to buy the tribute to the C7.R race cars, and the 500 examples for US customers sold quickly. Some fans, such as the owner of the 2016 Z06 C7.R Edition on the right, took their appreciation to new levels by copying the race car's graphics and sponsor stickers. The C7.R on the left is the real race car. (Photo Courtesy Nigel Scott Dobbie)*

### *Paying Respects to the Factory Race Team*

The last time Chevrolet paid its respects to the Corvette Racing team was in 2009 with the GT1 Championship Editions. Offered in black or yellow, these Corvettes were a hit with buyers and today are one of the most-collected models from the C6 Corvette era. With the new Z06 C7.R package, Chevrolet again showed its respect for the factory racer with a new appearance package that made this car one of the star attractions at any Corvette Corral on the Tudor United SportsCar Championship series.

The Corvette Z06 began its rollout to customers in late 2014 as a 2015 model and, despite the late start, the Z06 surprised all by having its largest total production year with 8,000 produced during the 2015 model year.

For 2016, the Corvette team retired the long-running Velocity Yellow exterior for a new shade called Corvette Racing Yellow. Along with the fact that Corvette Racing won its class at the 2015 24 Hours of Le Mans, it seemed a special celebration edition was in order.

*The black Z06 C7.R Editions were outfitted like their Corvette Racing Yellow counterparts. For an even bolder look, this black C7.R Z06 has the aftermarket Jake graphic instead of the matte-black version that came with the car. (Photo Courtesy Keith Valone)*

### *Corvette Z06 C7.R Edition Features*

The Corvette Z06 C7.R Edition started shipping to customers in the fourth quarter of 2015. With a figure matching the LT4's 650 hp, Chevrolet planned for a total of 650 Corvette Z06 C7.Rs to be produced with 500 for the United States and the other 150 for export. All C7.R Editions included the Z07 Performance package (enhanced aerodynamics, Michelin Pilot Super Sport Cup tires, and Brembo Carbon Ceramic Brakes) and were offered in both coupe and convertible Z06 configurations with either the 7-speed manual or the 8-speed automatic transmission. The special edition was offered only in 3LZ trim, and buyers could select the exterior in Corvette Racing Yellow or black. The 650 Z06 C7.Rs all came with their own unique sequential VIN to ensure collectability in the future.

New for 2016, the B92 hood featured the visible carbon fiber weave on the island or stinger area, and the Jake logo was created with a matte black overlay. The black stripe was carried over the roof with a matte silver stripe that proclaimed the car as the C7.R Edition. The two-tone Carbon Flash metallic/matte black racing stripe was carried to the rear, where it terminated at the rear spoiler. The coupe versions could be ordered with either the standard painted top or the visible carbon fiber top.

The exterior of the car also featured the visible carbon fiber ground effects package, black wheels with a yellow accent stripe, and yellow brake calipers. The grilles and vents were finished in Spectra Gray Metallic.

The convertibles featured the silver racing stripe integrated into the fabric of the otherwise black convertible top. On the driver's side, "C7.R Edition" appeared in the same silver color as the stripe.

Inside the C7.R limited-edition package was a black leather interior with suede microfiber accents and yellow stitching, a high-gloss version of the carbon fiber interior trim package, and competition sport seats with suede microfiber steering wheel and shifter. The C7.R logo was both embossed and embroidered into the seat backs and the word "Edition" was laser-etched into the seat, which was a first-time use of the laser etching process on a Corvette. The C7.R Edition came with Corvette Racing sill plates, and a numbered C7.R Edition dash plaque featured the number of class

*Corvette Racing's mascot, Jake, was back on the hood of the 2016 Corvette Z06 C7.R Edition with a unique matte black graphic laid over the new B92 hood's visible carbon fiber weave. His popularity with race fans now spanned two generations of Corvettes. (Photo Courtesy Gerald Corbo)*

*RPO ZCR complemented the Corvette Racing Yellow exterior with the yellow stripe black aluminum wheels and yellow brake calipers. This Z06 C7.R also has the Z07 Performance package, evident by the carbon ceramic brake rotors and Michelin Pilot Sport Cup 2 tires. (Photo Courtesy Keith Cornett)*

*Corvette designers used a combination of embossing and embroidery to display the C7.R's logo on the headrest of the Competition Sport Seats. Further accents come from the yellow stitching on the black and suede interior. (Photo Courtesy Keith Cornett)*

wins at the 24 Hours of Le Mans (7) as well as the number of championships won by the Corvette Racing team (10).

Each 2016 Corvette Z06 C7.R Edition also came with an indoor car cover from Covercraft that depicted the real Corvette C7.Rs, complete with official racing graphics.

### Introduction to Corvette Enthusiasts

At the National Corvette Museum's bash in April 2015, the Corvette Yellow Z06 C7.R Edition Coupe was unveiled by Corvette Racing program manager Doug Fehan and C7.R driver Tommy Milner. Parked end to end with Corvette Racing's number-4 C7.R, the C7.R Limited Edition Z06 was immediately mobbed by a crowd trying to get a closer look at the new car.

In June 2015, a black Z06 C7.R Edition Convertible made its debut at the 2015 Bloomington Gold Corvette Show at the Indianapolis Motor Speedway.

"Corvette Racing's legacy and technology were significant influences on the development of the Corvette Z06, and the new C7.R Edition honors the direct link between the race car and the production model," said Harlan Charles, Corvette product and marketing manager. "It also advances Chevrolet's plan to offer special-edition models that offer a unique, personal ownership experience, which become important parts of Corvette's legacy."

Corvette designers used a matte black racing stripe that was carried over the roof and onto the rear deck. In the middle of the roof graphic, "C7.R Edition" appears reversed in gloss black. (Photo Courtesy Peter Panagis)

Chevrolet took the very first 2016 Corvette Z06 C7.R Edition to Barrett-Jackson's Las Vegas auction in September 2015. The car was sold for a cool half-million dollars with the proceeds going to the College of Creative Studies, a design school in Detroit. (Photo Courtesy Keith Cornett)

The interior the Z06 C7.Rs received a healthy dose of suede that served a number of purposes including keeping drivers firmly planted in their seats. The suede-covered steering wheel and manual gear shift did not become slippery in the driver's sweaty hands. (Photo Courtesy Keith Cornett)

### *Pricing and Production*

The Corvette Z06 C7.R Editions required the Z06 3LZ package and were ordered with ZCR RPO, which was priced at $23,055 ($24,150 for convertibles). Preliminary MSRP for the C7.R Edition Coupe started at $111,400, and that didn't include the $995 delivery fee.

Official production started in mid-September 2015, with the first models reaching their new owners in early October. The model was a sell-out. The Z06 C7.R Edition was limited to 650 total examples with 500 for the United States and the other 150 assembled for export. The model breakdown was officially listed as 570 coupes and 80 convertibles.

## 2016 Corvette Z06 C7.R Edition Production Breakdown

| Model | Color | 7-Speed Man | 8-Speed Auto | Total |
|---|---|---|---|---|
| Coupe | Yellow | 129 | 234 | **363** |
| Coupe | Black | 67 | 140 | **207** |
| **Total** | | **196** | **374** | **570** |
| Convertible | Yellow | 13 | 31 | **44** |
| Convertible | Black | 14 | 22 | **36** |
| **Total** | | **27** | **53** | **80** |
| Combined | Yellow | 142 | 265 | **407** |
| | Black | 81 | 162 | **243** |
| **Total** | | **223** | **427** | **650** |

## C7 Corvette Z06 and C7.R Race Car Introduced Together

So closely linked were the C7 Corvette Z06 and the Corvette Racing C7.R race car that Chevrolet introduced them to the world together in January 2014 at Detroit's North American International Auto Show.

Many of the design and aerodynamic features from the C7.R could be found on the C7 Corvette Z06. Both cars shared the production-based aluminum frame built at the Bowling Green assembly plant. The C7.R was powered by a competition-mandated 5.5L naturally aspirated V-8 engine with the same direct injection fuel-saving technology that was found on the LT4 production V-8, and both cars utilized dry sump oil systems.

The race cars were 3 inches wider than the Z06 and showcased race-size versions of the Z06's front aerodynamic splitter and side rocker panel. Both cars had rear brake-cooling ducts along with the air-cooling ducts built into the top rear fenders for drawing air to cool the rear differential and transmission. While the street Corvette generated downforce with larger spoiler winglets and an adjustable wickerbill rear spoiler, the C7.R relied on a large mounted rear wing for racing, which provided greater handling and stability for the race car at high speed.

"Corvette Racing sets the gold standard for technology transfer between the track and street," said Corvette chief engineer Tadge Juechter in the official C7.R press release. "We are continually taking what we learn in competition and applying it to improve production Corvettes—which then make better race cars. As a result, the new Corvette Z06 is the most track-capable production Corvette ever while the new C7.R is poised to be even more competitive on the race circuit."

***The C7 Corvette Z06 and Corvette Racing's C7.R were designed and introduced together at the 2014 North American International Auto Show. The early introduction allowed the C7.R to homologate to race in 2014. (Photo by Keith Cornett)***

***Developed exclusively for the Corvette Z06 C7.R Edition was a custom car cover from Covercraft that replicated the racing livery of the Corvette C7.R race cars. The cover is so realistic that it once fooled Corvette Racing program manager Doug Fehan, who saw a covered Corvette at the National Corvette Museum and wondered why one of the C7.R race cars was in Bowling Green without his knowledge. A closer look revealed it was just a cover. (Photo Courtesy Keith Cornett)***

CHAPTER 4

# CORVETTE SPECIAL EDITIONS

In 1982, Chevrolet released the first special-edition Corvette that was special because Chevrolet made it so. Its two previous special-edition Corvettes from 1978 were created to celebrate two real events: Corvette's 25th anniversary and pacing the Indianapolis 500. The 1982 Collector Edition came about as a marketing idea. Billed as a way to celebrate the end of the C3 generation, its real function was to give Corvette buyers something new and special to keep sales strong before the C4 generation arrived.

Since that first model, Chevrolet has envisioned a number of models over the years that were created to be special and, in many cases, were limited in production. The collector edition model has seen several iterations over the years toward the end of each generation. Chevrolet also used two special editions to help launch the C7s. Others in this chapter include special lines of cars created for specific purposes, such as the Corvette Challenge race cars or the Hertz Rent a Cars.

***These Corvette special editions were built for a variety of reasons, and Corvette enthusiasts can't get enough of them. (Photo Courtesy Robert Castro)***

These special editions are enjoyed by enthusiasts for their exclusiveness as well as the low production numbers and, in many cases, serialized production meant collectors snapped them up. As time progresses, these special editions become more special every day.

## 1982 COLLECTOR EDITION HATCHBACK COUPE

The C3 Corvette run, which lasted from 1968 to 1982, was a generation of both innovation and a fight for Corvette's survival as fuel regulations clamped down on performance and budgets for updates became scarce. Through it all, the Corvette persevered with gradual updates to styling while engineers grappled with wringing whatever performance possible out the venerable 350-ci V-8.

*Chevrolet first introduced the fastback design on the 1978 Corvette, but it still took five years before the car was fit with a hatchback window. Access to the rear area forever changed the Corvette design. Every coupe since then has a rear window that opens. (Photo Courtesy Charles Kwiatkowski)*

| | |
|---|---|
| Base MSRP | $22,537.59 |
| Model Availability | Coupe |
| Engines | L83 Cross-Fire |
| Features | Exclusive exterior and interior colors, graphics, badging |
| Production Numbers | 6,759 |

*The 1982 Collector Edition helped maintain interest in the last C3 Corvettes despite knowledge that a new C4 Corvette was coming in 1983. It was very successful and showed Chevrolet again that customers would pay for the exclusivity of a special-edition model. (Photo Courtesy Hal Gurman)*

After a 14-year run, the C3 generation was officially coming to an end. A new Corvette was just around the corner. The year before, Chevrolet had opened a new Corvette assembly plant in Bowling Green, Kentucky. The 1981 Corvette was built simultaneously in St. Louis and Bowling Green through the end of the model year and starting in 1982, all Corvettes would be built in Kentucky.

To close out the C3 era, Chevrolet offered a Collector Edition for 1982. Finished in an exclusive silver-beige exterior, it featured unique, graduated stripes applied on the hood bulge and from the front side quarter vents to the rear of the car. The graduated graphics had the appearance of the paint fading to another color. Pinstriping was also applied to the top of the front and rear quarter panels. Exclusive to the Collector Edition was the 1967-styled fin aluminum wheels, and the rear window finally became a working hatchback.

The Collector Edition's interior was the most luxurious as far as C3 Corvettes go. Matching the exterior, the interior's silver-beige leather interior featured graduated striping on the door panels and seats. Designers selected premium "luxury" carpeting that provided a contrast to the silver-beige upholstery. Removable bronze-color glass panels (CC1), rear window defogger (C49), white letter Goodyear Eagle GT performance tires sized in P255/60R15 (QXH), and U75 power antenna were included in the Collector Edition package. Special Collector Edition badges were affixed to the hood, rear fuel door, and steering wheel.

To avoid the possibility of people passing off standard 1982 Corvettes as Collector Editions, a Corvette Collector Edition Coupe was identified with an ID number in the VIN. For the Collector Editions, the sixth digit in the VIN was 0. Chevrolet produced the Collector Edition "as needed," so the cars were not given sequence numbers.

### 1982 Improvements

Improvements on the 1982 model included new cross-fire injection, which would be the first fuel-injection V-8 or "fuelie" since

The wheels on the Collector Edition are as unique as the rest of the car. Based on the Stingray's cast-aluminum spinners, the new wheel forgoes the three-pronged spinner and uses a center cap cover much like that found on the 1967 Corvette. The center cap shows off the 1982 Corvette's crossed-flags logo. (Photo Courtesy Noel Carboni)

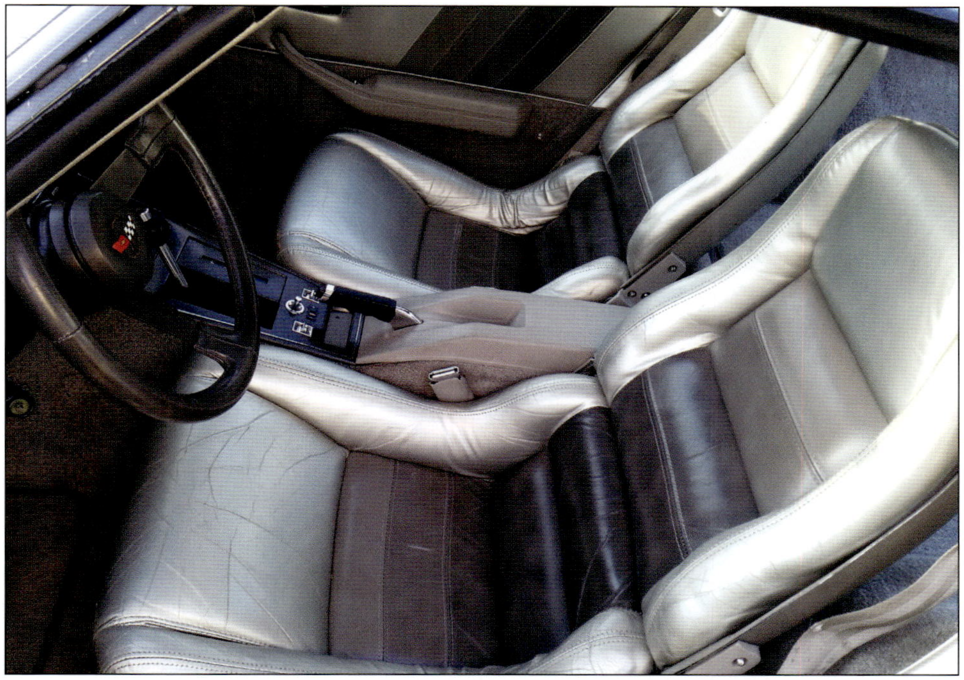

The 1982 Collector Edition's graduated paint theme was also carried into the interior. Silver-beige striped door panels and multi-colored seats help to tie it all together. (Photo Courtesy Charles Kwiatkowski)

To celebrate the end of an era, designers worked to create a sports car that was both elegant and unique. The interior was done in hues of beige and silver; Chevrolet worked with suppliers to color match the leather interior to exact specifications. The result is one of the most unique Corvette interiors ever. (Photo Courtesy Chris Jarrett)

1965. The twin electronic throttle body injectors added an additional 10 hp for a total of 200 hp. The only transmission that came with the L83 was a 4-speed automatic.

An optional lightweight fiberglass mono-leaf spring was introduced in 1981, and it became standard on all 1982 models. The main benefit of a composite spring versus steel was the weight savings: the composite spring weighed 7 pounds versus the 40-pound steel springs. Chevrolet offered the heavy-duty nine-leaf spring as the Gymkhana Suspension (RPO FE7). It also included the 1⅛-inch front anti-sway bar and a 7/16-inch anti-sway bar in the rear.

Chevrolet also boasted about the new production process that Corvettes would undergo at the brand-new Bowling Green assembly plant. A multistep plan for painting Corvettes was developed utilizing the new state-of-the-art paint facility at the Bowling Green plant. For the first time, Corvettes received a final clear-coat finish to protect the paint and add a final layer of defense against the sun's UV rays.

*In addition to the side graphic, Chevrolet designers added the graduated graphic scheme to the hood. They decided the design still needed something more, so pinstripes were added to nearly every curve and outline on the 1982 Collector Edition. In fact, reproduction kits come with a total of 39 separate graphics to faithfully replicate the special edition. (Photo Courtesy Noel Carboni)*

### Price and Production

If you looked at sales numbers in the latter half of the C3's run, you would think the car to be very popular indeed. In 1977, the Corvette set a record for sales with 49,213 sold, and two years later in 1979, Corvette broke the 50,000 barrier, closing at 53,807.

The base price of the Corvette had been steadily increasing and finally broke $20,000 for the first time in 1982. Pricing of Corvettes had actually doubled from 1978's MSRP of $9,351.89 to $18,290.07 in 1982, a necessary increase to keep the model alive and fund work on the next-generation C4.

Sales in 1982 were 25,407 units, of which 6,759 were Collector Editions. The Collector Editions accounted for 26 percent of all 1982 Corvettes. Unfortunately for Chevrolet, sales dropped off a whopping 15,199 from 1981's total of 40,606, making 1982 the lowest sales year since 1971. While the price of the Collector Edition ($4,247.52 above the base price of the 1982 Corvettes) may have contributed to slower sales, 1982's sales decline was most likely tied to a number of factors, including lack of a manual transmission and public knowledge of an all-new Corvette coming the following year.

*Remembering the issues with offering a limited-quantity 1978 Indy 500 Pace Car Replica, Chevrolet built an unlimited number of Collector Editions, but the special edition was built "only as needed" to satisfy customer orders. (Photo Courtesy Keith Cornett)*

*Jerry Palmer designed the 1982 Corvette, and one of the new technologies in exterior design was a method of printing graduated-tone color effects on pressure-sensitive film. Working with 3M, Palmer created a graduated stripe from the side vents to the rear wheels. (Photo Courtesy Charles Kwiatkowski)*

## The 1982 Cross-Fire V-8

Corvette engines continued their difficult evolution through the late 1970s and the early 1980s. As cars got heavier due to safety requirements and EPA standards for fuel economy continued to increase, performance suffered. Switching from carburetion to fuel injection was almost a requirement for getting additional power for the car while also meeting MPG standards set by the federal government.

Corvette chief engineer Dave McLellan was also in the process of designing a new Corvette from the ground up. One of the hallmarks of the C4 Corvette's design was the wedge shape with the low-angled hood. Because the hood height was lower on the C4 than the C3 Corvette, a new engine was required that could fit into both a C3 and the new C4.

Engineers cobbled together from the GM parts bin an updated 5.7L engine that became the RPO L83, known better by its marketing moniker cross-fire injection. The top of the engine used two Rochester 48-mm throttle bodies for a combined flow of 750 cfm on an aluminum manifold. Based on Cadillac's digital fuel-injection (DFI) unit, the two fuel injectors were controlled electronically by an updated version of GM's Computer Command Control unit, which monitored engine operations including throttle position, coolant temperature, engine vacuum, ignition timing, and oxygen sensors and could then adjust to deliver up to 80 "squirts" per second instead of the 10 on the previous unit.

The increase in performance was minimal with the cross-fire injection providing an increase of 10 hp for 200 hp at 4,200 rpm and peak torque at 283 ft-lbs of torque at 2,800 rpm. Peak torque comes on the low end with the L83 due to the porting on the intake manifold. The L83 delivered the highest engine output of any small-block Chevy V-8 since 1973.

Cross-fire injection was around only two model years before it was replaced with tuned port injection, but the L83 provided a quick and reliable start for Chevrolet engineers to bring back fuel injection.

**The 5.7L Cross-Fire V-8 could propel the 1982 from 0–60 mph in 8.1 seconds and down the quarter mile in 15.9 seconds at 86 mph. That's pretty slow by today's standards, but in 1982 the Corvette was America's fastest production car. (Photo Courtesy Keith Cornett)**

**The L83's cross-fire injection faced some undue criticism when it first came out. The public complained that it was difficult for back-yard mechanics to tune and nearly impossible to upgrade for an increase in horsepower and torque. However, the low-profile engine was actually a trial run for the new 1984 Corvette. (Photo Courtesy Keith Cornett)**

## 1988–1990 CORVETTE CHALLENGE/ESCORT GT FACTORY RACE CARS

The introduction of the fourth-generation Corvette in 1984 was a game changer for the brand. Not only did its great looks and driver-centered interior bring in new customers, but the car soon developed a reputation among racers as being the real deal on the track. The Corvette's winning formula consisted of an aerodynamic body mounted to a stiff chassis with a powerful V-8 engine, rigid suspension, and the game-changing anti-lock brakes. The potent combination gave the Corvettes an advantage over most cars in its class. Corvettes soon started showing up at Sports Car Club of America (SCCA) track events and, more often than not, came away with the win.

### *SCCA Showroom Stock Domination*

In 1984, the premier SCCA Showroom Stock event was a 24-hour endurance race called the The Longest Day. It was held at Nelson Ledges road course in Garrettsville, Ohio. Started in 1979, the event quickly gained the attention of those in the car business, as the track was just 100 miles from Motor City. The previous year saw Chevrolet bring out its new Camaro, and Porsche its 944.

John Greenwood, Dave Heinz, and Rod Millen entered a BFGoodrich–sponsored 1984 Corvette for the June event. A favorite of the crowd, it qualified in second place and, once the race started, its excellent fuel economy put it in the lead where it remained for 9 hours until mechanical issues dropped the car to 24th place. For the next four years running, this would be the only SCCA Showroom Stock race where the Corvette would not finish first.

The C4 Corvette platform attracted many professional race teams, including the likes of Morrison Motorsports, Rippie Racing, Bakeracing, and Powell Motorsports. Chevrolet was eager to help these teams further the development of the cars for racing, which resulted in feedback on wear and durability back to the engineers in Detroit.

The Corvettes dominated SCCA competition through 1987, and often, the only real competition came from other Corvettes in the race. Over the next three years, the Corvette went 19–0 and won every Showroom Stock race starting with the Playboy Challenge, then the SCCA Showroom Stock GT, and finally the Escort GT Endurance Series. The Corvettes won them all.

| Base MSRP | $33,043 (1988) |
|---|---|
| Model Availability | Coupe |
| Engines | L98 |
| Features | Special RPO, race-prepped cars have a special interior badge |
| Production Numbers | 56 (1988); 60 (1989); 23 (1990) |

***The number-5 1989-spec EDS Corvette Challenge Race Car was driven by the 1988 series winner, Stu Hayner. Hayner would also participate in the successful 24-Hour Endurance World Speed Record attempt with the 1990 Corvette ZR-1. (Photo Courtesy Ed Baumgarten / ©Mid America Motorworks)***

### *A New Corvette-Only Racing Series*

While this winning streak may have been fun to watch for Corvette fans, it quickly became a nightmare for the SCCA. As other marques, such as Porsche, threatened to withdraw their support to the SCCA, the organization finally relented and placed the Corvette on the banned list following the 1987 season.

Enter John Powell, owner of Powell Motorsports and operator of Canada's premier driving school. Powell organized a Camaro and Firebird racing series in Canada and brought the idea of a Corvette-only series to SCCA officials. As Powell's vision included support from Chevrolet along with sponsors offering up a $1 million purse, the SCCA sanctioned the Corvette Challenge Race Series.

Initially, Chevrolet was only lending its name to the series but eventually it provided monetary support. Sponsors included Mid-America Designs and its founder Mike Yager, along with Goodyear and Exxon. Powell's "Million Dollar Corvette Challenge" was given a place on the schedule and in 1988 ran 10 1-hour races as support races for Cart (Indy Car), NASCAR, and Trans Am races.

### *Chevrolet Offers a Factory-Built Corvette Race Car*

Chevrolet produced 56 identical Corvettes in 1988 for the series. Each Corvette was equipped with a unique 270-hp V-8 that was numbered and sealed before installation in the car at the Bowling Green factory. The Doug Nash 4+3 transmission and the Z51 Performance Handling package were also standard, along with six-way power driver's seat, side window and side mirror defog system, and the blue-tint-glass removable roof panel. The only differences between the cars were the exterior colors. Each Challenge Series Corvette had a unique sequence number and was also identifiable by the RPO B9B, officially known as the Challenge Powertrain.

*The Corvette Challenge Series made a stop in July 1988 at the Meadowlands in New Jersey, which served as a support race for the main event, the CART series. The Meadowlands Grand Prix was marketed as the Corvette Challenge Race for the Malcolm Konner Cup. (Photo credit: © Bill Erdman)*

*The Corvette Challenge Racing Series afforded both experienced drivers and up-and-comers a chance for seat time. The number-70 Corvette Challenge racer was sponsored by Malcolm Konner Chevrolet and featured the female driver Desire Wilson who had formerly campaigned in F1 and IndyCar. (Photo Courtesy Keith Cornett)*

To get the series moving, Gary Konner of Malcolm Konner Chevrolet placed the initial first order for the 56 Challenge Corvettes. Once these Corvettes were in the order system, teams and drivers began making commitments to get one of the cars. Each one of the 1988 Challenge Corvettes cost $33,043.

Of the 56 Corvettes produced, 48 were then sent to the Protofab race shop in Wixom, Michigan. One of the principals at Protofab at the time was Gary Pratt of Pratt & Miller. Protofab was selected by series organizer Powell Motor Sports to prepare the cars for racing. Each team paid $15,000 for the race prep that also included the entry fee for the season.

Each Corvette Challenge Race Car had a full roll cage and an onboard fire suppression system installed. Racing seats and five-point safety harnesses were also added. Enhancements to the car included Bilstein shocks, PBR brake pads and cooling components, and a low-restriction exhaust system. The cars

*Because the Corvettes were all outfitted identically with the same engines, racing was extremely competitive, and the winner often was the driver who could keep his or her car away from getting mixed up with others. The number-6 Corvette can be seen with damage to its rear bumper at the Meadowlands Grand Prix. (Photo credit: © Bill Erdman)*

rode on lightweight Dymag magnesium wheels with half-tread-depth Goodyear street tires.

The race graphics on the 1988 Challenge Race Cars were somewhat basic in nature, but at the time it represented a unified livery across the field to emphasize the "stock" nature of the series. Designed by the series organizers, the overall livery consisted of numbers on the front quarter panels, the main sponsors represented with large graphics on the front and rear of the cars, and smaller logos of other sponsors on top of the stock exterior color. During the race prep, specific Corvette Challenge emblems replaced the standard C4 Corvette emblems.

### *The 1988 Corvette Challenge Series*

The first race of the season was held on May 1, 1988, in Dallas, Texas, and the races were shown on a fledging cable channel called SpeedVision. Following the 10-race series, Stu Hayner was the series champion.

The series featured a number of up-and-coming drivers, including Andy Pilgrim, Paul Tracey, Boris Said, Tommy Kendall, Lou Gigliotti, Mark Dismore, Bruce Jenner, Scott Lagasse, Bill Cooper, Stu Hayner, Randy Ruhlman, Jeff Andretti, and Jimmy Vasser.

Because the Corvettes' performance was so closely matched, many races were decided by tenths of a second. To win, it took great driving and, in many cases, aggressive moves and "trading paint" to get to the front of the pack. The fans loved it and Chevrolet, sensing that the series was selling cars, signed on for a second year with the telecasts of the races moving to ESPN.

***The 270-hp racing engines were built in Flint and were equalized and sealed. Special paint was added to certain engine bolts and under a special light, the series officials could determine if they had been tampered with. (Photo Courtesy Ed Baumgarten / ©Mid America Motorworks)***

### *Corvette Challenge Returns for 1989*

The Corvette Challenge Series returned for its second year in 1989 and the season was expanded from 10 races in 1988 to 12 races. Chevrolet constructed 60 identical Corvettes with RPO R7F (1989 Challenge Vehicle), which came with the ZF 6-speed transmission and the FX3 adjustable suspensions. Of the 60 Challenge Corvettes, only 29 were converted for racing. The Corvettes were powered by a sealed and equalized 300 hp engine that was leased to the teams. The original engines were pulled and the corresponding race engines installed at the Powell Development America race shows in Wixom, Michigan.

***Once the Corvettes were completed at the Bowling Green assembly plant, they were sent to Protofab Engineering in Wixom, Michigan, where each received its racing and safety components. Even in race form, the 1988 Challenge Corvettes retained most of their stock interiors. (Photo Courtesy Ed Baumgarten / ©Mid America Motorworks)***

***The Corvette Challenge Race Cars were well documented with each race-prepped car receiving a plaque certifying it was outfitted for racing. The first plaques in 1988 were from Protofab while 1989's plaques came from Powell. (Photo Courtesy Ed Baumgarten / ©Mid America Motorworks)***

*Chevrolet leased racing engines to the teams for the series, and sealed replacement engines were also provided throughout the season as need. Following the final race of the 1988 season, Chevrolet removed the racing engines and returned the numbers-matching factory original L98 engines to the cars. (Photo Courtesy Ed Baumgarten / ©Mid America Motorworks)*

*One of the key supporters who helped get the Challenge Series off the ground was Mike Yager and Mid America Designs (now Mid America Motorworks). His early support helped lure other major sponsors, such as Goodyear and Exxon. Major sponsors were rewarded with large logos on every single Challenge car in the series. (Photo Courtesy Ed Baumgarten / ©Mid America Motorworks)*

*The number-1 1989-spec EDS Corvette Challenge Race Car was driven by the 1988 series winner, Stu Hayner. Hayner would also participate in the successful 24-Hour Endurance World Speed Record attempt with the 1990 Corvette ZR-1. (Photo Courtesy Keith Cornett)*

*The Corvette Challenge Series generated several firsts with its onboard monitoring program, including the first to synchronize telemetry with in-car TV for commercial broadcast and the first use of onboard electronics to enforce the series rules. (Photo Courtesy Ed Baumgarten / ©Mid America Motorworks)*

*The red number-3 Corvette was the overall winning car during the 1989 series. The Corvette was piloted by Bill Cooper and the Valley Chevrolet Team of Wilkes Barre, Pennsylvania. Cooper had 8 podium finishes including 3 wins in 10 races with the number-3 car. So dominant was Cooper that the championship was won with 2 races left in the series. (Photo Courtesy Corvettes at Carlisle)*

## 1988 Corvette Challenge Edition Information

Although the Corvette Challenge Race Car was a spec series with identical Corvettes, the cars were offered in multiple colors (some rarer than others), and those that were converted for the track and raced are considered the most valuable today.

### 1988 CORVETTE CHALLENGE COLOR INFORMATION

| Original Color | Number Produced | Number Converted |
|---|---|---|
| Red | 14 | 12 |
| Black | 4 | 3 |
| White | 25 | 24 |
| Yellow | 4 | 4 |
| Gray | 3 | 2 |
| Dark Blue | 4 | 3 |
| Dark Red | 2 | 2 |
| **Totals** | **56** | **50** |

### 1988 CORVETTE CHALLENGE PRODUCTION INFORMATION

| | |
|---|---|
| Cars produced: | 56 |
| Cars converted for racing: | 48 |
| Cars raced: | 46 |
| Cars raced all races: | 22 |
| Cars that won a race: | 6 |

### 1989 CORVETTE CHALLENGE COLOR INFORMATION

| Original Color | Number Produced | Number Converted |
|---|---|---|
| Red | 12 | 6 |
| Black | 12 | 5 |
| White | 12 | 8 |
| Charcoal | 12 | 6 |
| Medium Blue | 12 | 4 |
| **Totals** | **60** | **29** |

### 1989 CORVETTE CHALLENGE PRODUCTION INFORMATION

| | |
|---|---|
| Cars produced: | 60 |
| Cars converted for racing: | 29 |
| Cars raced: | 27 |
| Cars raced all races: | 10 |
| Cars that won a race: | 9 |

### 1990 ESCORT WORLD CHALLENGE COLOR INFORMATION

| Original Color | Number Produced | Number Converted |
|---|---|---|
| Red | 7 | [illegible] (maybe 2) |
| Black | 3 | N/A |
| White | 5 | 4 |
| Yellow | 5 | 3 |
| Dark Red | 1 | N/A |
| Turquoise | 1 | 0 |
| Quasar Blue | 1 | 0 |
| **Totals** | **23** | **8** |

### 1990 ESCORT WORLD CHALLENGE PRODUCTION INFORMATION

| | |
|---|---|
| Cars produced: | 23 |
| Cars converted for racing: | 8 |
| Total cars raced: | N/A |

### TEAMS THAT RACED CONVERTED CARS

| | |
|---|---|
| Rousch Racing: | 1 car (red) |
| Tommy Morrison Racing: | 3 cars (white) |
| Kim Baker Racing: | 3 cars (yellow) |
| Powell Racing: | 1 car (white) |

Specifications had changed from the previous year, allowing for more performance from the cars, and now they were much louder thanks to new side exhaust systems. An external oil cooler and a new data acquisition harness were part of the upgrades along with window nets. The data acquisition harnesses allowed series officials to monitor a car's engine performance. Each race, 10 random Corvettes were selected for monitoring to ensure the engines were operating correctly and not modded. An added benefit of the data acquisition harnesses was that viewers on ESPN got a look inside the race cars via full-functioning gauges displayed on the screen.

Another improvement for the series' sophomore year was a change in the rules that offered more flexibility for the graphics on the car. Teams were now free to pursue their own individual sponsorships. These sponsorships were reflected on the cars' liveries.

The final race of the 1989 season was held in St. Petersburg, Florida, as a

***Modern-day racing fans can still see Challenge Corvettes in action; they now qualify to race in various vintage series, including the Sportscar Vintage Racing Association (SVRA). (Photo Courtesy Ed Baumgarten / ©Mid America Motorworks)***

support race for the St. Pete Grand Prix. Bill Cooper in the number-3 Corvette Challenge Race Car was the season champion and took home $167,000 in prize money.

Although the series was more popular than ever, Chevrolet was forced to bow out of the series, and it was canceled. Following the final race in St. Pete, Chevrolet impounded all the race cars, removed the race engines, and reinstalled the 245-hp L98 V-8s that were original to the car.

### *SCCA Extends Invitation for the 1990 Escort World Challenge Series*

During the two years that Corvette was absent from the Showroom Stock GT series, Porsche and the other manufacturers caught up with the C4 Corvette's performance. While it looked like the end for C4 Corvettes racing in the SCCA, Corvettes were invited to participate in the new 1990 Escort World Challenge Series.

Although Chevrolet was officially out as the series sponsor, it continued to support the efforts of the racing teams and built a 1990 Corvette expressly for the World Challenge Series. A total of 23 World Challenge Corvettes were built. Wearing the RPO R9G, only approved teams were allowed to order. The R9G Corvettes featured the base 5.7L L98 V-8, and the 6-speed manual transmission with FX3 suspension was included in the package. Of the 23 R9G Corvettes built, only 8 were converted for racing.

The World Challenge was much like the previous showroom stock series. These were mostly stock vehicles with limited modifications. Corvettes raced against a diverse field that included Camaros, Saleen Mustangs, and Nissan 300 ZXs, to name a few. But most of the entrants were Corvettes, and they won every race in the Escort series.

Corvettes continued to dominate the competition during the 1991 SCCA World Challenge GT Series, but Chevrolet was done with building vehicles for the series. The last three years marked an exciting time for Corvette motorsports enthusiasts, and the efforts resulted in many firsts for the Chevrolet Corvette.

## 1996 COLLECTOR EDITION

From the 1984 Corvette through the final C4 Corvette, America's sports car only improved with age, and the final year of the C4's wedge-shaped body style was its exclamation point. During the 13 model years that made up the C4 Corvette generation, many advances were made.

| | |
|---|---|
| Base MSRP | $38,475 (coupe), $46,310 (convertible) |
| Model Availability | Coupe, Convertible |
| Engines | LT1, LT4 |
| Features | Unique exterior, badges, wheels |
| Production Numbers | 5,412 |

***The 1996 Collector Edition was the second Chevrolet special-edition package to celebrate the end of a generation. No limits were imposed on the Collector Edition production since Chevrolet used the model to maintain a high interest from buyers who might otherwise have waited for the new 1997 C5 Corvette. (Photo Courtesy Joshua S. Phelps / JSP Photography)***

*Chevrolet helped spread the development costs of the 1996 Grand Sport's one-year-only 330-hp LT4 by offering it as an option for the 1996 Collector Edition. The Grand Sport name remained on the LT4, and it was paired with the mandatory 6-speed manual transmission. (Photo Courtesy Joshua S. Phelps / JSP Photography)*

But a new Corvette was on the horizon and everybody and their brother knew it was coming in 1997. As new Corvette models go, speculation was high that the C5 Corvette would exceed the performance of the current car as past models had done. It was also expected to have a sleek new redesign. As interest dropped off the current model, Chevrolet turned to its tried-and-true formula to offer a special edition to keep interest up through the end of the generation.

From the two 1978 Corvette special editions and the 1982 Collector Edition, Chevrolet knew that its customers would pay a premium for a special edition, and they knew that it could help sell cars during the final year of a generation.

Most Corvette enthusiasts thought that a Collector Edition would be a given for 1996, considering it was the end of the generation. After all, Chevrolet had offered a C3 Collector Edition in 1982 that turned out to be very popular with 6,759 sold and accounting for 26 percent of all 1982 Corvettes built. However, the Corvette design team was going in a different direction and had already pitched the idea for the Grand Sport, a limited-edition tribute to Zora Arkus-Duntov and his 1963 Corvette Grand Sport race cars.

The 1996 Grand Sport would offer functional performance upgrades, including a new engine. But with only 1,000 Grand Sports planned, the costs for the upgrades were just too much for a limited run.

### Conceived Over Coffee

Former Corvette engineer John Heinricy spoke to a group of Corvette Grand Sport owners during an event at the National Corvette Museum in the summer of 2000 and recounted how the Collector Edition Corvette had been conceived.

As the story goes, Corvette chief engineer Dave Hill and Heinricy met up at the coffee pot one day and were discussing the problem of how to bring the Grand Sport to life. The upgrades they wanted for the Grand Sport were costing too much, and the marketing department was saying that only 500 to 1,000 Grand Sports could be sold. Marketing was also concerned about the impact the new 1997 C5 Corvette would have on sales.

It was then that they came up with the idea to offer two special editions in 1996; the Collector Edition would be the mass version with an unlimited quantity offered while the Grand Sport would be limited to 1,000, since that's what marketing believed it could sell.

Sebring Silver was a new color that was going to be ready for production in 1995, so John Cafaro sketched the 1996 model with the new silver exterior, along with silver ZR-1–style wheels, silver brake calipers, and a special Collector Edition emblem. Marketing liked the idea, and the company held off using the silver color that was slated for 1995 so that it would be offered exclusively with the 1996 Collector Edition.

### 1996 Corvette Collector Edition Features

The Silver Collector Editions were offered either as a coupe or convertible model and ordered with RPO Z15, which added $1,250 to the MSRP. It included the LT1 300-hp V-8 mated exclusively to the automatic 4-speed transmission and came with black Corvette-lettered brake calipers. Convertible Collector Editions featured a black soft top only.

Interiors for the Collector Editions were offered in three standard colors:

*Sebring Silver marked the return of a silver exterior for the 1996 Corvette and was exclusive to the Collector Edition. With Chevrolet bringing the Grand Sport name from 1963 back for the 1996 Grand Sport, it was fitting to bring the Sebring Silver color, which debuted in 1963, back as well. (Photo Courtesy Joshua S. Phelps / JSP Photography)*

Like the previous 1982 Collector Edition Corvette, the 1996 also received custom badges. (Photo Courtesy Keith Cornett)

Only 399 coupes and 141 convertibles received the Torch Red leather interior. The red interior LT4 convertibles are the rarest of the 1996 Collector Editions with just 68 examples produced. (Photo Courtesy Keith Cornett)

black, light gray, and red. Depending on the color of the interior, contrasting stitching with "Collector Edition" along with a small Chevrolet bowtie logo was sewn into the headrest.

The standard 1996 C4 crossed-flags circle logo was modified with the words "Collector Edition" and the Chevy bowtie on the right side of the flag; the left side retained the checkered-flag design. Larger emblems were found on the hood and on the rear fuel door, while each side had a smaller version on the front quarter panels above the centerline. The silver-painted ZR-1–style wheels also had the Collector Edition logos as special center caps.

While the 330-hp LT4 engine was developed specifically for the 1996 Grand Sports, Collector Edition buyers could select the upgraded engine as an option, which added $1,450 to the cost. By selecting the LT4 V-8, those buyers automatically got the ZF 6-speed manual transmission.

### Price and Production

The MSRP for the 1996 Collector Edition coupe started at $38,475, and the convertibles topped $46,310. Sales of the 1996 Collector Editions were strong with the combined total of 5,412 units built, accounting for 25 percent of all 1996 models. Of those, a total of 4,031 Collector Edition coupes were

### 1996 Collector Edition Coupe

| Model | Black | Light Gray | Torch Red | Totals |
|---|---|---|---|---|
| LT1 300-hp V-8 | 1,046 | 1,201 | 235 | 2,482 |
| LT4 330-hp V-8 | 751 | 625 | 164 | 1,540 |
| **Totals:** | **1,797** | **1,826** | **399** | **4,022** |

### 1996 Collector Edition Convertible

| Model | Black | Light Gray | Torch Red | Totals |
|---|---|---|---|---|
| LT1 300-hp V-8 | 472 | 367 | 73 | 912 |
| LT4 330-hp V-8 | 244 | 157 | 68 | 469 |
| **Totals:** | **716** | **524** | **141** | **1,381** |
| **Combined Totals:** | **2,513** | **2,350** | **540** | **5,403** |

A 1996 Collector Edition coupe is one of the featured cars in the collection of Corvettes on display at the National Corvette Museum. (Photo Courtesy of the National Corvette Museum)

The 1996 Corvette's gauge cluster evolved from the digital design featured in the early C4 Corvette. Like all Corvettes in the generation, the 1996 Corvette interior was very driver focused with a center console orientated toward the driver. (Photo Courtesy Joshua S. Phelps / JSP Photography)

sold along with 1,381 convertibles. Corvette owners love to know how rare their Corvettes are, and the production statistics for the Collector Edition allow us to break it down by model, engine, and interior color.

#### *Enhancements for 1996*

Even as the C4 Corvette was ending its reign and the new 1997 Corvette along with a new Gen III V-8 engine were just around the corner, Corvette engineers continued to build and refine the performance of the car in ways other than the introduction of the LT4 engine.

New to 1996 was the optional Selective Real Time Damping, which replaced the FX3 Selective Ride suspension from 1995. Known as RPO F45, sensors on all four wheels monitored the ride quality and made adjustments to find the optimal damping mode for the special shock absorbers. The system was capable of adjusting each individual shock every 10 to 15 milliseconds, which translated approximately into 1 foot of road traveled at 60 mph.

The other major news for Corvette performance in 1996 was the return of the Z51 Handling package, which was offered from 1984 to 1990 and replaced the coupe-only Z07 package that was similarly designed for competition driving and autocross events. The package offered Bilstein shocks, stiffer front and rear springs, and thicker sway bars. A 3.07:1 axle ratio was specified if ordering the Z51 with an automatic transmission. Finally, the Z51 option mandated 17-inch wheels sized with P275/40ZR17 Goodyear tires.

### 1996 GRAND SPORT

As Chevrolet prepared to close out the C4 generation, thoughts turned to how to keep sales up in 1996 when the all-new C5 Corvette would be debuting in 1997. The Corvette team had some ideas and pitched a special edition with unique styling as well as functional mechanical changes.

Corvette designer John Cafaro had been drawing sketches, and the styling department eventually settled on a blue car with a white stripe and black wheels. Earlier drawings depicted the car with a painted white "mustache," along with a blue fabric soft top and blue door handles. The red hash marks on the driver-side fender was a callback to the legendary Grand Sport Racers of the 1960s; accordingly, the new special edition would be called the Grand Sport.

Marketing wasn't initially hot on the examples it was shown in 1993. It found the design too polarizing and believed that only 500 to 1,000 of the cars could be sold. At 1,000 units, the costs for making the performance changes were too expensive for such a low volume.

| Base MSRP | $40,475 (coupe), $47,940 (convertible) |
|---|---|
| Model Availability | Coupe, Convertible |
| Engines | LT4 |
| Features | Custom exterior, badges, wheels, exclusive engine, unique VIN |
| Production Numbers | 1,000 |

***The 1996's Z16 Grand Sport RPO was the ultimate one-year Corvette special edition and it attracted a wide range of buyers, from those interested in the higher-performance capabilities to collectors who appreciated the bold looks, low volume, and rare one-year-only options. (Photo Courtesy Amanda Kossina / Kossina Creative)***

The Corvette team then came up with the idea to offer two special editions for 1996. The Collector Edition would be the high-sales-volume model, and the Grand Sport would be the limited-edition model with the performance changes the team had been pushing for.

### *Chevy Ups Performance for Final Year*

On the mechanical side, the challenge was to improve handling and performance, but with such a limited budget for a one-year car, the opportunity to develop a new engine wasn't feasible, especially with the new LS1 right around the corner. And any parts for suspension and brakes needed to come from existing parts and be available off the shelf.

To increase performance, the engineering team set out to use some old racer tricks on the existing 300-hp LT1 V-8 that included increasing air and fuel flow. With a new aluminum head design, high-flow fuel injectors, new roller rockers for additional valve lift, and a new camshaft, the redline increased from the standard LT1's 5,700 rpm to the 6,300 rpm for the new LT4.

For better handling, the team used the ZR-1's five-spoke wheels (now painted black) fitted with Goodyear Eagle GS-C tires. On all coupe models, the tires were sized P275/40ZR17 fronts and P315/35ZR17 rears. To keep the wider tires tucked under the car, the coupes required the use of an Export Flare on the rears. Only the coupe models received the ZR-1-sized tires, as they were too big to fit into the trunk of the convertible models. Instead, the Grand Sport convertibles received P255/45ZR17 fronts and P285/40ZR17 for the rears.

### *Bringing the Grand Sport to Life*

Making the car on a limited budget meant there would be some give and take with the original concept and going with what could be accomplished. The original white body stripes were to be painted and then matched to the bumper with the white mustache design. As the bumpers were painted off the car, there were issues with aligning them to the body stripes, so the white mustache was gone and the white body stripe became a decal. The Admiral Blue fabric top was canceled because the color was not matching the paint. Eventually, a white convertible top was chosen. The door handles' inexpensive metal was difficult to paint and took too long, so that idea was scrapped as well. We did hear that one Grand Sport convertible exists with the prototype blue door handles!

Because the black brake calipers were visible through the Grand Sport's five-spoke black aluminum wheels, it was important for them to look good. Unfortunately, the stock calipers just would not hold paint. Like the door handles, the stock calipers were manufactured out of an inexpensive metal casting, resulting in a surface that was resistant to paint adhesion. The Corvette team worked with the vendor, who utilized a different metal that resulted in a stronger, heat-resistant caliper.

*From an appearance standpoint, the new 330-hp V-8 was nearly identical to the LT1 300-hp V-8. To differentiate the new engine, Chevrolet dressed up the powerplant with a red aluminum intake manifold, red ignition wires, and a black fuel-injector cover adorned with "Corvette" in red letters. (Photo Courtesy Keith Cornett)*

*Making the 1996 Corvette Grand Sport even more appealing to collectors was that the special editions had their own special VIN sequence. After the ZR-1s finished production in 1995, Chevrolet wanted to ban the practice for being too costly. Members of the Corvette team successfully argued that it was needed to make the Grand Sports "even more special." (Photo Courtesy Keith Cornett)*

***The 330-hp LT4 added 30 hp and 5 extra ft-lbs of torque that could propel the Grand Sport 0–60 mph in 5.2 seconds and run the quarter mile in 13.7 seconds at 105.1 mph. (Photo Courtesy Amanda Kossina / Kossina Creative)***

***A unique feature found only on the C4 generation was the Corvette's clamshell hood that offered easy access to the engine bay, tires, and brakes. The rear-lifting glass hatchback has become a mainstay of Corvette design and has been included on every Corvette Coupe since it was first introduced in 1982. (Photo Courtesy Andrew Eisemeier)***

### *Lucky Breaks*

During a C4 reunion at the National Corvette Museum in May 2015, Corvette engineer and test driver John Heinricy recounted some of the lucky breaks that fell the engineering team's way. These breaks allowed the team to add additional performance content when normally that would not be an option with any kind of one-year-only powertrain warranty.

For better handling, they had the ZR-1-sized tires but nothing else for the suspension. For 1996, Heinricy said, there just happened to be an initiative to look at new shock absorbers, so they went with a new supplier named Delphi.

The ZR-1 tires stuck too far out of the wheelwells during testing. They could be modified, but it would be too much work. By collaborating with the wheel vendor, they were able to make an inexpensive change to their tooling, and the wheels were then modified to better fit the wider tires under the coupes.

A new OBDII certification meant that all Chevy motors had to be updated for the 1996 models, so the LT4 could be pushed through without additional costs. That same OBDII certification is one of the main reasons the ZR-1 ended production in 1995: It was deemed too costly for the LT-5 to be certified.

### *Pricing and Production*

The 1996 Corvette Grand Sport was sold as RPO Z16, and the option added $3,250 to the MSRP of $37,225 for the coupe or $2,880 on top of the $45,060 MSRP for convertibles. Interior color choices were either black or red/black.

All Grand Sports featured the Admiral Blue with white body stripe, red hash marks, and black ZR-1–style wheels. All were powered by the 330-hp LT4 V-8 and all were available only with the ZF 6-speed manual transmission.

Performance junkies could also opt for the Z51 Performance Handling package ($350), which added Bilstein shock absorbers, stiffer springs, and front and rear stabilizer bars. The Z51 was offered only on coupes. Another hot option was the F45 Selective Real Time Damping System, which monitored and adjusted the suspension every 10 to 15 milliseconds.

As expected, Chevrolet built and sold 1,000 Grand Sport models; of those, 810 were coupes and 190 were convertibles. The Grand Sports represented 4.6 percent of total 1996 production.

#### A Breakdown of the Body Style, Interior Color, and Suspension Package

| **Body** | **Interior** | **FE1** | **F45** | **Z51** | **Total** |
|---|---|---|---|---|---|
| Coupe | Black | 197 | 206 | 190 | 593 |
| Coupe | Red/Black | 40 | 91 | 86 | 217 |
| Convertible | Black | 76 | 61 | 0 | 137 |
| Convertible | Red/Black | 42 | 11 | 0 | 53 |
| **Total:** | | **355** | **369** | **276** | **1,000** |

*The interiors for the Grand Sport were either all black or a two-tone red/black combination with red leather seats, door panels, and lower console. For convertibles, the interior color also surrounded the boot. The red interiors were selected by only 27 percent of Grand Sport buyers. (Photo Courtesy Keith Cornett)*

*It's a very rare trick to pull off the kinds of performance upgrades that the Chevrolet team offered on the limited-edition Grand Sport, especially coming at the end of a generation. With off-the-shelf parts and the help of vendors, the 1996 Corvette Grand Sport became the grand finale for the C4 generation. (Photo Courtesy Andrew Biesemeier)*

### *The End of the Fourth-Generation Corvette*

The year 1996 was the rare year that two separate special-edition Corvettes were offered at the same time. With the introduction of the C5 Corvette coming in 1997, these two special editions and the other changes Chevrolet implemented did their jobs and kept buyers' interest in the 1996 models. Sales climbed to 21,536, a modest increase of 3.8 percent above the 20,742 Corvettes sold in 1995.

A total of 366,227 Corvettes were built during the C4 generation, a testament to the vision of Corvette chief engineer Dave McLellan, who completely transformed the brand and disrupted the sports car market with the introduction of the technically advanced C4 Corvette in 1984. McLellan retired in 1992 after production of the 1 millionth Corvette, and Dave Hill led the crossed-flags into the next generation.

*The 1996 Grand Sport's striking design is one of the most popular color combinations offered by Chevrolet. With its distinctive Admiral Blue paint, white center stripe, and red hash marks, it's a timeless look that was adopted by the new C7 Grand Sport in 2017, as well. (Photo Courtesy Amanda Kossina / Kossina Creative)*

In the end, the 1996 Grand Sport was a sort of redemption for Zora Arkus-Duntov, whose lightweight Grand Sport program was killed by GM corporate for violating the AMA racing ban. Even after General Motors learned of it, Duntov somehow managed to get the five completed Grand Sport race cars into private hands, where they were raced before owners finally figured out how rare (and valuable) they would become. Three decades later, that same company recognized those cars that never should have been with the commemorative 1996 Grand Sport.

## 2008 ZHZ HERTZ COUPE (RENTAL) / 2009 ZHZ HERTZ CONVERTIBLE (RENTAL)

What's a great way to get people behind the wheel of an automobile for an extended test drive that, best of all, they pay for? The answer for Chevrolet was to sell its halo sports car to Hertz Rent a Car, achieving a car sale and marketing purpose. For many of the people who would rent a sports car, it was their first experience driving a Corvette.

In the summer of 2008, Hertz Rent a Car announced it was teaming up with Chevrolet to offer the Corvette ZHZ, an exclusive, limited-edition version of the iconic American sports car. The Corvette ZHZ was included in the Hertz Fun Collection, which featured a variety of sporty vehicles available for rent in key metropolitan markets across the county. The Hertz Fun Club program garnered considerable attention when it reintroduced the Carroll Shelby black and gold Mustang GT-H, just like it had back in 1966. Other Fun Club cars included a Nissan 350Z Convertible, Hummer H3, and the Jeep Wrangler.

The initial list of cities offering the Hertz Fun Club included Miami, Orlando, Fort Lauderdale, Tampa, Palm Beach, Fort Myers, Dallas, Houston, Boston, San Diego, Las Vegas, Los Angeles, Seattle, Portland, San Francisco, Oahu, Maui, Nashville, Charlotte, Charleston, Philadelphia, Dulles, Phoenix, Denver, and Newark.

| Base MSRP | $59,540 (coupe),<br>$64,290 (convertible) |
|---|---|
| Model Availability | Coupe, Convertible |
| Engines | LS3 |
| Features | Exterior yellow with black stripe, badging, embroidery |
| Production Numbers | 875 |

***The C6 Corvette coupe and convertible gave new meaning to Hertz Rent a Car's Fun Club. The Corvettes generally rented for $100 to $200 per day, and most locations had a mileage limit of between 100 and 150 miles. (Photo Courtesy Trevor Freeman)***

### *The ZHZ Corvette Coupe and Convertibles*

The Hertz Corvette ZHZs were rolled out over two years with 500 coupes produced during 2008 and 375 convertibles produced at the beginning of the 2009 model year. The specialty rentals were exclusively offered in Velocity Yellow with a black body stripe, the color combo appropriately matching the Hertz corporate logo.

The Corvette ZHZ was equipped with the standard 436-hp LS3 coupled to the 6-speed paddle shift automatic transmission and was fully optioned with dual mode exhaust, Magnetic Selective Ride Control, and larger cross-drilled brake rotors. A 2LT Ebony interior featured embroidered ZHZ center consoles, floor mats, and a Hertz ZHZ emblem on the front fenders.

*Genuine Corvette Accessories*, Chevrolet's official aftermarket parts and accessories catalog, played a large part in accessorizing the ZHZ rentals. Included was the Ultimate Appearance package, featuring the screen mesh on the side coves, exhaust plate, and front grille. Other accessories featured were the body-color rear license plate frame, underhood blanket and lamp kit, as well as the full-width spoiler and body-color door handles. Seven-spoke forged aluminum chrome wheels completed the build.

### *What's Not Included*

In terms of features, the ZHZ is actually a stripped-down version of the retail Corvette: no seat/mirror memory, no Heads-Up Display (HUD), no in-seat heating, and no control buttons on the steering wheel.

The first 2008 ZHZ Coupe came off the assembly line on April 21, 2008. The Corvettes were built in daily batches, and their production was mixed with other coupes, so the VIN were not in sequence. The final 500th ZHZ Corvette was completed on June 20, 2008. The 2009 Corvette ZHZ convertibles did have their own VIN sequence, which started at 1G1YY36W195200001 and ended at 1G1YY36W195200375.

During their service as rental cars, the Corvettes were outfitted with the Hertz NeverLost navigation system. Average rental fees ran between $100 and $200 depending on location and demand.

***Chevrolet Dealership Completes Conversions***

The ZHZs were assembled in Bowling Green as standard 2LT Velocity Yellow Corvettes and then were sent to Bob Hook Chevrolet in Louisville, Kentucky, where the dealer-installed ZHZ options were added. Bob Hook Chevrolet was selected to perform the conversions because it was the GM accessory distributor in Kentucky and had the space to warehouse the parts and perform the conversions.

Each of the Corvettes underwent a secondary assembly process through which its standard wheels were removed and polished seven-spoke wheels were added. The accessory rear spoiler was installed, and then the body graphics and mesh screens were installed.

The Corvettes were rotated through the Chevy dealership, with transports bringing in unprepped vehicles while the finished ZHZs were loaded up and taken back to Bowling Green to be shipped to various

***The 2008 Corvette ZHZ coupes arrived first at select Hertz locations and then expanded with the convertible lineup in 2009. The black racing stripe flows across the sports car from front to back, over the coupe's removable roof panel. (Photo Courtesy Travis Raczynski)***

***The "Hertz Yellow" Corvette's black stripe and seven-spoke wheels provided the backdrop for many photos in the early days of social media. Videos of vacationers with their ZHZ Corvettes can still be found on YouTube. (Photo Courtesy Trevor Freeman)***

***The interiors and standard equipment were limited on the rental Corvettes with just the standard Ebony offered. The console lid showed a yellow ZHZ logo, and Hertz normally offered the rentals with its in-car GPS system called NeverLost. (Photo Courtesy Trevor Freeman)***

*The clever people who came up with the RPO name "ZHZ" for the Rent a Car package must have been science nerds as well. Hertz is also a scientific unit of frequency, known by the symbol "Hz." (Photo Courtesy Trevor Freeman)*

*With a run of 875 units, the sports car migrated from "Manager's Special" rental to collectible Corvette within just a year or so of being produced. Following their service, they were auctioned in mass batches at a Florida wholesale auction. (Photo Courtesy Travis Raczynski)*

Hertz locations throughout the country. The coupes took about 10 hours each to convert. The convertibles shipped with the polished wheels and took only 6 hours each to prep.

### *Rentals Sold to Consumers*

In the summer of 2009, the first Hertz Corvette ZHZs ended their service as rentals and were sold through the dealer-only Manheim Auto Auctions in Florida. The Corvettes had on average 22,000 to 25,000 miles and were in "driver" condition, with some scratches and worn interiors. Auction watchers reported the average sales to be in the low $30,000s.

A couple of ZHZs that had been stored with virtually no rental miles went through the big auction houses, such as Barrett-Jackson and Mecum.

### *Buyer Beware*

Just the fact the car was a rental would turn off many buyers. After all, the saying "don't be gentle, it's a rental" was even more true when you were handed the keys to a 436-hp sports car. Countless ZHZs were crashed during their rental service, including one that spectacularly took out eight other cars in Philadelphia.

The Corvette ZHZs also became magnets for those who wanted to drive a Corvette to the local drag strip or participate in high-performance driving events. YouTube is full of examples of people goofing off in the yellow rentals. A couple of our favorite stories include a man who taught his daughter how to do donuts in a Corvette ZHZ convertible, and an early YouTuber who rented a ZHZ and installed a temporary nitrous system for a night at the track.

## 2009 COMPETITION SPORT

In 2009, the global economy was in the middle of a financial meltdown that pundits would soon call the Great Recession. Millions of Americans

| | |
|---|---|
| Base MSRP | $55,655 (coupe), $77,500 (Z06) |
| Model Availability | Coupe, Z06 |
| Engines | LS3, LS7 |
| Features | Exterior color, gray wheels, graphics, exclusive engine cover |
| Production Numbers | 72 |

*Inspired by Corvette owners who enjoy autocrossing and other high-performance driving education (HPDE) events, the Corvette design team created the 2009 Corvette Competition Sport, which packaged race-focused options and appearance cues in the lightest and most powerful versions of the Z51 coupe and Z06 models. (Photo Courtesy Dawn Jobe / DJ Carbon Flash Photography)*

***Along with the Z51 Performance package and the NPP dual exhaust, the Competition Sport Coupe included exclusive features from the Z06, including the differential oil cooler and tall spoiler. The Heads-Up Display (HUD) was made available for the first time on a 1LT-equipped coupe. This was the most powerful and track capable Corvette coupe in the 2009 model lineup. (Photo Courtesy Dawn Jobe / DJ Carbon Flash Photography)***

***Because the Competition Sport was marketed with the track enthusiast in mind, Chevrolet tied in Corvette Racing's mascot, Jake, the skull with the Corvette crossed-flags-logo eyes. Jake was placed on the B-pillar of the exterior and inside on the seats and console lid. (Photo Courtesy Travis Raczynski)***

***The Competition Sport Corvettes made their public debut in March 2009 at the 12 Hours of Sebring. The number-02 Z51 Coupe in Blade Silver served as one of the official track cars and was used to give hot laps around the track at speeds of up to 140 mph to fans (including the author) during breaks in the races. (Photo Courtesy Keith Cornett)***

saw their home values drop as the subprime mortgage bubble burst. The ripple effect across multiple sectors of the economy was enormous, and soon major pressure was brought to bear on the Big Three automotive manufacturers. With General Motors running out of cash and obligations mounting, the company entered into a government-ordered Chapter 11 Bankruptcy reorganization in June 2009.

The Chevrolet Corvette, long considered a secondary or non-primary vehicle, saw its sales drop by 50 percent to only 16,956 in 2009 versus the 35,310 Corvettes sold in 2008. The one bright spot for Corvette had been the introduction of the 638-hp Corvette ZR1, which had an MSRP of $105,000 (but most were up-optioned models that sold for $118,000 or more). Chevy went on to sell 1,415 Corvette ZR1s in its inaugural year.

It was against that backdrop in January 2009 that Chevrolet announced a new special-edition Corvette package known as the Competition Sport with production planned for the spring. A few weeks later, General Motors also announced the limited-edition 2009 GT1 Championship models. Customers not swayed or able to purchase the new 2009 Corvette ZR1 now had a choice between two very different special-edition Corvette models.

### *The 2009 Corvette Competition Sport*

Chevrolet made the announcement of the new package through its dealer network instead of through a public reveal of the car. The move to make a low-key announcement for a special-edition Corvette package during the same week as Detroit's 2009 North American International

***The 2009 Corvette Competition Sport and 2009 GT1 Championship Corvette were total opposites when it came to planned functionality, but one item the two special editions of 2009 shared was the tech-pattern engine covers on top of the 430-hp LS3 V-8s. The only difference was that the CSR had red lettering and the GT1 Corvettes were painted yellow. (Photo Courtesy John Dunlap)***

***Following its public reveal at the Mobil 1 12 Hours of Sebring in March 2009, Corvette enthusiasts got their next look at the Competition Sport models during the National Corvette Museum's Birthday Bash in April 2009. (Photo Courtesy Travis Raczynski)***

Auto Show was curious considering the amount of automotive press that regularly attends the show. But it was also a sign of the times that the company didn't want to be seen as marketing a new special-edition Corvette created for track use just weeks after General Motors had accepted billions in financing from the government and US taxpayers.

The Competition Sport Racer (CSR) Corvettes were available in either a base 1LT coupe with 436 hp or as the base-level 1LZ Z06 with 505 hp. The package was offered in two colors per model, with the Z51 coupe models outfitted in either Blade Silver or Arctic White and the Z06s available in Blade Silver and black. Chevrolet's official press release proclaimed the Competition Sport was aimed for Corvette owners who attended driving schools and track events; every model was uniquely identified with a customer-installed racing number decal that matched the build sequence of the series.

Regardless of exterior color, every Competition Sport came with Competition Gray exterior stripes, Competition Gray painted aluminum wheels, and gray headlamps. Corvette Racing's mascot Jake (the skull with the Corvette crossed-flags logo as eyes) was featured on the exterior of the B-pillar along with "CSR" to signify Competition Sport Racer.

### For Corvette Owners Who Track Their Cars

Under the hood, the Competition Sports had their own special engine covers in a graphic pattern with red lettering. Inside the cabin, an Ebony interior was accented with Titanium-colored stitching. The Jake mascot and CSR monogram were prominently featured with Titanium-colored embroidery on the seat headrests and on the center armrest. Corvette Racing pedals from the Genuine Corvette Accessories catalog completed the look.

The Competition Sport featured gray headlamps that contrasted the silver and white exteriors of the Z51 coupe but complemented the Competition Gray full-length body stripe. It was the first package to offer contrasting-colored headlamps.

One of the main selling features of the Competition Sport model in the coupe form was that several performance options that racers relied on could be purchased together in the base model configuration. Previously, options such as HUD were available only in the 2LT or 3LT trim packages. The coupe CSR model came configured with the Z51 Performance package and also included the 6-speed manual transmission, NPP dual performance exhaust, oil differential cooler, Heads-Up Display, red-painted brake calipers, and the Z06's tall spoiler.

### Track Days Serve as Inspiration for the CSR Corvette

The Z06 CSR model was offered with the same mechanicals as the standard Z06 model, making this a stickers version in the truest sense.

The Corvette team was inspired to create the Competition Sport package after attending High Performance Driver Education (HPDE) events with the National Corvette Museum. After talking with fellow attendees and seeing how much they enjoyed using their Corvettes at these events, the team created the Competition Sport package for enthusiasts who brought their Corvettes to track events, autocross competitions, and driving schools.

In addition to using the lightest versions of the Z51 coupe and the Z06, track-inspired features of the CSRs included race numbers on the doors for identification at driving events. The Corvette Racing accessory pedals came recommended by the driving instructors at Spring Mountain Motorsports Ranch for improving heel-toe shifting. The tall Z06 spoiler helped create additional downforce, and the Competition Gray wheels helped to hide brake dust.

### *Price and Production*

The Z51-equipped 1LT coupe version was priced at $55,655, while the Z06 1LZ model was listed for $77,500, including destination charges. During the 2009 model year, Chevrolet produced 72 Competition Sport Corvettes.

The CSR coupes represented just .6 percent of coupe production, and the CSR Z06 production was just 20 cars out of 3,471 Z06s built for .6 percent of total Z06 production. Overall, the 72 Competition Sport Racers made up just .4 percent of 2009 Corvette production.

The Corvette CSR was its own package and was listed as "Complete—without options." But one silver Z51 coupe was delivered with the optional dual roof package.

These Corvettes are so rare they hardly ever become available. Two low-mileage examples were sold at auctions in 2016 with the number-42 CSR Z51 coupe selling for $37,000 and the number-38 Corvette Z06 CSR

*Corvette designers chose Competition Gray aluminum wheels instead of bright chrome or a black design because the gray helps to better hide the brake dust generated during track events. The Competition Gray theme was carried across the model with full-length racing stripes and gray headlamps leading the way. (Photo Courtesy Keith Cornett)*

## Z51 Production Numbers Breakdown

| CSR Model | Color | Quantity |
|---|---|---|
| Z51 Coupe | White | 13 |
| Z51 Coupe | Silver | 39 |
| Z06 | Black | 10 |
| Z06 | Silver | 10 |
| **Total:** | | **72** |

*Most High Performance Driver Education (HPDE) and autocross events require a number on the car for identification, so each of the 72 Competition Sports came with their own unique door number based on the sequence of production. The Corvette design team knew that not everyone would want the numbers on their cars, so they were included with the car for the owner to install. (Photo Courtesy Keith Cornett)*

*The track-inspired Corvette Z06 Competition Sports are one of the lowest production special-edition models ever made with just 20 total CSR Z06s produced, 10 in black and 10 in Blade Silver. The model is big on the qualities collectors covet: high performance and limited production. These models became collectibles the minute they were built. (Photo Courtesy Dawn Jobe / DJ Carbon Flash Photography)*

fetching $66,000. The number-02 CSR shown in some of these photos sold at the Barrett-Jackson Scottsdale auction for $46,200.

## 2011 Z06 CARBON EDITION

To understand the significant changes made for the 2011 Corvette Z06, we first need to look at what's been going on with Corvettes over the past few years.

The C6 generation started in 2005 with the standard coupe and convertible, producing 400 hp from the 400-hp 6.0L LS2 V-8 engine. In 2006, the sixth-generation version of the Corvette Z06 was released. Powered by a naturally aspirated 7.0L V-8, the 505-hp engine was available exclusively for the Z06. Accolades were plentiful, and it was the Corvette to have for track enthusiasts. Not only did the Z06 establish itself as a bonafide track car, a total of 22,162 Z06s were sold in the first three years with sales peaking at 8,159 in 2007.

| | |
|---|---|
| Base MSRP | $90,960 |
| Model Availability | Z06 |
| Engines | LS7 |
| Features | Exterior colors, carbon fiber aerodynamics, graphics, embroidery |
| Production Numbers | 252 |

The Corvette team breathed new life into the now venerable Corvette Z06 during the 2011 model year. The Carbon Edition name is derived from its carbon fiber raised hood and black carbon fiber aerodynamics that include side rocker panels, front splitter, and a ZR1-style body-color rear spoiler. With a host of performance parts and additional weight savings, the Carbon Edition Z06 was a formidable sports car. (Photo Courtesy Chad B. Hall)

*In 2004, a painted carbon fiber hood was featured on the Commemorative Edition Corvette Z06. Chevrolet reintroduced it for the 2011 Carbon Z06. It became known as RPO B92 and was offered in successive years as a $2,500 stand-alone option. Not only was it lightweight but underneath was also fully visible carbon fiber. The hood weighed just 14 pounds compared to 26 pounds for the standard Z06 hood. (Photo Courtesy Keith Cornett)*

*The cabins of the Carbon Editions were covered in suede, and the Ebony interior featured contrasting thread in either orange or blue, depending on the exterior color. A unique center was added to the Carbon Edition's steering wheel and custom door sills. (Photo Courtesy Keith Cornett)*

*The 50th anniversary of Corvette's first class win at the 24 Hours of Le Mans was in 2011. Chevrolet celebrated the anniversary exclusively on the Carbon Edition with special dealer-installed Euro-style door graphics. The track maps at the bottom represent Milford Proving Grounds, Road Atlanta, Willow Springs, Spring Mountain, and Virginia International Raceway. (Photo Courtesy Keith Cornett)*

### *Corvette Z06 Competing with Grand Sport and ZR1*

As the Z06 was enjoying its status as the tip of the spear, Corvette engineers were busy on two very different Corvette models that would chip away at the Z06's sales from both ends. In 2009, Chevrolet introduced the 638-hp Corvette ZR1, boasting its own exclusive powerplant, the supercharged 638-hp LS9 V-8, capable of reaching 205 mph. In 2010, the new mid-level Grand Sport model took its place in the Corvette lineup, sporting the Z06's wide-body in both coupe and convertible versions and priced below the Z06.

It was also during this time that the global economy took a nosedive. Automakers were particularly hard hit, and Corvette's sales fell from 35,310 in 2008 to 16,956 in 2009 and would further tumble to 12,194 in 2010. The Corvette Z06 sold just 518 copies in 2010, and enthusiasts were worried that the once-great performance model would be cannibalized by sales of the Grand Sport and ZR1.

Chevrolet heard those pleas and arranged to have several Corvette ZR1 performance parts flow down to the Corvette Z06, which provided most of the capabilities of the ZR1 without the six-figure MSRP. Also benefiting the Z06 was the recent work from Corvette Racing in developing its GT2 race car the previous year. With the 2011 Corvette Z06 Carbon Edition, the transfer of technology from racing to production was never more apparent. Chevy utilized the prominent theme of track-to-street technology transfer to announce the 2011 Corvette Z06 Carbon Limited Edition.

"Designed to further incorporate technology developed through racing, the Corvette Z06 Carbon Limited Edition is a tribute to the 50th anniversary of Corvette's first race in the 24 Hours of Le Mans," said Jim Campbell, Chevrolet general manager, in the official press release. "With a limited production of 500 units, this car is a must-have for the true Corvette collector and driving enthusiast."

## The Carbon Z06 Production and Color Breakdown

| Color | Quantity |
|---|---|
| Inferno Orange | 86 |
| Supersonic Blue | 166 |
| **Total:** | **252** |

*Two new colors, Inferno Orange and Supersonic Blue, were used for the 2011 Carbon Editions. This Inferno Orange 2011 Carbon Edition show car wore VIN number 013 and was one of two cars used to debut the special edition to the public in March 2011 at the 12 Hours of Sebring. (Photo Courtesy Keith Cornett)*

### *Z06 Carbon Limited Edition Features*

Combining the Z06's lightweight body and 505-hp naturally aspirated LS7 with the Magnetic Selective Ride Control and braking found on the ZR1, the Corvette Z06 Carbon Edition was hailed as the best balanced track Corvette yet. Tadge Juechter, Corvette chief engineer, stated, "For technical tracks like Laguna Seca, the Z06 Carbon could shave up to 3 seconds off the Z06 lap time."

Mechanically, for the first time on the Z06, the Carbon added Magnetic Selective Ride Control, Brembo carbon ceramic brakes with dark gray metallic calipers, and enhanced cooling. Black 20-spoke 19-inch front/20-inch rear wheels carried Michelin PS2 tires.

On the exterior, the Z06 Carbon was produced in two colors: Inferno Orange and Supersonic Blue. The body changes included black headlamps and mirrors, a ZR1-style body-color spoiler, body-color door handles, carbon fiber raised hood, and black carbon fiber rockers and splitter. For track events, customer-installed Eurostyle numbers came with each car.

Inside the Z06 Carbon were Ebony leather and suede complemented by matching blue or orange seat stitching. A unique steering wheel and sill plates were in place, as well as logoed headrests. Suede was used throughout the interior, including on the steering wheel, shifter, seat inserts, armrests, and doors.

### *Carbon Z06's Z07 and CFZ Options*

General Motors knew the options that made up the package would be in demand. For ease in ordering, the company packaged most of Carbon Z06's components into two new RPOs that could be ordered together or separately on any Z06.

The optional Z07 Performance package included the mechanical upgrades found on the Z06 Carbon: brakes, ride control, and chassis

## Bookend Carbon Editions for Rick Hendrick

The first regular-production 2011 Corvette Z06 Carbon Edition was offered for sale at Barrett-Jackson's 2010 Palm Beach auction, and it sold for $297,000 with the proceeds going 100 percent to charity. Chevrolet dealer and NASCAR team owner Rick Hendrick purchased the right to buy the very first Carbon Z06 and, once production was ready to start, he chose Inferno Orange for VIN 001.

Hendrick also worked with General Motors to buy the final Carbon Z06, VIN 252. What's special about this car is that it was painted black, making it the only 2011 Carbon Z06 that was not Inferno Orange or Supersonic Blue. Another unique feature is the reversed Eurostyle number on the sides of the car. The regular color scheme for the graphic is black lettering, but General Motors prepared a special silver version that shows up very nicely on the black Z06. And, finally, the black Z06 holds the LS7 that Hendrick assembled himself at GM's Performance Build Center in Wixom, Michigan, as part of the Engine Build Experience.

***Longtime Chevrolet dealer, NASCAR team owner, and Corvette enthusiast Rick Hendrick owns both the first and last 2011 Carbon Editions. The final Carbon Edition was specially painted black as he has been known to favor the color on his Corvettes. Hendrick also participated in the Engine Build Experience, assembling the 505-hp engine that went into that very car. (Photo Courtesy the National Corvette Museum)***

## 2011 Corvette Z06 VIN Number 001

In commemorating the 50th anniversary of Corvette's first class win at Le Mans, General Motors built a very special one-of-one tribute to the 1960 Briggs Cunningham Corvette. VIN 001 shares the same exterior cues as the first Corvette to win at Le Mans, including the twin stripes over the hood, roof, and trunk and the number 3. A special graphic on the B-pillar features a 50th anniversary logo and the dates 1960 and 2010.

The Arctic White Corvette Z06 is equipped with both the Z07 Performance package and the CFZ black carbon fiber package. Unique are the side-view mirrors painted in Cyber Gray instead of the black that comes on the Carbon edition. These gray mirrors match the Cyber Gray wheels.

As a fundraiser for the National Corvette Museum, the car was auctioned at the 2011 Barrett-Jackson auction in Scottsdale, Arizona. The car was signed by famous racers Dick Thompson and Dick Guldstrand. The winning bid was $210,000.

***Briggs Cunningham took three 1960 Corvettes to the 24 Hours of Le Mans and came home with a class win, the first ever for Corvette. Chevy kicked off the 2010 Bash event at the National Corvette Museum with a special unveiling of an Arctic White/ blue-striped 50th anniversary tribute to those vintage racers featuring the VIN 001 Corvette Z06. It was later auctioned to support the National Corvette Museum. (Photo Courtesy Keith Cornett)***

and cooling upgrades. The Z07 also included the Competition Gray 20-spoke wheels.

RPO CFZ was the package for the carbon fiber aerodynamics found on the car. The enhanced aerodynamic components included the black carbon fiber rockers, splitter, and roof panel with the full-width body-color spoiler.

### Pricing and Production

Corvette's product marketing manager, Harlan Charles, announced the 2011 Corvette Z06's MSRP at $90,960, and if you selected all the option boxes, a loaded 2011 Z06 Carbon Edition sold for $99,925. Chevrolet limited the Carbon Edition to just 500 units, but production reached only half that number with 252 Carbon Editions produced. The Carbon Z06 package was ordered with the RPO ULZ and added $15,705 to the Z06 MSRP of $74,305. With the destination charge, the 3LZ-equipped version started at $98,130. Chevrolet built 252 Carbon Z06s out of the total 904 Z06s built in 2011.

The two RPOs created from the Carbon Z06 sold very well: 535 Z06s were equipped with the CFZ ($3,995) and 540 were optioned with the Z07 Performance Package ($9,495). Chevrolet did not release how many Z06s were optioned with both RPOs.

### Production Delays Plague Rollout

The 2011 Carbon Z06 package made its public debut in March 2010, and it was announced then that initial production was to start later that summer. The Carbon Z06 would be delayed though the end of the year. Chevrolet officially revealed the Carbon's MSRP just before Thanksgiving and announced that the car would start production in early first quarter 2011. The first regular production Carbon Z06 was built in late February, and the rest followed in early March.

## 2013 427 CONVERTIBLE

With the 2013 model year being both the 60th anniversary of the Corvette as well as the C6's final year of production, it was widely anticipated that Chevrolet would offer something special for Corvette enthusiasts.

Taking a cue from customer requests to put the 505-hp LS7 V-8 engine into a convertible model, Chevrolet didn't disappoint when it offered a special one-year-only model called the 2013 Corvette 427 Convertible Collector Edition. The 427 Convertible was unveiled along with a special new 2013 60th Anniversary package during Detroit's North American International Auto Show in January 2012.

### The Corvette 427 Convertible Collector Edition

The 427 Convertible was a unique model in the Corvette lineup that played up the historic combination of convertibles powered by 427 big-blocks similar to those of the late 1960s. In this modern version, the 427 was a potent 7.0L small-block. Combining the modern technology of the performance-oriented Z06 and ZR1 models with the steel frame of the Corvette Grand Sport, the 427 Convertible was the fastest and most capable convertible model in Corvette's history.

| | |
|---|---|
| Base MSRP | $76,900 |
| Model Availability | 427 Convertible |
| Engines | LS7 |
| Features | Exclusive engine and body combination, badging |
| Production Numbers | 2,552 |

*The 427 Edition was created based on feedback from customers who wanted a convertible Z06. The Z06's chassis was aluminum, and a convertible version wasn't feasible for a one-year model. But engineers could put the 505-hp LS7 into the steel chassis of the Grand Sport Convertible. While not a true convertible Z06, the 427 Edition satisfied most of those wanting a 505-hp performance-oriented drop-top. (Photo Courtesy Keith Cornett)*

*The heart of the 427 Convertible package is the 505-hp LS7 that was codeveloped with the Le Mans–winning GT1 racing engine. Both featured lightweight titanium connecting rods and intake valves, high-flow cylinder heads, and a dry sump oil system. The LS7 engine was assembled by hand at GM's Performance Build Center in Wixom, Michigan. (Photo Courtesy Keith Cornett)*

*With its low mass and high power output, the 427 Convertible was marketed as one of the fastest and most capable convertibles in the world. Its worthy performance statistics included 0–60 mph in 3.8 seconds, a quarter-mile time of 11.8 seconds, lateral acceleration of 1.04 g on the skid pad, and a top speed of more than 190 mph. (Photo Courtesy Keith Cornett)*

"The 2013 model year would be historic for Corvette, marking its 60th anniversary and the final year for the current 'C6' generation," said Chris Perry, vice president of global marketing and strategy for Chevrolet. "We couldn't think of a more fitting way to celebrate these milestones than bringing back one of the most-coveted combinations in the brand's history—the Corvette convertible and a 427–cubic inch engine."

The new Collector Edition Convertible was powered by the 427-ci 7.0L LS7 from the Corvette Z06. Rated at 505 hp and 470 ft-lbs of torque, it was at the time the most powerful engine ever installed in a production Corvette convertible. The new model came only with a 6-speed manual transmission and was available in all exterior and interior colors and 2LT, 3LT, and 4LT trim levels.

Other performance options on the 427 Convertible included the Z06's driveline and rear axle system, standard Magnetic Selective Ride Control, and a rear-mounted battery. The new model rode on standard 19-inch and 20-inch ZR1-style Michelin PS2 tires with the lightweight machine-face cup wheels. Black cup wheels or chrome ZR1-style wheels were optional.

The 427 Convertible also featured several carbon fiber components to help with weight reduction, including the carbon fiber raised hood that was first introduced on the 2011 Z06 Carbon Edition. It also included carbon fiber Z06-style fenders and carbon fiber floor panels. Buyers could also choose to add the "CFZ" carbon fiber front splitter and rocker panels. This diet brought the 427's curb weight to 3,355 pounds. Combined with the 505-hp LS7, the power-to-weight ratio was 6.64, or 1 horsepower for every 6.64 pounds of vehicle mass. That's better than the more expensive sports cars, such as the Porsche 911 Turbo S Cabriolet (6.90) and the Ferrari California Convertible (8.31).

As for the official numbers, Chevrolet claimed that the 427 Convertible was one of the fastest convertibles in the world with an estimated 0–60 mph of 3.8 seconds, quarter-mile performance of 11.8 seconds, lateral acceleration of 1.04 g, and a top speed of more than 190 mph.

### Corvette 60th Anniversary Package

Available on all 2013 Corvette models, including the new 427 Convertible, was the new 60th Anniversary package featuring an Arctic White exterior with a Blue Diamond leather-wrapped interior with suede accents. Convertible models also featured a blue top.

The 60th Anniversary package included a ZR1-style rear spoiler, special badging, gray-painted brake calipers, and the 60th logo on the wheel center caps, steering wheel, and seat headrests. An optional graph-

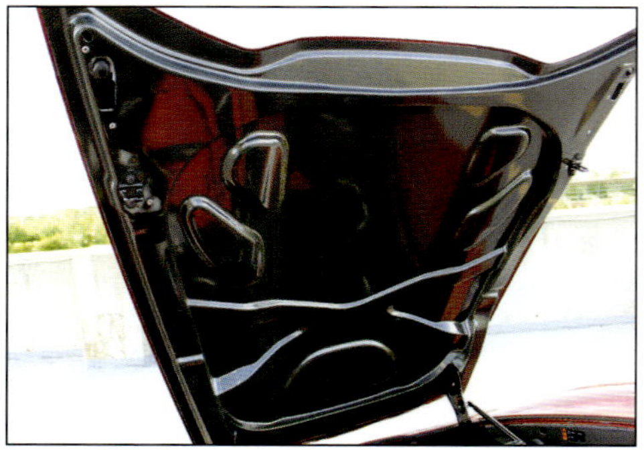

*The 427 Convertible featured several carbon fiber component upgrades to reduce weight. Included was the carbon fiber raised hood first introduced on the 2011 Carbon Z06, and the Z06's carbon fiber fenders and floor panels. Optional carbon fiber front splitter and rocker panels were also available for $2,995 (these were included in the 60th Anniversary package). (Photo Courtesy Keith Cornett)*

*The 427 Convertible was a special-edition model that could also be ordered with the special-edition anniversary package. The 60th Anniversary Edition came in Arctic White with Pearl Silver Blue racing stripes. (Photo Courtesy Richard Straker)*

*With a curb weight of 3,355 pounds, the 505-hp engine gave the 427 Convertible a power-to-weight ratio of 6.64:1 or 1 horsepower for every 6.64 pounds of mass. Chevrolet claimed that it was a better power-to-weight ratio than that of the Porsche 911 Turbo S Cabriolet and the Ferrari California. (Photo Courtesy Keith Cornett)*

*Buyers of the 427 Convertible could also select the 427 Heritage package, which included the modern rendition of the classic 427 hood stinger stripe and 427 logos sewn into the floor mats. A total of 691 were ordered at an additional cost of $1,195. (Photo Courtesy Keith Cornett)*

### 2013 Corvette 427 Convertible Production Breakout

| | |
|---|---|
| **Total 427 Convertibles** | **2,552** |
| Options: | |
| 60th Anniversary Edition | 1,088 |
| With 60th Anniversary Graphics | 897 |
| 427 Heritage Graphics | 691 |

ics package added a new Pearl Silver Blue full-length racing stripe and, for convertibles, a tonal stripe stitched into the convertible top, which extended the graphic theme over the roof.

All 2013 Corvettes featured the 60th Anniversary badges on the front and rear as well as the waterfall panel on convertibles. The 60th logo also appeared on the instrument panel gauge cluster and the door sills.

### First 427 Convertible Offered for Charity

Chevrolet followed up the announcement of the 2013 Corvette 427 Convertible and the 60th Anniversary package by offering VIN 001 for sale two weeks later at Barrett-Jackson's 2012 Scottsdale Auction.

Chevrolet, with Hendrick Motorsports owner Rick Hendrick and four-time NASCAR Sprint Cup Champion Jeff Gordon, offered the winning bidder the opportunity to take delivery of the first retail production 427 Convertible with VIN 001 when it started production later in the year. Proceeds for the Corvette would go 100 percent to benefit the AARP Drive for Hunger.

The Corvette was purchased by well-known collector Ron Pratte, who paid $600,000 for the VIN 001 car.

*With the addition of the 427 Convertible for the 2013 Corvette model lineup, Chevrolet offered no less than seven separate Corvette models for the C6 Corvette's swan song. (Photo Courtesy Keith Cornett)*

### *Pricing and Production*

The new model had its own specific VIN starting with 570000. A total of 2,552 Corvette 427 Convertibles were built at an MSRP of $76,900.

Of the 2,552 427 Convertibles produced, 143 were exported. Canada received the most with 84, followed by 53 to Europe and 6 to the Middle East.

## 2014 STINGRAY COUPE AND CONVERTIBLE PREMIERE EDITIONS

The launch of any new Corvette brings a significant amount of attention from the public and the press, and the newest Corvette was no different, as Chevrolet managed to build the reveal of the C7 Corvette Stingray into a frenzy. Finally, after months of teasing videos, spy shots, and social media leaks, the newest and latest sports car, reborn as the Corvette Stingray, was unveiled in Detroit on January 13, 2013, ahead of the 2013 North American International Auto Show.

### *The Corvette Stingray Returns*

The C7 Corvette was completely redesigned, and only two small parts carried over from the previous generation. The 2014 Corvette was the most powerful standard Corvette ever conceived. With 460 hp and 465 ft-lbs of torque, it was equipped with the most fuel-efficient engine ever to power the Corvette. It had an EPA-rated 17-mpg city and 28-mpg highway fuel economy rating achieved with the Gen V small-block LT1 V-8 with Active Fuel Management, which deactivates 4 of the 8 cylinders when in ECO mode.

Buyers could choose a 6-speed automatic transmission with paddle shifts or a new 7-speed manual transmission with Active Rev Technology that assisted the driver in providing the perfect revs during shifts. The Z51 package offered an electronic limited-slip differential (eLSD), dry sump oil system, differential and transmission cooling, as well as a unique aerodynamics package for high-speed stability.

Equipped with the Z51 Performance package, the new C7 Corvette had a 3.8 second 0–60 mph estimate, and a quarter-mile time of 12 seconds at 119 mph! In addition to the acceleration stats, the new Corvette could brake from 60 mph to 0 at 107 feet and sustain 1.03 g while cornering.

For many, the C7 Stingray finally righted the perception that Corvettes had poor interiors with a new handcrafted high-tech cockpit featuring luxurious Napa leather, microsuede, real aluminum, and carbon fiber trim. Long the bane of customers and auto journalists, the C6 Corvette seats were replaced with two new versions: the standard GT Touring seat or an optional Competition Sport seat featuring larger bolsters and carbon fiber trim.

| Base MSRP | $75,760 (coupe), $77,450 (convertible) |
|---|---|
| Model Availability | Coupe, Convertible |
| Engines | LT1 |
| Features | Limited production, unique VIN, accessory wheels, interior badge |
| Production Numbers | 1,050 |

***Chevrolet staggered the production of the Corvette Stingrays with the coupe model starting several months ahead of the convertible model. Chevrolet introduced the 2014 Corvette Stingray Convertible Premiere Edition in the fall of 2013. (Photo Courtesy Larry Greenwalt)***

The public was captivated by the new Corvette, but Chevrolet wasn't quite done with the surprises. In the summer of 2013, just a few months before the new C7 Corvette coupes would begin shipping, a new limited-edition version of the Corvette Stingray was announced.

### *The 2014 Corvette Stingray Premiere Edition Coupe*

The announcement of the 2014 Corvette Premiere Edition Coupe came during the National Corvette Museum's celebration of the 60th Anniversary Corvette on June 28, 2013. The new launch edition Corvette Stingray was limited to 500.

The first 500 Corvette Stingray Premiere Editions were all Laguna Blue Metallic Coupes with the 3LT Brownstone suede interior. The Corvettes featured the suede-wrapped interior trim and carbon fiber packages. Each of the coupes was equipped with the Z51 Performance package and included Magnetic Selective Ride Control, the variable-tuned performance exhaust system, and the visible carbon fiber roof.

All the Premiere Edition Coupes were optioned with the 7-speed manual transmission. The very first Premiere Edition, number 001, was built with the 6-speed automatic transmission.

The 2014 Premiere Edition Coupes were among the first C7 Corvettes produced. Specific exterior design cues featured on the coupe version included Laguna Blue color, Torque chrome wheels, and the black hood stinger graphic. (Photo Courtesy Mike Bridges)

The sports cars showcased some of the new official accessories from GM's Genuine Corvette Accessories catalog that were created for the new C7 generation of Corvettes, including wheels, sill plates, and floor mats. (Photo Courtesy Mike Bridges)

Advancements in the Stingray's interior included a major upgrade in the infotainment system with an 8-inch retractable touch screen as well as the use of premium materials that blend well together. The Premiere Editions included Napa leather, microsuede, brushed aluminum, and carbon fiber. (Photo Courtesy Mike Bridges)

The Premiere Edition coupes and convertibles also served as a way for Chevrolet to highlight the new C7 Corvette parts and accessories line from the official Genuine Corvette Accessories catalog. These official Corvette aftermarket items were included on the Premiere Editions: Torque chrome wheels, Stingray sill plates, center caps, and floor mats. (Photo Courtesy Mike Bridges)

***Only the top Corvette dealers received an allocation for one of the Premiere Editions. Many sold their allocation immediately while other dealers chose to use the car as a draw in their showrooms. (Photo Courtesy Larry Greenwalt)***

***For the return of the C7 Corvette Stingray, Chevrolet introduced two new colors, Laguna Blue and Lime Rock Green. These served as the colors for the Premiere Editions. The new colors were named after famous racetracks frequented by Corvette Racing, repeating a similar color-naming scheme that Chevrolet used in the 1960s for Corvette colors. (Photo Courtesy William Norman)***

The Premiere Edition also featured a bevy of accessories that served to showcase some of the new customizing options of the C7 Stingray available through the *Genuine Corvette Accessories* catalog. Featured on the 2014 Corvette Stingray Premiere Edition were 19/20-inch Torque five-spoke chrome aluminum wheels, the black stinger hood stripe, Stingray interior sill plates and wheel caps, and custom Corvette-branded luggage from Thule.

To ensure these launch editions were truly special, each of the 500 Corvette Stingray Premiere Editions had a unique VIN number starting with 300001, and the sequence number was also shown on the exclusive dash plaque commemorating the limited-edition model.

***The Corvette finally got the interior it deserved, and designers put much effort into improving the seats, recognizing this is the main point of contact the driver has with the car. Chevrolet finally offered two seating choices: a GT seat for all-around comfort and a Competition Sport seat with more aggressive side bolstering that provides greater support on the track. (Photo Courtesy Larry Greenwalt)***

The Premiere Editions could not be ordered from the factory. They were built and then shipped to a select group of dealers based on their previous Corvette sales volume. The dealers could decide to take the car or pass on it, but most did take the offering, as it was hard to turn down a saleable unit during the initial launch of the C7.

The MSRP for the Premiere Edition Coupe was $75,760, and the car was offered to dealers only in the United States, Canada, and Mexico.

### *The 2014 Corvette Stingray Premiere Edition Convertible*

When Chevrolet first began production of the C7 Corvettes in August 2013, it rolled out the coupe versions for the first couple of months and then the convertible Stingrays began production in the fall of 2014.

As Chevrolet was rolling out the first 2014 Corvette Stingray Premiere Edition Coupes, it was believed that a Premiere Edition Convertible would follow. Chevrolet made the announcement official with a press release on November 26, 2013, featuring the Premier Edition Convertible as part of a gift guide for Corvette enthusiasts.

Like the coupe, the Corvette Stingray Premiere Edition Convertible was a top-of-the-line 3LT with the Z51 Performance package, variable-tuned performance exhaust system, and Magnetic Selective Ride Control. The Stingray convertible was also outfitted with suede leather trim, carbon fiber accents, Torque five-spoke chrome aluminum wheels and Stingray center caps, unique Stingray logo sill plates, and the five-piece luggage branded with the Corvette logo. Unlike the coupe, which was Laguna Blue, the Premiere Edition Corvette Stingray Convertibles were Lime Rock Green with the Brownstone interior.

***The luxurious Brownstone leather-wrapped interior was available only with the 3LT trim package. With the upgrades and performance options, the Premiere Editions retailed for more than $20,000 above the base non-Z51 model. (Photo Courtesy Larry Greenwalt)***

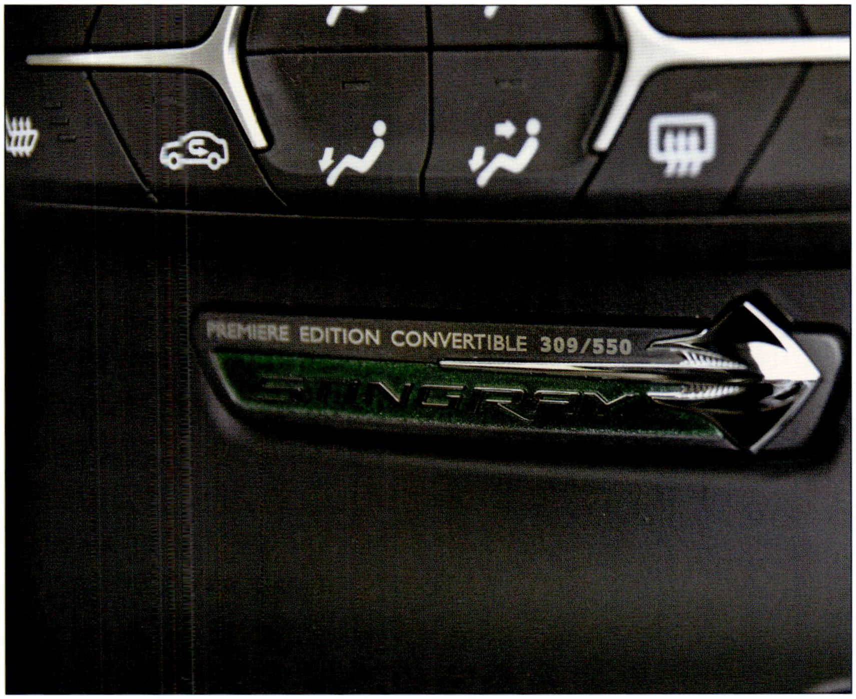


***The Premiere Editions were the first special editions of the C7 era, and to appeal to those who like limited-production Corvettes, Chevrolet offered color-matched dash plaques that labeled total production and the individual Corvette's build sequence number. (Photo Courtesy Larry Greenwalt)***

The Premiere Edition Corvette Stingray Convertible had an MSRP of $77,450 and only 550 were produced. The limited-edition convertible has a unique VIN sequence and interior dash plaque. The Corvettes were available in early 2014 and were distributed only to the volume-selling Chevrolet dealers, as was the coupe.

## 2015 DESIGN PACKAGES: ATLANTIC AND PACIFIC STINGRAYS

Over the years, Chevrolet has produced many special and limited Corvettes. Most are dedicated to certain themes, such as the anniversary Corvettes, pace car replicas, or collector editions. For 2015, Chevrolet offered two design packages for the Corvette Stingray.

In the C6 era, Chevrolet produced many different special editions in the later production years, and the new design packages for the C7 Corvette were intended to offer even more choices to Corvette buyers. Think of the design packages as a "check-the-box" feature that used predetermined options to set up the Corvette Stingray as either a luxury grand touring convertible or a race-inspired coupe.

The cars were designed to represent the differences in automotive styling between the east and west coasts of the United States. The Atlantic and Pacific Design packages were first introduced in November 2013 as design concepts during the SEMA automotive show in Las Vegas. A few months later in April 2014, the two design concepts were revealed during the new-model rollout at the National Corvette Museum's Bash event, where it was announced they would join the 2015 Corvette lineup.

"One of the design goals for the Corvette Stingray was to provide customers with the flexibility to tailor the car to their personality," said Kirk Bennion, Corvette exterior design manager. "The Atlantic and Pacific Design packages were originally designed to showcase how the Stingray could be configured as a luxury sport GT car or as a high-performance motorsport car."

### *The Atlantic Design Package*

The Atlantic Convertible is a GT luxury open-top cruiser reminiscent of a private jet. It was available only in the Z51 configuration and could be ordered in all colors with a 2LT or 3LT interior. The front splitter was styled after the Z06 molded splitter. Elements also included Shark Gray exterior vents, hood stinger graphic, and tonneau inserts.

Chrome five-spoke Torque wheels (19 inches in the front and 20 inches in the rear) came with new Stingray-script center caps and logo valve stem caps. Finishing touches also featured a Stingray underhood liner and floor mats, custom-molded splashguards, and the custom Corvette luggage set.

The Atlantic Design Package was ordered with RPO ATI and required a Z51 Convertible in either 2LT or 3LT equipment groups. The package cost an additional $6,350.

| Base MSRP | $71,245 (coupe), $75,505 (convertible) |
|---|---|
| Model Availability | Coupe, Convertible |
| Engines | LT1 |
| Features | Specific colors and accents, accessory wheels |
| Production Numbers | 17 Atlantic Stingrays; 97 Pacific Stingray |

***Corvette designers like to talk about the ability to configure the C7 Corvette Stingray, and that's the heart of the Design Package. The Atlantic is the refined cruiser while the Pacific represents a racier appearance. (Photo Courtesy Keith Cornett)***

***It's no accident that Corvette designers like to compare the Corvette to a private jet. Like in a jet, the Corvette's cockpit is driver centered; passengers are surrounded by a luxurious Kalahari-wrapped leather interior. (Photo Courtesy Keith Cornett)***

***The Pacific Design Package***

The Pacific is the bookend to the Atlantic Convertible, and its styling was drawn from the West Coast's unique culture of speed and style. For those who enjoy taking in driving events, the Pacific was the perfect Stingray to bring to HPDEs and autocrosses. The Pacific Design Package was offered only in the Z51 configuration and was limited to four colors: Torch Red, Arctic White, Blade Silver, and Shark Gray.

Whatever the color, the Pacific Design Package featured Satin Black full-length racing stripes with the "CFZ" Carbon Fiber Ground Effects package, a Carbon Flash rear spoiler, and the visible carbon fiber roof panel. Satin Black Z51 aluminum wheels were highlighted with a red stripe and Stingray center caps. Red brake calipers, along with black outside mirrors and exterior badges, helped tie together the different design elements that contrasted and highlighted the four exterior colors.

The Pacific Design Package on the inside came with Competition Sport Seats in either red or black, a carbon fiber interior trim, and Stingray door sill plates and floor mats. Custom molded splashguards and a rear license plate frame wrapped up the package.

The Pacific Design Package was ordered with RPO PFI and required a Z51 Coupe in either 2LT or 3LT equipment groups. The package cost an additional $7,090.

***Production Shortage Brings Change***

The C7 Corvette Z06 began production in the fall of 2015, and the new 650-hp Corvettes were much in demand while sales of the Stingray showed no sign of slowing down. During the fall and winter, Chevrolet was still dealing with many constraints (or low inventories of selected options) in ordering some of the popular options found on both cars, including the visible carbon fiber roof panels, carbon fiber ground effects, and interior carbon fiber trim. Even the Z51s were under constraint at one time or another during the year.

Chevrolet directed many of the scarce options to go first to Z06 buyers, and the Design Packages were pushed back until spring of 2015. Even then, Chevrolet was unable to offer the CFZ carbon fiber side rockers, and they were removed from the package. Only the first Atlantic edition was said to have been shipped with the side skirts.

The first Atlantic edition was completed on March 27, 2015, and the first two Pacific editions were delivered on May 5, 2015. So much time had passed between the initial introductions and the announcement that dealers could start ordering the cars that many buyers simply forgot they were even available.

Of course, that led to low production numbers; again, something that collectors of special-edition Corvettes love to see. Only 17 Atlantic Stingray Convertibles were built, and the Pacific Stingray Coupes would end with a final tally of 97.

*The chrome Torque wheels with Stingray center caps from the* **Genuine Corvette Accessories** *catalog give the Atlantic a sense of movement even when it's standing still. The wheels were previously featured on the 2014 Premiere Editions. (Photo Courtesy Keith Cornett)*

*West Coast design comes to the Stingray with a two-tone black and adrenaline red leather interior with Competition Sport seats. The red stitching on the steering wheel, shift boot, and door panels further enhanced the Pacific's interior. (Photo Courtesy Keith Cornett)*

*Check the box and select your color. That's how easy Chevrolet made outfitting a Corvette with the Atlantic or Pacific Design packages. Buyers could also add many other options to fully customize their Corvettes. (Photo Courtesy Keith Cornett)*

## Grand Turismo Concept

When the Atlantic and Pacific Design concept cars made their initial public debuts at the 2013 SEMA show, they were joined by a third concept called the Gran Turismo. For those who grew up playing video games, Gran Turismo was the widely popular driving game for Sony's PlayStation.

Chevrolet worked with Gran Turismo's designers to tease the upcoming launch of the C7 Corvette on January 13, 2013, by first showing a camouflaged 2014 Corvette Stingray in *Gran Turismo 5*. The game even let you download and "drive" the car nearly two months before the reveal date. As Sony's game developers were modeling the car for the game, Chevrolet designers set out to create a real-life Gran Turismo Corvette.

What they showed at SEMA was a Satin Blue C7 with gloss racing stripes running from the revised hood vents across the roof and down the rear deck and ending on the carbon fiber rear wing. Up front, yellow-tinted headlamps flanked each forward corner of the car. The carbon fiber theme carried on throughout the car from the carbon fiber hood and extractor to the carbon fiber rockers and front splitter. Out back there was a carbon fiber diffuser surrounding four square-ish exhaust tips.

Back up front was a racing-inspired front tow hook and custom front grille. Custom front fender and rear quarter vents adorned the sides. Inside were custom Competition Sport Seats wearing driver and passenger racing harnesses. A flat-bottom steering wheel helped drivers get through the twisties with ease. A leather-wrapped safety belt bar and rear braces rounded out the custom interior touches.

*The first test drives of the C7 Chevrolet Corvette appeared in digital form in the Sony PlayStation 3 game* **Gran Turismo 6**. *With the 2014 Corvette Grand Turismo Concept, Chevrolet returned the favor by making a real-life version of the Corvette that is played in the video game. (Photo Courtesy Keith Cornett)*

*The Gran Turismo shows the wild side of the C7 Corvette Stingray with race-inspired yellow-tinted headlights, a one-of-a-kind rear spoiler, and the dark blue GT6 exterior. (Photo Courtesy Keith Cornett)*

## 2016–2017 DESIGN PACKAGES: TWILIGHT BLUE, SPICE RED, AND JET BLACK SUEDE RPOS

The Corvette team expanded on the Atlantic and Pacific Design packages and in late 2015 offered three new design package RPOs to choose from: Twilight Blue, Spice Red, and Jet Black Suede. The exterior and interior designers collaborated to provide three packages that followed a select theme, offering customers multiple exterior choices of unique color combinations and accessories. The three design packages would return for the 2017 model year and include the new Grand Sport models.

The design packages made outfitting the Corvette as easy as checking the box to select the design package's RPO and the exterior color to get started. The packages were offered on both coupes and convertibles but required the 3LT (Stingray and Grand Sport) or 3LZ (Corvette Z06) equipment group. As the packages were design oriented, buyers could also order their choice of transmission as well as any of the performance options including Z51 or Z07.

### *Twilight Blue Design Package (RPO ZLD)*

Twilight Blue consisted of four color options: Shark Gray, Blade Silver, Arctic White, and Night Race Blue and was accented with Shark Gray vents and chrome badges. Convertibles received a blue top and Shark Gray tonneau inserts. Stingrays were outfitted with the Polished Motorsport Wheel, Grand Sport featured the Machine Aluminum Wheels, and Z06 came with Pearl Nickel Blade Wheels.

Inside the car was a special "dipped" Twilight Blue interior, meaning the entire interior from the dash down was the same color. The interior also featured Mystic Blue stitching and included the carbon fiber interior trim plate around the gauge cluster.

One of the unique options for the Twilight Blue package was an optional tricolor red, white, and blue stripe that ran from the crossed-flags badge down the center of the car.

The Twilight Blue Design Package was priced at $3,500 with 371 total packages sold in 2016 and 231 in 2017.

| | |
|---|---|
| Base MSRP | $69,140 (coupe), $73,140 (convertible), $92,350 (Z06 coupe), $96,340 (Z06 convertible) |
| Model Availability | Coupe, Convertible, Z06 Coupe, Z06 Convertible |
| Engines | LT1, LT4 |
| Features | Specific colors and accents, dipped interior, wheels |
| Production Numbers | 2,168 |

***New for 2016, the Spice Red Design Package had three new choices for setting up a Corvette Stingray or Z06 simply by checking a box. The design packages were available on all Corvette models and body styles. (Photo Courtesy Michael Whited)***

***Chevrolet accessorized the Twilight Blue Package with an optional full-length red/white/blue body stripe (RPO DUP) as shown during its introduction in 2016. Just 83 Corvettes ordered the tricolor stripe in 2016, and for 2017 the total was 71. (Photo Courtesy Keith Cornett)***

*The Spice Red interior choice provided buyers an alternative to the bright Adrenalin Red interior much the same way the Long Beach Red exterior offered an alternative to Torch Red. (Photo Courtesy Michael Whited)*

*One of the differences in the package was that the wheels were customized to the model. A Spice Red Package on a Corvette Z06 added the Pearl Nickel Z06 blade wheel. The Stingray received a polished motorsports wheel. (Photo Courtesy Michael Whited)*

*The interior of the Twilight Blue Design Package is where this special edition got its name. The 3LT's (Stingray) or 3LZ's (Z06, shown) trimmed seats, dash, and door panels were Twilight Blue leather. (Photo Courtesy Tony Sgro)*

### Spice Red Design Package (RPO ZLE)

Spice Red's four exterior color choices were Long Beach Red, Shark Gray, Blade Silver, and Arctic White. Convertibles featured the new Spice Red top. Shark Gray vents were three of the four colors, while Long Beach Red Corvettes had black vents. Wheels choices were the polished motorsport wheel for Stingrays, machine aluminum wheels for the Grand Sport, and Pearl Nickel blade wheels for the Z06. The Z06 version came with Spice Red brake calipers.

The Spice Red interior was new in 2016 and was likened to a more luxurious red than the bright Adrenaline Red. The darker red interior complemented the equally darker Long Beach Red exterior. Like the Twilight Blue package, it also featured a dipped interior, which is said to harken back to the days when Corvettes offered single color combinations, such as a red Corvette with red dipped interior or a blue Corvette with blue dipped interior.

The Spice Red Design Package was priced at $3,000 for RPO ZLE. A total of 535 were made in 2016, and 307 were offered in 2017.

### Jet Black Suede Design Package (RPO ZLG)

The Jet Black Suede Design Package was built with JEt Black, Blade Silver, Arctic White, or Torch Red interiors; convertible models featured a black convertible top. The wheel options for the Black Suede package were Satin Black with the red stripe. This was new in 2016; all previous black wheels up to that point had been offered as a high-gloss black. Red calipers were also offered on each of the models along with Carbon Flash badges.

The package's interior was also a departure from the two dipped interiors. The black suede was similar to the 2016 Z06 C7.R edition with its black with black suede and gray stitching. The seat inserts and armrests were also done in black suede as was the steering wheel and shift boot. Also new for the 2016 version was the high-gloss carbon fiber instrument trim panel as compared to the satin-finish offered on the other two design packages.

The Jet Black Suede Package was priced at $3,995 for RPO ZLG. A total of 454 were built in 2016, and 270 were built for 2017.

*The 2016 Jet Black Suede was offered in four exteriors and featured a black convertible top, Carbon Flash badging, and an optional Satin Black hood graphic. Wheels for the design package were Satin Black with a red stripe. (Photo Courtesy Keith Cornett)*

### 2016 Design Package Production

| MODEL | Twilight Blue | Spice Red | Jet Black Suede |
|---|---|---|---|
| Stingray Coupe | 105 | 128 | 85 |
| Stingray Convertible | 152 | 196 | 76 |
| Z06 Coupe | 43 | 127 | 43 |
| Z06 Convertible | 71 | 84 | 50 |
| **Totals:** | **371** | **535** | **454** |

### 2017 Design Package Production

| MODEL | Twilight Blue | Spice Red | Jet Black Suede |
|---|---|---|---|
| Stingray Coupe | 33 | 34 | 29 |
| Stingray Convertible | 29 | 31 | 10 |
| Grand Sport Coupe | 71 | 84 | 77 |
| Grand Sport Convertible | 48 | 47 | 33 |
| Z06 Coupe | 19 | 75 | 98 |
| Z06 Convertible | 31 | 36 | 23 |
| **Totals:** | **231** | **307** | **270** |

## 2017 GRAND SPORT COLLECTOR EDITION

As Chevrolet was planning the C7 Corvette's fourth year of production, it managed to pull off a double surprise for enthusiasts and buyers for the 2017 model year. A Corvette Grand Sport model and a limited collector edition would be offered.

The introduction of the 2017 Corvette Grand Sport at the Geneva Motor Show caught nearly everyone by surprise, except for a casual leak on social media by Corvette Racing driver and Chevrolet European ambassador Oliver Gavin. Gavin shared an itinerary for the Geneva Motor Show and said he was looking forward to the Grand Sport reveal the next day.

On March 1, 2017, Gavin did, indeed, join Corvette chief engineer Tadge Juechter, Corvette production manager Harlan Charles, and interior design manager Ryan Vaughn in unveiling the Grand Sport Coupe in its Collector Edition package.

"Today, the Grand Sport marries the naturally aspirated engine from the Corvette Stingray with the important technologies from the Z06. Things like aerodynamics, cooling, braking, and tires. The result is an incredibly capable car both on the street and on the track," said Juechter.

| | |
|---|---|
| Base MSRP | $80,190 (Grand Sport Coupe), $84,190 (Grand Sport Convertible) |
| Model Availability | Grand Sport Coupe and Convertible |
| Engines | LT1 |
| Features | Gray exterior with exclusive interior color, badging, graphics, embroidery |
| Production Numbers | 935 |

*Although the 2017 Corvette Grand Sport wore the collector edition name for the C7 era, it's different from those offered in 1982 and 1996. The 2017 option was the first time a collector edition was limited to a fixed production count. The previous two collector edition models had been designed for mass consumption. (Photo Courtesy Howard Brown Photographic)*

### *The Historic Grand Sport Model Returns for C7*

The 2017 Corvette Grand Sport would become known as the best of both worlds: the perfect combination of the previously introduced C7 models, the Stingray, and the Z06. The potent merger resulted in a lightweight architecture with a track-honed aerodynamics package, along with Michelin Sport Cup 2 tires and a naturally aspirated LT1 V-8 with 460 hp. With the optional Z07 Performance Package, the Grand Sport took driving to a new level.

The Grand Sport, like the Stingray and Z06, was offered as either a coupe or convertible and with a choice of the 7-speed manual or 8-speed paddle-shift automatic transmission. Brembo offered the stopping power in the form of the standard two-piece steel rotors or the Z07's carbon ceramic rotors. The cup wheels were lightweight 19-inch fronts and 20-inch rear aluminum alloys and were fitted with the super-wide 335 Michelin Pilot Super Sport Cup 2 summer tires.

The Grand Sport's suspension included Magnetic Selective Ride Control as standard equipment. The Electronic Limited-Slip Differential (also standard) improved stability and responsiveness, which improved steering feel, handling, and traction. The Grand Sport was capable of 1.05 lateral g's in its standard configuration and an incredible 1.2 lateral g's with the Z07 Performance Package.

The Corvette Grand Sport models also featured specific front fender inserts, a Z06-style front grille, and wider rear fenders. The Grand Sport was offered with a Heritage Package, which included the hash mark fender graphics in six different colors with the hash mark detail carried into the interior, along with matching aluminum trim.

### *2017 Corvette Grand Sport Collector Edition*

When Chevrolet took the stage at the Geneva Motor Show to introduce the newest Corvette in the C7 lineup, it used the occasion to premiere the limited collector edition version of the car to make its first public appearance.

Like the Grand Sports, Collector Edition Corvettes have graced showroom floors during periods in Corvette's long history. What was different from the 1982 and 1996 version was that those editions came at the end of a generation, while the new Collector Edition was offered during the inaugural year of the Grand Sport.

The 2017 Corvette Grand Sport Collector Edition was offered either as a coupe or a convertible. Watkins Glen Gray Metallic, a new color for 2017, was exclusive to the Collector Edition. It featured a set of bold Tension Blue hash mark graphics on the front fenders as well as Satin Black full-length stripes and black aluminum wheels. Inside, the cockpit had the exclusive Tension Blue interior. Representations of the 1963 Corvette Grand Sport were embroidered on the seat headrests.

Like all recent special editions, the 2017 Grand Sport

***Despite the bold Tension Blue interior, the Collector Edition's Matching Tension Blue hash marks appear more subdued against the Watkins Glen Gray Metallic. Black wheels and matte black hood graphic accentuate the dark appearance. (Photo Courtesy Keith Cornett)***

***The 2017 Corvette Grand Sport was the perfect combination of the Z06's lightweight and aerodynamic wide-body and the Stingray Z51's chassis with the naturally aspirated 460-hp LT1. But don't call it a Z51: The Grand Sport received many standard upgrades with the Z06's aerodynamics, grille, and upgraded suspension. (Photo Courtesy Howard Brown Photographic)***

***The Corvette team went bold by offering the bright Tension Blue leather and Black Suede–wrapped interior available exclusively on the 2017 Grand Sport Collector Edition. It's one of the few Corvette models whose design is instantly recognizable. (Photo Courtesy Howard Brown Photographic)***

Collector Edition featured its own VIN. That build sequence number was displayed inside on a specially designed dash plaque that features a representation of the number 002 1963 Grand Sport roadster campaigned most famously by George Wintersteen.

*Every Collector Edition shows its build sequence number on a plaque in the interior. This 2016 Corvette Grand Sport Collector Edition is number 111 of the 935 produced. The plaque features a rendition of the original 1963 Corvette Grand Sport roadster known as chassis number 002. (Photo Courtesy Howard Brown Photographic)*

### *Pricing and Production*

The Z25 RPO for the Collector Edition added $4,995 to the cost of a 3LT-equipped Corvette Grand Sport coupe or convertible, and the official MSRP started at $80,190 for the coupe and $84,190 for the convertible. The ultimate Grand Sport Collector Edition Corvettes were equipped with the Z07 Performance Package for an additional $7,995. A total of 184 Grand Sport Collector Editions were optioned with the Z07 Performance Package.

The Collector Edition package was limited to 1,000 models with 850 for buyers in the United States and 150 for export. Chevrolet built the Collector Edition on sold orders only and production was initially planned to run between October 2016 and February 2017. However, production was extended to the end of the model year due to continued availability. When the 2017 model year production wrapped, the model was just short of being a sellout with a total of 935 Collector Editions built.

The model counts were 784 for the coupe and 151 for the convertible. Since the totals were different than initially planned, it also slightly changed the export numbers from 150 to 142.

*The Grand Sport model sold exceptionally well in its inaugural year. Of the total 32,782 Corvettes produced in 2017, Grand Sport production was 11,958 (36.2 percent) versus 13,551 Stingrays (41.3 percent) and 7,273 Z06s (21.2 percent). The 935 Collector Editions represented just 2.9 percent of all 2017 Corvette production and 7.8 percent of all Grand Sports. (Photo Courtesy Ken Pauley)*

*Like all previous first VIN C7s, Chevrolet auctioned the first retail production 2017 Grand Sport Collector Edition with VIN 0001 during the Barrett-Jackson April 2016 Palm Beach sale in South Florida. Unlike the previous four C7s that were all purchased by Rick Hendrick, the first Grand Sport Corvette sold for $170,000 to auto dealership owner David Flynn with 100 percent of the sale's proceeds donated to the Karmanos Cancer Institute in Detroit. (Photo Courtesy Keith Cornett)*

## Grand Sport Collector Edition Corvette Breakdown

| Option | Coupe | Convertible | Total |
|---|---|---|---|
| 7-Speed Manual | 173 | 27 | 200 |
| 8-Speed Automatic | 611 | 124 | 735 |
| Z07 Performance Package | 157 | 27 | 184 |

## Grand Sport Collector Edition Exports

| Destination | Coupe | Convertible | Total |
|---|---|---|---|
| USA | 667 | 126 | 793 |
| Canada | 50 | 11 | 61 |
| Japan | 5 | 0 | 5 |
| Mideast | 17 | 0 | 17 |
| Europe | 45 | 14 | 59 |
| Mexico | 0 | 0 | 0 |
| **Totals** | **784** | **151** | **935** |

## Grand Sport Corvettes Through the Years

Corvette enthusiasts will know that this was the fourth time since 1963 that Chevrolet had built a Grand Sport model. In 1963, five Grand Sports were built as racing prototypes, and when Corvette's chief engineer Zora Arkus-Duntov was busted for going against the corporate racing ban, he made sure the cars went out the back door and got in the hands of the top Corvette racing teams and drivers at the time. These cars went on to dominate America's racetracks for the next few years and were commonly known as the Cobra Killers. Today, these five Grand Sports are considered to be among the most valuable Corvettes on the planet.

Chevrolet next brought the Grand Sport name back for one year only in 1996 as a special edition to mark the end of the C4 generation. Offered with a special one-year-only LT4 V-8 engine with 330 hp, Chevrolet built 1,000 of the cars, and it was the first time that the now-famous livery of blue with white stripes and hash marks on the fender appeared on the Corvette.

The C6 Grand Sports were very common during their 2010–2013 model run, and the car eventually gained more than 50 percent of the market share of the six different Corvette models offered at the time. Introduced in 2010, the Grand Sport received the great wide-body look of the Z06 Corvette with the LS3 430-hp V-8 from the base coupe. Unlike the Z06, it was offered both as a coupe and convertible model on the standard Corvette chassis.

The popularity of the C6 Grand Sport Corvette during the C6 generation had many asking for a C7 version of the same as soon as the Stingray came out. The Corvette team said that the 2017 Corvette Grand Sport was another example of listening to customers and then delivering those Corvette dreams.

***The Corvette Grand Sport was introduced on the racetrack in 1963, and the C7 Corvette Grand Sport lives up to that tradition. As technology transfer improves the Corvette from one generation to the next, the Grand Sport featured a host of performance technologies inherited from the factory race car, including aerodynamics, cooling, braking, and tires. (Photo Courtesy Keith Cornett)***

CHAPTER 5

# LIMITED REGULAR PRODUCTION CORVETTES

This next section represents some of the most popular and important cars during Corvette's 65-year history and each one tells a story. These Corvette models and special options were featured years before Chevrolet ever considered building a special edition just for the sake of calling it special. These models, options, and packages are special-edition Corvettes in their own right. Without these Corvettes in our history, we wouldn't have the cars we have today.

The men and women who transformed the Corvette from its original idea made huge technological leaps in automotive performance in the first 25 years of the brand's existence. Their contributions were critical to solving the problems of the day. From those challenges, the Corvette helped usher in new technologies that have become standard today, such as advanced materials for saving weight, fuel injection, cold air induction, and disc brakes.

During Corvette's early years, racing played a huge role in the development of the car. As Corvette evolved over the years, history shows that it was made better by racing the model, while at the same time having to live within the confines of the industry's ban on supporting racing. It's hard to imagine what might have been possible had there not been a ban on manufacturers' support of racing, if Corvette's engineers and designers had been allowed to compete on racing's world stage.

*These historic Corvettes are the reason we celebrate the Chevrolet Corvette today. (Photo Courtesy Andrew M. Taylor)*

## 1953 CORVETTE

"The Corvette was a little thing I started. I went to a sports car race in Watkins Glen. That's where I got the idea for the Corvette," said Harley J. Earl.

For Corvette fans, the story of the Corvette is a fairy tale come true. The convergence of a brilliant concept executed with the right people at the right time. It's the birth of an automotive legend and an American icon that is as popular as ever some 65 years later.

The 1953 Corvette was everything that GM styling boss Harley J. Earl envisioned. A two-seat sports car with the same wheelbase as a Jaguar XK120, it would be wrapped in an exotic fiberglass body and finished with plenty of chrome and whitewall tires as was the style of its creator. (Photo Courtesy Corvettes at Carlisle)

### *Father of the Corvette*

Harley J. Earl, the brilliant creative force behind General Motors, not only knew what people wanted in an automobile but, in his position as vice president of GM's Styling Department, could order up designs of any

| Base MSRP | $3,498 |
|---|---|
| Model Availability | Roadster |
| Engines | Blue Flame 6-cylinder |
| Features | First year release, limited production |
| Production Numbers | 300 |

Every legend has a starting point. For the Chevrolet Corvette, the fuse was lit on June 30, 1953, when the first of 300 Polo White Roadsters were completed in a warehouse in Flint, Michigan. (Photo Courtesy the National Corvette Museum)

*The first Corvette was priced at $3,498 but was nearly impossible to order the first year because Chevrolet limited who would get one. Many went to executives in the company as well as Hollywood stars, such as John Wayne. This policy of exclusivity held back sales in 1954; many people who had expressed interest in buying a 1953 Corvette were turned away. (Photo Courtesy Corvettes at Carlisle)*

*As the Chevrolet Corvette made its way from concept to production, examples of the American two-seater were shown around the world. The Polo White and Sportsman Red Corvette roadster is shown here at the Paris Motor Show in October 1953. (Photo Courtesy the Revs Institute, The George Phillips Collection)*

idea that caught his attention. Earl was a man of firsts in the automotive industry: The first to do clay models, the first to utilize designers for coordinating interiors and colors, and the first to create the concept car. As a showman, Earl took his creations on the road with his GM Motorama car shows that traveled across the nation. Earl had recently unveiled his 1951 Buick Le Sabre, featuring the common jet aircraft cues that his cars were famous for in the 1950s.

To promote the Le Sabre concept, Earl took it to Watkins Glen, a racetrack in the Finger Lakes region of New York, in September 1951, where it would serve as the pace car for the race. There, he saw the small European sports cars racing on the track. Briggs Cunningham, who later took three Corvettes to Le Mans in 1960, supposedly joked with Earl, asking why he hadn't brought a car he could race.

With the American economy beginning its boom phase following World War II, the design chief had already taken note of the enthusiasm for the small two-seat sports cars that were being purchased by GIs recently returned from service in Europe. Dealerships, including New Jersey's Malcom Konner, were starting to sell British sports cars from Triumph, MG, and Jaguar. For Earl, a two-seat sports car from General Motors would offer an alternative to these European brands. But which division should build it? Sharing his ideas was then–Cadillac Chief Engineer Ed Cole, who believed a car like that should be inexpensive and use off-the-shelf parts to keep costs down. Earl thought the sports car could be just the thing to project a new image for Chevrolet. Sales were down nearly 40 percent from 1950–1952 sales, and its model lineup was anything but imaginative at the time.

### *Fiberglass in the Automotive Industry*

At the same time that Earl was showing off the experimental Le Sabre, the plastics industry was undergoing its own revolution as innovators looked for new uses for what was called glass-reinforced plastic (GRP), commonly referred to as fiberglass. A number of companies were experimenting with the new material, and the use of the material on cars caught the attention of the major automotive manufacturers. In November 1951, General Motors set up its own plastics department under the Parts Fabrication Group in GM Engineering.

In February 1952, *Life* magazine published an article on the future of plastics showcasing Glasspar Corporation's *Alembic I* fiberglass car. Glasspar began in the fiberglass boat business in the late 1940s, but company founder Bill Tritt wanted to expand his growing business into cars. Several of the pictures accompanying the *Life* article showed a pre-painted translucent body highlighted with dramatic lighting so that it appeared to glow. Another image was of seven men standing on the front of the car to highlight the strength of the material. In March 1952, Glasspar and the *Alembic I* were shown to GM executives, including Harley Earl, who took note of the glass-reinforced plastic body and the possibilities the lightweight material offered.

About the same time as the *Life* magazine article, another designer was building a sports car that utilized a fiberglass body. Designed by Howard "Dutch" Darrin and produced by Kaiser, a small automotive manufacturer based in Warren, the Kaiser Darrin roadster made use of fiberglass as its body and became the first American sports car to use fiberglass.

***Just hours before the 1953 Corvette's introduction at GM's Motorama, the original Corvette emblem was swapped because the original crossed-flags design contained the American flag. GM's legal team rejected the emblem design. The American flag cannot be used on a commercial product. A new design was quickly rendered with a red flag containing the Chevrolet bowtie and the fleur-de-lis (a nod to Louis Chevrolet). The original badge is on display at the National Corvette Museum. (Photo Courtesy Keith Cornett)***

### *Designing the First Corvette*

After Earl's return from Wakins Glen, Project Opel was chosen as the name for the new sports car, which gradually took shape on the ninth floor of the GM building in the Body Development studio. Robert McLean, a graduate of Caltech and a sports car enthusiast, started the design with the rear of the car first and then found the dashline where the Blue Flame V-6 engine would eventually be placed. At the time, McLean's design was considered somewhat revolutionary because the engine was located 3 inches lower and 7 inches farther back than in any previous Chevrolet. The design came close to achieving a 50/50 weight distribution, and the lower center of gravity improved the car's handling. McLean's final design featured a 102-inch wheelbase, the same as the Jaguar XK120 that Earl was fond of at the time. Chevrolet's director of research and development, Maurice Olley, sketched out details of the basic chassis and suspension while Joe Schemansky designed the car's interior.

But even as McLean was designing the car on paper, Earl's own contributions to the design were apparent. The Opel's wraparound windshield came from Earl's 1951 Le Sabre, as did the soft convertible top that was hidden when the top was down. He wanted clear headlight covers but had to settle for the now-familiar mesh that covered the 1953's headlights.

On June 2, 1952, Harley Earl presented the Corvette to GM executives. Arranging the display at the GM Proving Grounds, the Polo White with red interior sports car was shown in a blacked-out room with special lighting that made the car shine like a pearl. Selling the board, he told them that the car was based on standard off-the-shelf parts from Chevrolet and simple to build. The executives loved it and approved the car for Chevrolet. Project Opel was green-lighted with the goal of completing the prototype in time for the 1953 Motorama. Two prototypes and a third car for engineering purposes were assembled by the end of the year. The completed fiberglass body, manufactured by GM's Parts Fabrication Group, weighed just 411 pounds, 200 pounds less than a comparable steel body.

### *The Corvette Receives Its Name and Crossed-Flag Logo*

Chevrolet's advertising agency, Campbell-Ewald, was tasked with finding an appropriate name for the sports car. The only requirement was that it had to start with a C. More than 300 names were reviewed, and for a while the name Corvair was considered.

One of those on the naming committee was an assistant advertising manager at Campbell-Ewald named Myron Scott. A veteran in the PR department who was responsible for new car photography press kits and the like, Myron was also known for creating the "All American Soap Box Derby." Looking for an appropriate name, Myron turned to the dictionary and under C found "corvette," a speedy pursuit ship in the British Navy. In later interviews, Myron said the name Corvette rolled off the tongue well and resonated with men who had served during World War II and were familiar with the light attack ships.

The Corvette was shown to GM executives in early January 1953, just four days prior to the GM Motorama in New York City. The only change requested was the logo that was featured on both the hood and horn that displayed a crossed-flags design consisting of a checkered flag and the American flag. Because use of the American flag on a commercial product was illegal, the redesigned crossed-flags featured a Chevrolet bowtie logo along with the fleur-de-lis that paid homage to Louis Chevrolet's French name (despite the fact that he was born in Switzerland). The new emblems were completed in time and attached to Chevrolet engineer car EX-122, the 1953 Motorama Corvette.

### *The 1953 GM Motorama*

On January 17, 1953, thousands of Americans saw the Chevrolet Corvette for the first time. The two-seater sports car became the star of GM's Motorama show at New York's Waldorf Astoria. More than 300,000 people stood in line to see the latest concepts from General Motors, and the Corvette display was a huge draw. Onlookers stood three and four people deep to gaze upon the car as it spun on a turnstile. Interest in the 1953 Motorama was so high that General Motors announced that they were taking the show to a number of cities across the country. It's estimated that 1.7 million Americans saw the Polo White roadster along with GM's other offerings in the traveling show that year.

One man in the audience at the Waldorf Astoria was a Belgian-born Russian engineer named Zora Arkus-Duntov. Duntov was so taken with the potential of the Corvette that he later wrote a letter to Chevrolet's chief engineer, Ed Cole. Cole, who was impressed with Duntov's ideas, hired him as an assistant staff engineer.

Realizing they had a potential hit, production of the Chevrolet Corvette was rushed from its planned 1954 launch to late 1953 to capitalize on the public's excitement for the car.

### *Building the Chevrolet Corvette*

Chevrolet initially planned for a total of 250 and later increased it to 300 cars to be built before the 1954 model year started. The first production Corvettes rolled out beginning June 30, 1953, with an MSRP of $3,734.55.

Chevrolet made some design changes between the building of the Motorama Corvette and what eventually became the first-year 1953 Corvette roadsters. Most notable was the position of the chrome trim on the side of the cars. On the Motorama Corvette, a chrome spear pointed downward, where on the production Corvettes it was changed to point upward. The Chevrolet script that was under the spear on the Motorama car was changed to be above it. Another interesting change was that the prototype Corvette came with external door locks, but when production started they left those off.

A former customer delivery garage at Van Slyke Avenue and Atherton Road in Flint, Michigan, was set up as the temporary assembly line. The space was small, and only six chassis could be worked on at any one time. The first car is reported to have taken three 16-hour days to be assembled. But as time passed, they began producing three cars per day.

A uniform design allowed workers to concentrate on putting the bodies together without the distraction of trim and equipment variations. All 1953 Corvettes were, therefore, Polo White with Sportsman Red interiors and equipped with a black canvas soft top, 6.70x15 whitewall tires, and a Delco signal-seeking radio. Also standard was a 5,000-rpm tachometer and a counter for total engine revolutions.

As each of the 300 Corvettes was hand-built, the entire production was like a giant pilot car run, with rolling changes and updates to the production process happening on an ongoing basis. It's said that the number 001 and

*Chevrolet first displayed the Corvette at the GM Motorama show in New York City's Waldorf Astoria in January 1953. GM placed listening devices around the displays to capture sentiment from the onlookers who praised the small convertible's great looks. Based on that feedback, the Corvette was rushed into production. (Photo Courtesy GM Media Archive)*

*The world's oldest Corvette is known as EX-122, the actual 1953 GM Motorama show car. Differences between the show car and the production 1953 included scoops on the top quarter panels and the chrome spear along the side that was pointed downward. Its owner, George Kerbeck of Kerbeck Corvette in Atlantic City, shows the car annually at Corvettes at Carlisle. (Photo Courtesy Keith Garrett)*

*As exciting as the first Corvette was, under the shiny fiberglass the first Corvettes were made mostly of off-the-shelf parts from various Chevrolets. The 6-cylinder Blue Flame was originally the passenger-car version of the 235-ci truck engine. After some performance upgrades, the 150-hp engine was the most powerful 6-cylinder Chevrolet had ever offered. (Photo Courtesy Keith Cornett)*

the number 300 Corvettes were similar in appearance but had many subtle differences as assembly techniques improved.

### The 1953 Corvettes Hit the Market

When the 1953 Corvette was first offered for sale, General Motors wanted the first 50 or so to be in the hands of VIPs and movie stars such as John Wayne, who received the number 051 Corvette in October 1953.

*All 1953 Corvettes featured the Sportsman Red interior, and only two options were available, AM Radio and a heater. Sports car fans liked the proportions of the Corvette, which was based on the same wheelbase as the Jaguar XK120, but most derided the 2-speed Powerglide automatic transmission despite the fact that Chevrolet mounted the shifter on the floor "like an authentic sports car." (Photo Courtesy Keith Cornett)*

*This 1953 Corvette was assigned GM engineering number EX-87, and it became the test bed, or mule as they are called, for various performance engineering tests. The car was used to test Chevrolet's first V-8 engines offered in the Corvette starting in 1955. (Photo Courtesy the Revs Institute, The Karl Ludvigsen Collection)*

A standing order issued to dealers in July 1953 from the central office proclaimed: "No dealer is in a position to accept firm orders for delivery of a Corvette in 1953." When the average sports car enthusiast learned that it was nearly impossible to buy a new Corvette, interest waned and many of the 300 Corvettes went unsold. General Motors wasn't too concerned; those unsold cars in many ways served as a centerpiece display for the dealer's showroom.

### Borrowed Driveline

To power the 1953 Corvette roadster, Chevrolet chose its Blue-Flame 235-ci 6-cylinder engine capable of 150 hp. To boost performance, the

*The Corvette is the longest continually produced sports car in automotive history, and its legacy has spanned more than 65 years. In 2009, a new milestone was reached when the 1.5 millionth Corvette was produced. (Photo Courtesy Keith Cornett)*

6-cylinder engine was fitted with a high-lift camshaft, a vacuum booster fuel pump, and three sidedraft Carter carburetors. The engine was coupled to a 2-speed Powerglide transmission, capable of a full-throttle upshift at 55 mph. The gear selector was mounted on the floor between the seats in sports car tradition and a shift pattern was embossed on the knob. Top speed was rated at 105 mph and 0–60 mph was 11 seconds.

Sports car enthusiasts who did get a Corvette found it to be underpowered, and its lack of a manual gearshift was a major drawback. Sophisticated buyers found the build quality to be crude and its lack of weather protection unforgivable. Its high price of $3,500 was nearly twice as much as what Earl was targeting.

Chevrolet's general manager, Tom Keating, and chief engineer, Ed Cole, struggled to define the Corvette's identity in that first year. But that was all about to change after the hiring of a new associate engineer in May 1953 by the name of Zora Arkus-Duntov.

Today, collectors who have one of these year-one roadsters appreciate the hand-built characteristics and the first-year provenance these cars bring. Of the 300 Corvettes built, its estimated that only 175 to 200 still exist. The oldest surviving chassis is the number 003 Corvette, which sold for $1 million in 2006.

***The 1953 Corvette remains a favorite of collectors due to the low production numbers and the provenance of owning the first-year, hand-built example of America's favorite sports car. 1953 Corvettes routinely sell for $250,000 to $350,000 at public auctions. (Photo Courtesy Keith Cornett)***

## Robert Morrison's Molded Fiber Glass Company

Perhaps no man was more influential in keeping the original concept of a fiberglass body on the Corvette than an Ohio businessman named Robert Morrison. After two decades as a Ford dealer, Morrison took over a failing plastics company and turned it around. In the early 1950s, his company, Molded Fiber Glass Company (MFG), was one of the largest and most successful plastics companies in the industry. Like others in the industry, he was looking to branch into the automotive field. In late 1952, a couple of representatives from GM's Fisher Body subsidiary came to see him, showing the drawings and asking about production. The Monday following the Motorama in New York City, two Chevrolet engineers came calling again, this time with revised plans to fit MFG's tooling. Robert promised to expand into a new building and fill it with the presses needed, and he even offered to redesign the parts to produce the strongest panels.

In early February 1953, Morrison traveled to Detroit, where a meeting was scheduled to plan production of the Corvette. There was a mix-up, however, and Morrison thought he was stood up. He ran into Elmore Gormsen, the head of purchasing for Chevrolet, who told him that Chevy was going to build the Corvette with steel bodies. Morrison was crushed. Figuring the Chevrolet deal was over, he met later that afternoon with the Kaiser engineers who ordered 500 bodies for the Kaiser Darrin sports car. Arriving home at 2:00 a.m., his wife told him that a man from Chevrolet had called and wanted Morrison to call him right away, no matter the time. Morrison made the call to Elmore Gormsen, who told him to "get that building because we've decided we're going to do the Corvette with a fiberglass body."

MFG had a $4 million contract to build 300 complete bodies by June 1. Morrison was officially in the car business. That night, his family celebrated, and Morrison's son says that it was the first time he and his sister tasted champagne.

For all his contributions, Robert Morrison was posthumously inducted into the National Corvette Museum's Corvette Hall of Fame in 2003.

***While Harley Earl was touting the benefits of fiberglass for rapid development, Molded Fiber Glass Company (MFG) owner Robert Morrison saw the potential of fiberglass for automotive purposes and actively worked with Chevrolet designers to produce the Corvette's fiberglass panels. Sixty-five years later, MFG is still producing composite panels for the C7 Corvette. (Photo Courtesy Molded Fiber Glass Companies)***

## 1957 CORVETTE WITH RPO 579D "AIRBOX"

The 1957 Corvette was a real turning point in Corvette's history. Following a mid-cycle redesign in 1956, the single headlight and coves design with the toothy chrome grille offering was back for its final year before the quad-headlight design would debut in 1958.

The Corvette was now a serious contender in SCCA races with "The Flying Dentist" Dick Thompson tearing up tracks with production Corvettes while many others were entered in professional sports car contests, including Sebring and Daytona. John Fitch and Walt Hansgen took first in class at the 1956 Sebring 12-hour race in the 1956 Corvette SR, aka *The Real McCoy.*

The sales mantra "Win on Sunday, Sell on Monday" was beginning to take shape for the Corvette, and engineers provided even more power with the arrival of fuel injection and a 4-speed manual gearbox for 1957.

*Zora Arkus-Duntov and John Dolza designed the initial fuel-injection system that would be manufactured by Rochester and offered first on the 1957 Corvette. The airbox gets its name from the special ductwork it uses for routing cooler air to the fuel-injection unit. (Photo Courtesy Keith Cornett)*

| Base MSRP | $4,697.82 |
|---|---|
| Model Availability | Convertible |
| Engines | 283/283 Fuel injection |
| Features | Exclusive engine and upgraded suspension package |
| Production Numbers | 43 |

*Corvette's performance was taken seriously in 1957. With a fuel-injected 283/283 V-8 and a 4-speed transmission, the airbox was Chevrolet's first cold air intake designed for the sports car and the RPO 579D was one of the building blocks for creating a factory-prepared race car. (Photo Courtesy Keith Cornett)*

### *Fuel Injection and One Horsepower per Cubic Inch*

Duntov spent a lot of time in the spring of 1956 working on the fuel-injection system. Ed Cole, now Chevrolet's general manager, wanted to have it available across the entire Chevrolet lineup because there were no new major updates in the design for the year. During this time, Duntov was injured in a Corvette crash at the proving grounds and wore a full body cast; he had broken his back in the mishap.

Despite his injury, Duntov collaborated with John Dolza, the head of GM's fuel-injection development group, and they came up with a workable system that was refined by famed NASCAR engine builder Smokey Yunick. GM's Rochester carburetor division would build the system and, while many thought it wasn't ready for prime time, the 1957 Corvette was the first GM vehicle to receive a Ramjet fuel-injection unit.

Chevrolet offered fuel injection on two versions of the 283 solid lifter V-8. The first was set up with 9.5:1 compression, which offered 250 hp at 5,000 rpm and 305 ft-lbs of torque at 3,800 rpm. The second had the Duntov cam and 10.5:1 compression and achieved 283 hp at 6,200 rpm and 290 ft-lbs of torque at 4,400 rpm.

The milestone horsepower level was lauded by Chevrolet (although Chrysler had surpassed the same benchmark a year earlier). In a number of classic advertisements, Chevrolet pointed out that the Italian and German cars didn't have the "exotic" and "high-tech" fuel system.

The three components that make mechanical fuel injection work are the air meter, fuel meter, and the intake manifold. The system basically relates air velocity to fuel flow and provides a constant flow of fuel directly to each of the eight cylinders. (Photo Courtesy Keith Cornett)

### *The First Corvette Factory Race Cars*

The knowledge gained from setting up the various production and concept Corvettes during the 1956 racing season paid dividends for what would essentially be the first Corvette that could be ordered from the factory and ready to go racing.

The first upgrade was to the 283/283-hp fuel-injection unit. A lesson learned from racing Bill Mitchell's 1956 SR2 at Nassau in December 1956 was implemented as RPO 579D (also referred to as 579E).

The fuel-injected units combined with the new 4-speed transmissions allowed Corvettes to dominate SCCA B-Production racing. The winning streak continued until 1962, when the Corvettes met a worthy adversary in Carroll Shelby and his Shelby Cobras.

All fuel-injected 1957 Corvettes had air cleaners attached directly to the air meter on the unit, and they drew air from the hot engine compartment. As the units didn't like the heat, engineers fabricated a fiberglass box to the left side of the engine compartment. Ductwork from a hole cut into the left side of the radiator support allowed fresh air into the airbox, which then fed

*Another first for Corvette that started with the 1957's RPO 579D was the practice of deleting options to discourage street use of the car. The radio in this 1957 was deleted as shown by the delete metal plate where the radio would be located. (Photo Courtesy Keith Cornett)*

*In 1957 only a few high-end sports cars used fuel injection. Duntov recognized the benefits that fuel injection offered, namely fuel management efficiency and delivery, and he correctly predicted that someday all cars would be fuel injected. (Photo Courtesy Keith Cornett)*

the cooler air directly to the fuel-injection unit. It was the first cold air intake system offered for the Corvette. The package also included an 8,000-rpm tachometer mounted on the steering column. To discourage use of the cars with the special engine package on the street, radios and heaters were deleted. The 43 airboxes were all installed during a production run in May 1957.

A total of 50 airboxes were fabricated and 43 were installed into 1957 Corvettes with the RPO 579D. It was a pricey option at $726.30 compared to the regular-production 283/283 fuelie that was priced at $484.20.

Also addressed for racing were the brakes and suspension, and Chevrolet had an option for that as well. RPO 684 added heavier front and rear springs, a wider-diameter anti-roll bar, firmer shock absorbers, tightened steering, limited-slip differential (positraction), finned cast-iron brake drums, and cerametalix brake linings. The heavy-duty chassis package added $780.10 to the 1957 Corvette's MSRP of $3,176.32, and 51 Corvettes left the factory equipped with the option.

One last RPO completed the factory race car prep, and it cost only $15.10. RPO 276 swapped out the production steel wheels for five rims sized 5.5 inches wide, a half inch more than the standard wheels so it could be fitted with 7.10/7.60x15 six-ply racing tires.

### *The First 4-Speed Manual Transmission*

As another surprise for sports car enthusiasts, Chevrolet also addressed the transmission availability for the Corvette. Three speeds were long considered acceptable for passenger cars, but a 4-speed transmission could offer the Corvette a tremendous advantage. Duntov wrote to his friends at Porsche and asked for suggestions for a 4-speed manual as early as 1954. While suggestions were forthcoming, the actual T-10 4-speed gearbox was developed by Chevrolet engineers.

Starting with a 3-speed T-85 from BorgWarner, they moved the reverse gear set and then were able to add the four synchronized forward gear sets. The ratios were the same as on the 3-speed transmissions but the additional fourth gear set was inserted between the first and second gears of the 3-speed. The RPO 685 cost $188.30 and was made available in early April of 1957. Only 664 Corvettes were built with the 4-speed manual.

### *Corvette Performance Unleashed*

Chevrolet's fuel-injected 1957 Corvettes were very fast for the era, and test results showed the 283/283 with the 3-speed manual and the 4.11:1 gears could rocket 0–60 mph in 5.7 seconds and do a standing quarter mile in 14.3 seconds at more than 90 mph. The car's top speed was said to be 132 mph.

At the 1957 Sebring, two production Corvettes finished 1–2 in GT and some 20 laps ahead of the Mercedes-Benz 300SL. Dick Thompson won the SCCA national championship in the B-Production category (even after the larger V-8 moved it into the new class).

As the final accolade for the important model year, a total of 6,339 Corvettes were sold in 1957, nearly double from the 1956 year. A total of 1,040 fuelies were built. With the Ford Thunderbird now out of the two-seat market, the Corvette owned the sports car class. Nobody was talking about canceling the Corvette now.

***Newly minted Chevrolet general manager Ed Cole wanted to roll out fuel injection across the Chevy lineup in 1957 as a new option. General Motors was the only manufacturer of the Big Three to offer mass-produced fuel injection during the era. (Photo Courtesy Keith Cornett)***

***Helping transmit the 283 hp into forward progress was BorgWarner's new T-10 4-speed manual transmission. The T-10 4-speed was offered in Corvettes through 1963, when it was replaced by the Muncie 4-speed. (Photo Courtesy Keith Cornett)***

***For the uninitiated, these painted steel wheels on an RPO 570D Corvette make the car plain. But those wheels are the first clue that these Corvettes were ordered with performance options that are more at home at the racetrack than on the street. (Photo Courtesy Keith Cornett)***

## 1963 CORVETTE GRAND SPORT RACERS

Perhaps the most celebrated Corvettes of all time, and also the most valuable, are five prototype race cars that never saw production. On the track, their record was mixed at best. But in the 1963 Corvette Grand Sports, Duntov saw a way to put Chevrolet in the winner's circle at the world's three major endurance sports car races: Daytona, Sebring, and Le Mans.

### *Born in Secrecy*

Following a tragic racing accident at the 1955 24 Hours of Le Mans, which killed 83 spectators and injured dozens more, automotive manufacturers became increasingly wary of promoting speed and racing. In 1957, members of the Automobile Manufacturers Association (AMA), led by General Motors, agreed to stop supporting organized automotive racing and marketing top speeds as a selling point. However, this was a gentleman's agreement, and many manufacturers found ways to circumvent or blatantly ignore the spirit of the agreement.

| Base MSRP | Never sold to the public |
|---|---|
| Model Availability | Coupe, Roadster |
| Engines | 327/360 fuel injection, 377/550 fuel injection |
| Features | Factory build race car |
| Production Numbers | 5 |

But the environment was different in 1962 than it had been when the ban was first put in place and General Motors was now enforcing it among its divisions. The US Department of Justice was starting to take notice of the automaker, which commanded 51 percent of all automotive sales in the United States. At 60 percent, it was likely that the government would force the company to break up, much like Standard Oil had several decades earlier. Racing not only encouraged sales; it also put a spotlight on the brands that were winning the races, and that was something GM chairman Frederic Donner wanted to avoid.

At the time the agreement was signed in 1957, Semon "Bunkie" Knudsen was head of Pontiac, and he was working to reinvent the brand. His solution was to go full force against the racing ban. "To hell with those guys," Bunkie said regarding the AMA ban. "I've got a division to save and we're going racing." After finding success and setting up Pontiac as a major performance brand in the 1960s, Knudsen moved to Chevrolet in 1961. Recognizing the prestige that would come from having a Chevrolet Corvette win the GT class at Le Mans, he and Duntov were on the same page.

The top-secret program began in early 1962 as Zora Arkus-Duntov received the go-ahead to begin work on what was referred to as the "Lightweight." To get around the AMA ban, Duntov planned to build five prototype lightweights, and then 125 would be produced and sold to customers, thereby homologating the sports car to production-based racing classes.

### *The Lightweight*

With experience from racing various European sports cars, including the Porsche 550 RS Spyder at the 1954 and 1955 Le Mans, Duntov knew he needed to shave weight substantially to compete on the world stage of racing. The goal was to get the car down to 2,000 pounds, about the same curb weight as the Shelby Cobra that made its public debut in April at the New York Auto Show. That meant the reduction of 1,100 pounds from the production Sting Ray Coupes.

***With a green light from Ed Cole, Duntov commenced "The Lightweight" project that saw the building of five racing prototypes that would weigh 1,000 less than the 1963 Corvette Sting Ray. The ultimate goal was building 125 to qualify for racing, but General Motors canceled the project as it violated the manufacturer's ban on racing. (Photo Courtesy Keith Cornett)***

*Grand Sport chassis number 002 is one of two Grand Sports with the roadster body. This car and the other roadster, GS chassis number 001, were purchased from General Motors in 1966 by Roger Penske. Penske immediately sold number 002 to George Wintersteen, who raced it in SCCA races in 1966. (Photo Courtesy Andrew M. Taylor)*

*Chassis number 004 was the most successful of the five Grand Sports in competition, and it was the first to bring home a checkered flag with a first-place finish at Watkins Glen in August 1963. (Photo Courtesy Peter Harholdt)*

The Lightweight was built with a seamless steel tubular chassis that was much stiffer than the production frame and weighed in 90 pounds less. In 1963, the Corvette received a new independent rear suspension and that followed over to the Lightweight, but many of the components were manufactured by hand to reduce weight. Trailing arms were drilled and aluminum was used for the differential housing, which shaved 100 pounds. Magnesium alloy wheels replaced the stock steel wheels. The car was fitted with a 36.5-gallon fuel tank and, as per Federation Internationale de L'Automobile (FIA) regulations, and contained a small trunk for the mandatory spare tire. A roll cage and racing seats were added and the interior was fully carpeted.

Although Duntov lost the battle of the split window with GM design chief Bill Mitchell on the 1963 production car, he got his way on the Grand Sport. The split window was cut out and replaced with a sheet of plexiglass for weight savings and increased visibility. The driver seating position was slightly different, but for the most part the Lightweight was nearly similar in design to the production Sting Rays.

As for powering the Lightweight, Duntov foresaw the need for a bigger-bore engine and settled on an aluminum block with 377-ci displacement. The special hemispheric cylinder heads allowed a larger intake and exhaust valve, and the valves were reworked to allow two spark plugs per cylinder. Dyno results put the engine's performance at 550 hp and 6,400 rpm with 500 ft-lbs of torque at 5,200 rpm. At the time, no other sports car or GT racer had this much power.

*Although a number of engines were featured in the Grand Sports during their racing careers, Duntov planned to use a 377-ci aluminum small-block with aluminum heads and the 58-mm Weber side-draft carburetors. (Photo Courtesy Keith Cornett)*

*Although the Grand Sport was all race car, it shared many components with the regular-production Corvette Sting Rays. The dash cluster in the number 002 Grand Sport was straight out of a 1963, although the center gauges were changed from silver to matte. (Photo Courtesy Andrew M. Taylor)*

***The Lightweights were technological marvels when first constructed in 1963. By 1967 standards, however, the car was considered outdated compared to the rest of the GT field it was intended to race against. Pictured is the number 004 Corvette Grand Sport at the 1967 24 Hours of Daytona. The car failed to finish its last major endurance race. (Photo Courtesy the Revs Institute, The Albert R. Bochroch Photographic Archive)***

***The Grand Sports found much success in their trips to the Bahamas. The number 005 Grand Sport shed another 300 pounds by removing its jacks and water pressure systems before the race. Now known as the Light-Lightweight, Roger Penske drove it to victory to win the 1964 Tourist Trophy. (Courtesy the Revs Institute, The Eric della Faille Photograph Collection)***

The Grand Sport made its first shakedown run at Sebring International Raceway in December 1962 with drivers Dick Thompson and Masten Gregory. The test was hidden from General Motors, as the Lightweights were accompanied by several production and experimental Sting Rays. While the team struggled with braking performance, the sheer speed of the cars was apparent from the beginning. After an initial six laps, the car never was slower than 3:17 and was within seconds of breaking the track record. A victory for Chevrolet at Sebring was now very much possible.

The Grand Sport test at Sebring was deemed successful, and the engineering team fitted Grand Sport's brakes with vented discs and wider rotors. A follow-up test was planned just after New Year's when the call came down from GM chairman Donner, who ordered Knudsen to cease the program immediately. While the dream of building 125 production cars for homologation appeared to be dead, the engineering team had already fabricated enough parts to build the five prototype cars, and the three coupes were completed before the 1963 racing season. The five Grand Sport prototypes are historically identified by their chassis number and range from 001 to 005.

### *The Grand Sport Makes Its Debut*

With the Grand Sports completed, Duntov loaned out the number 004 chassis to the Grady Davis Gulf Oil Racing team with Dick Thompson. The number 003 chassis was sent to Chevrolet dealer Dick Doane. As the cars were prototypes and were never homologated, they were classified in the SCCA as C-modified and would compete against other prototype race cars. Not knowing how the cars would be received and wanting to hold back some firepower, Duntov pulled the 377-ci V-8s and replaced them with standard 327/360 fuel-injected production engines before the cars were loaned out.

The first Grand Sport to see action came at Marlboro on April 7, 1963. It would not go well. A faulty fuel injector left Thompson standing on the starting grid. He saw a fifth-place finish and several third-place finishes later on, but the car had more than its share of issues and failed to finish several races. One of the key issues affecting the car was the aerodynamics.

***As the Lightweight program developed, the individual Grand Sports evolved in their engineering and each would be unique in its own way. The number 005 Grand Sport was built at 7/8's scale and was equipped with a 54-gallon fuel tank. Jim Hall developed a rapid refueler system that could fill the larger gas tank faster than a Corvette with the regular 36-gallon tankers could be filled. (Photo Courtesy Peter Harholdt)***

Under full throttle, the front end exhibited noticeable lift, which became an ongoing battle that was never truly solved. The one bright spot for the number 004 car was a first-place finish at Watkins Glen in August 1963 with Dick Thompson taking the overall win. He finished fourth in C-modified at the end of the season.

As two of the five Grand Sports were racing throughout 1963, Duntov was monitoring their progress and continuing to refine the cars based upon his observations along with input from the drivers and teams. Following the 1963 SCCA season, the cars were returned to the Chevrolet tech center in Warren and prepped for their biggest challenge yet: going head to head with Carroll Shelby's Cobras.

### *The 1963 Corvette Z06 Meets Carroll Shelby's Cobra*

In early 1963, Carroll Shelby's new Cobras were tearing up the tracks and had beaten the new 1963 Corvette Z06s handily at Riverside in January despite Chevrolet putting the cars into the hands of some of the most capable drivers of the time. Adding to the defeat was Ken Miles, running in second place behind former Corvette racer Dave MacDonald in the Cobras, who pulled into the pits for a drink of water. Once all the Corvettes went by, he proceeded to pass them all again to finish in second place.

With the Cobras weighing nearly 1,100 pounds less than the fuel-injected Sting Ray, the Z06 would never have the power-to-weight advantage enjoyed by Shelby's race cars. After watching the Z06s being thrashed throughout the year, Duntov turned to the Grand Sports and formulated his plan for revenge.

### *The Grand Sports' Finest Hours*

Following the SCCA Nationals, the last big event on the racing schedule for the year was the Nassau Speed Week races in the Bahamas. To compete with the Cobras, Duntov equipped the three Lightweight coupes with the 377-ci aluminum race engine featuring the distinctive 58-mm Weber carburetors mounted on top. The three Grand Sport Coupes were sent to John Mecom, who put together a top-notch team of drivers for the 1963 Nassau Speed Week, including A. J. Foyt, Roger Penske, Jim Hall, Augie Pabst, and Dick Thompson.

Despite the cars being prototypes, organizers allowed them into the production race events, where they finished in the top 10 in the Governor's Cup race, handily beating the Cobras. The Corvettes did not win any of the three major Speed Week races, but they did finish considerably higher than the Shelbys. The Grand Sports had some problems, including differential cooling issues. As luck would have it, a Chevrolet engineer who had booked a last-minute vacation to the Bahamas just happened to be traveling with several external passenger-car transmission coolers in his suitcase that were fitted to the rear decks of the Grand Sports to cool the rear differentials. Another vacationing Chevrolet engineer, who was asked about the cars from a member of the press, is said to have replied, "You realize, of course, that you are talking to a man who isn't here." The Corvette Grand Sport found success in the Bahamas with Duntov finally handing it to Carroll Shelby and his Cobras.

***Chassis number 001 was released to Roger Penske in 1966, and he campaigned the car in the 1966 12 Hours of Sebring. Driven by Dick Thompson and Dick Guldstrand, the Grand Sport held its own against the more exotic Ferraris and Porsches. A collision with another entry resulted in heavy suspension damage and the car was forced to retire. (Photo Courtesy Corvettes at Carlisle)***

### *End of the Never-Never Corvette*

The cars returned to Chevrolet and preparations began for the 24-hour

***Traco was a popular choice for replacement racing engines. The number 002 Grand Sport shows off a L88-spec engine. Traco's shop was located two doors down from Dick Guldstrand's garage in California. (Photo Courtesy Andrew M. Taylor)***

endurance race at Daytona in January 1964. To counter the aerodynamics of Daytona's high banks, Duntov prepared chassis numbers 001 and 002 as roadsters to compensate for the Grand Sports' front-end lift. As preparations were underway, the ax fell once again as General Motors found out about the racing efforts in Nassau. This time, they made sure that all the tooling for the Grand Sports was destroyed, effectively orphaning the five original Lightweight racers and ending the dream of production.

Duntov responded by putting the number 003, 004, and 005 Grand Sports into the hands of privateer racers. This time the cars were powered by an iron-block version of the 377-ci engines. John Mecom received number 003. Grady Davis and Gulf Oil took the number 004 car but sold it within a couple of months to a Texas Chevy dealer and racer named Delmo Johnson Jr. The number 005 Grand Sport was sent to Jim Hall, who immediately sent the car to Roger Penske to race. The roadsters were hidden inside Chevrolet until 1966.

The three coupes were raced throughout 1964, with the number 004 chassis competing in the Mexican Carrera de Coasta a Coasta race while the number 003 and 005 cars headed once again to the Bahamas for the 1964 Speed Week races. There the coupes were raced for another couple of years and saw competition at Sebring and Daytona as well as the other major tracks. The Grand Sports were considered old by race car standards in 1965 as Ford's GT40 and Ferrari's 250 LM took to the scene.

#### *One Last Try*

The two roadster Grand Sports were finally let go in early 1966 with Penske buying both cars and then selling the number 002 car to his friend, a gentlemen racer named George Wintersteen.

Penske was convinced that Chevy's new big-blocks were the way to go and used one of the 427-ci Daytona Mystery Motors that Duntov had been offering to select racers out the back door. With an eye on Sebring, Dick Guldstrand supervised the race preparation and helped beef up the suspension to handle the extra weight from the big-block V-8. Aerodynamics was addressed with a spoiler added to the lower front and the fairing behind the driver removed. With Dick Thompson behind the wheel, the Grand Sport Roadster led the Fords and Ferraris early in the race when the car was forced off-road, breaking its oil pan and ending the race after just 65 laps. Penske sold the number 001 roadster not long after.

Having experience behind the wheel of the number 005 Coupe Grand Sport, Wintersteen saw the number 002 Corvette Grand Sport Roadster as a cheap way to go racing in 1966. The prototype race car was now doing battle with Lolas and McLarens, but Wintersteen was game. In his final race, he finished ninth overall. He sold the car for $6,700, a decision he would later regret.

Just three years after the birth of the Lightweights, they were considered obsolete and slowly disappeared from competitive racing. The cars became relics and were sold and resold, but eventually the five cars found their way into the hands of collectors who recognized the special role the cars played in Corvette history. Today, the cars are considered the most valuable of all Corvettes with the number 002 roadster being the most rarest car available. It was sold in 2009 for an undisclosed price reportedly north of $5 million.

## 1963 CORVETTE Z06

The first 10 years of the Corvette were heralded by its spectacular

| Base MSRP | $6,070.45 (coupe), $5,855.45 (convertible) |
|---|---|
| Model Availability | Coupe, Convertible |
| Engines | L84 |
| Features | Exclusive performance package |
| Production Numbers | 199 |

***Although built for racing, some Corvette Z06s saw limited or no track action and were used as daily drivers. This white 1963 Corvette Z06 tanker served as the daily driver for Mickey Thompson. Thompson was a race car builder and driver and was known for becoming the first American to break the 400-mph land speed barrier. (Photo Courtesy Jeff Romm / Corvette Mike)***

***Corvette chief engineer Zora Arkus-Duntov stands next to the 1963 Corvette Sting Ray Sport Coupe. Known as the Godfather of the Corvette to enthusiasts, he turned Harley Earl's 155-hp two-seat boulevard cruiser into a world-class sports car. It's hard to imagine what the Corvette would have become without his guidance. (Photo Courtesy the Revs Institute, The Karl Ludvigsen Collection)***

introduction at the 1953 Motorama in New York. The car found slow acceptance in its first few years and even faced cancellation, but by 1956 the Corvette started selling and would mark the start of an 11-year sales run, each year better than the last.

Duntov distinguished the Corvette as both a mellow boulevard cruiser in its base form and a thunderous factory-built SCCA racer at its most extreme. With the change in body styles looming for the 1963 model year, Duntov pushed the envelope again to take the standard Corvette to its performance limits.

### Bill Mitchell's Corvette

Design of the new Corvette fell to design chief William "Bill" Mitchell, who succeeded Harley Earl after his mandatory retirement at the end of 1958. One of the first projects he undertook as design chief was XP-87, which would become the 1959 Stingray Racer. Larry Shinoda provided much of the design, and the body was fitted on Duntov's 1957 SS test-mule chassis. Mitchell took the car racing by personally financing much of the project, and Dick Thompson drove the car to two consecutive class championships in 1959 and 1960. After the car was retired from racing in 1960, Mitchell detuned it and added a windshield and passenger seat. The Stingray Racer was displayed as an experimental show car.

Work on the new Corvette started as early as 1959, but it was made easier with Mitchell's initial mandate. Mitchell was so enamored with the design of the Corvette Stingray Racer that he told the designers to make it look like the Stingray Racer. Combining elements of the Stingray Racer and the aborted Q-Corvette Coupe by Bob McLean, designers produced a prototype of the next Corvette. Codenamed XP-720, the fastback

***The Z06's 327/360-hp fuel-injection engine was essentially carried over from 1962. The fuel pump was upgraded from a geared unit to a wobble-plate fuel pump. The fuelie's plenum chamber was cosmetically improved with a finned cover featuring Chevrolet's crossed-flags logo. An airbox mounted on the driver's side brought fresh air to the fuel-injection unit. (Photo Courtesy ProTeam Corvette Sales)***

***All 1963 Corvette interiors were practically the same whether you were driving the 360-hp Corvette Z06 or the 250-hp base Corvette Sting Ray. The Z06 included the radio delete option, so there is no cutout for the radio on the instrument panel. (Photo Courtesy ProTeam Corvette Sales)***

***RPO Z06 was created for racing, and most of the Z06s sold would see competition on the track. When the RPO first became available, you had to be an accomplished racer to order the car. The number-6 Corvette Z06 was campaigned by Don Yenko in the 1965 12 Hours of Sebring. (Photo Courtesy Keith Cornett)***

***Although initially part of the Z06 special equipment package, the 36-gallon fuel tank ended up as its own option. This 1963 Corvette Z06 is one of 63 total Corvettes to have the RPO N03 tanker option. (Photo Courtesy ProTeam Corvette Sales)***

Corvette Coupe most notably featured a split rear window much like that from the Olds Golden Rocket show car of 1956 and one that had been considered briefly for the 1958 Corvette.

For Mitchell, that split window represented the signature design of the car. With Duntov pushing back on the function versus design, Mitchell was adamant that it stay, to the point of threatening to withhold resources to Duntov's engineering staff unless he got his way. Ed Cole got involved and agreed with Mitchell that the window would stay (at least for the first year).

### Improvements for 1963

At the heart of the new Corvette was a new frame design that weighed about the same as the previous generation's X-member frame but was torsionally stronger, a characteristic required for the new rear suspension as well as the larger and more powerful engines that would be coming. The 1963 Corvette also had double the amount of steel reinforcements (82 pounds of steel versus 48 pounds) and included a new birdcage design supporting the windshield, doors, and roof.

The 1963 Corvette debuted with a rear independent suspension, an important advancement over the previous solid-axle cars. Utilizing half-shafts and a transverse leaf spring from the CERV 1 engineering concept car, the suspension offered a significant difference in unsprung weight and improved the handling of the car. Also improving the handling was the optional hydraulic power steering, while bigger brakes offered more stopping power.

### The 1963 Corvette Z06 Package

With the Corvette dominating SCCA racing since it first won the B-Production championship in 1957, it was only natural that the new Corvette Stingray have a ready-to-go race package straight from the factory. That package was RPO Z06.

Initially available only as a coupe, the Z06 package started off with the most powerful engine in the Corvette lineup, the 327/360 fuel-injected L84 V-8 coupled with a close-ratio 4-speed transmission, positraction, and the limited-slip differential with choice of axle ratios. A 36-gallon fuel tank and aluminum knock-off wheels were initially included in the $1,818.45 Special Performance Group package. At some point, the package dropped the 36-gallon fuel tank (but still offered it as RPO N03 at a cost of $202.30) and the knock-off wheels, which were delayed through 1964 due to casting

***No less than six Corvette Z06s entered the 1963 12 Hours of Sebring. Among the drivers for the Corvettes are a who's who of Corvette racing legends, including Dick Thompson, Don Yenko, A. J. Foyt, and the team of Delmo Johnson and Dave Morgan who would take the number-3 1963 Corvette Z06 to 2nd place in class behind a Shelby Cobra and 16th in the race overall. (Photo Courtesy the Revs Institute, The George Phillips Collection)***

*Some of the common characteristics of Corvette Z06s with a racing history are the painted steel wheels, side-mounted exhaust, and removal of the front chrome bumpers. Of course, a Corvette Z06 with numbers on the body is also a good clue. The AP stands for the SCCA's "A" production class. (Photo Courtesy Keith Cornett)*

*Dr. Dick Thompson, aka "The Flying Dentist" (on the right), was one of the most accomplished race car drivers in North America, and he won multiple SCCA championships in Corvettes. In 2009, the 88-year-old Corvette Hall of Fame member was reunited with one of his previous race cars, the 1963 Corvette Z06 known as Gulf One that was sponsored by Grady Davis and Gulf Oil. The former race car sold for a cool $1 million at Mecum's 2009 Kissimmee auction. (Photo Courtesy Keith Cornett)*

*The 1963 Corvette was a special performance equipment package designed for racing. Elements included the 327/360-hp fuel-injected engine, 4-speed manual transmission, and power brakes with dual circuit master cylinder. Metallic brakes, backing plate air scoops, and a heavy-duty suspension were also included. (Photo Courtesy Keith Cornett)*

*Of the 199 Corvette Z06s produced in 1963, this black Z06 stands out from the other 198 cars. It's currently the only fully documented convertible known to exist. The Convertible Z06 was originally owned by a GM engineer who was a model builder for Duntov. (Photo Courtesy Tony Avedisian)*

issues. The last change allowed the Z06 package for convertibles, and just one Z06 Convertible was produced. With the deletions of the tanker fuel tank and knock-offs, the package was re-priced at $1,293.95.

Brakes were a major emphasis, and the new Z06 came with oversized transversely finned brake drums with internal fans. Large elephant ear scoops directed cool air over the sintered-metallic brake linings while a power booster used a dual-circuit hydraulic system to apply the brakes. The brake shoes were lined with a material known as Cerametalix rather than the regular sintered-lined option.

The Z06's suspension was also made race-ready with heavy-duty springs, dampers, and a front anti-roll bar that was 20 percent larger than standard.

Chevrolet's Corvette was now ready to compete with the best from Europe. Unfortunately, its eventual nemesis would come from a Texan named Carroll Shelby.

### Corvette Versus Cobra

On Saturday, October 13, 1962, the 1963 Corvette Z06 saw its first competition during a support race for the Sports Car Grand Prix at Riverside, California. Three Z06s were built and offered to successful drivers known to the Chevrolet team: Bob Bondurant, Jerry Grant, and Dave MacDonald. They picked up their cars in St. Louis and drove them to California as their break-in. A fourth car was already in California with Mickey Thompson and would be driven by Doug Hooper. As a side note, Thompson attempted the first installation of Chevrolet's new Mark II big-block in a Corvette, but he reverted back to the 327 fuelie due to concerns over the reliability of the new engine. Because of the newness of the car, it would be run in the provisional X-Production class.

Another race-car builder also had two sports cars entered for the race that were also classified as X-Production: Carroll Shelby and his Shelby

Cobras, powered by the Ford Fairlane's 260-hp V-8. The Corvettes had a displacement advantage with the 327 fuelies, but the Cobras weighed nearly 1,100 pounds less.

The four Corvettes and two Cobras battled throughout the race with Corvette and Cobra exchanging the lead. Attrition on both sides took its toll on the new sports cars, and Doug Hooper eventually won that first race. Duntov had seen the future and knew that once Shelby solved the reliability of the car, it would be a force to be reckoned with.

The Shelby Cobras would have another go at the Corvette Z06s at Riverside in January 1963, and this time it was no contest. Dave MacDonald joined the Shelby team, and he and Ken Miles took first and second place; the Corvette took third.

The SCCA classified the Cobra in A-Production, where it ran circles around the competition in the 1963 SCCA season. The defeat of the Corvettes by the Cobras was a demoralizing loss, but sales didn't seem to suffer; the Corvette had already earned its racing bonafides and could stand on its own.

### *Price and Production*

With the introduction of the new Corvette Sport Coupe and Convertible, sales soared and a total of 21,513 Corvettes were produced. The RPO Z06 saw 199 examples produced, all coupes except for one lone convertible model, and these 199 represented just .9 percent of total production.

In all, 63 Corvettes were optioned with the 36-gallon tanker. Today, these Corvettes command top dollar at auction due to the equipment package and the fact that they were all built with the one-year-only split-window design.

## 1967–1969 CORVETTE L88

There is perhaps no more hallowed RPO in the 65-plus-year history of the Corvette than the L88 engine package that was offered from 1967 to 1969. Just 216 of these specially equipped Corvettes were released into the wild. Powered by the thunderous yet underrated 427/430-hp V-8 and packaged with a host of heavy-duty options, they tore up the drag strips and won matchups from streetlight to streetlight in cities and small towns across America. Corvettes with RPO L88 also competed on the world stage of sports car races including the 24 Hours of Le Mans, the 24 Hours of Daytona, and the 12 Hours of Sebring. For Duntov, the L88 engine represented a complete competition-ready Corvette package that was for sale at your local Chevrolet dealer.

### *Duntov's Progression of Power*

The L88 was the natural progression of the successful Mark IV big-block V-8 engine program that grew from Mystery Motors. The L88 began making its way into various race cars in early 1963 to stock cars to Mickey Thompson's Z06s at the 1963 Daytona 250-mile race during Speed Weeks. With the Sting Rays still heavier than the 427/425 V-8–powered Shelbys (which were underrated as well, with Dyno tests showing 480 hp out of their race engines), the new Mark IV engines at least gave the Corvette a fighting chance. Chevrolet first started producing the Mark IV engines in January 1965, starting with the L78 396/425-hp V-8. In 1966, a 427/450-hp V-8 was initially released and then revised downward to 427/425 hp "to satisfy insurance company concerns," and finally in 1967 came the Tri-Power L71 427/435-hp V-8.

The second-generation Corvette design was scheduled to be retired after 1966 and a new Corvette based on the Mako Shark show cars would be introduced for 1967. Delays and changes in the design pushed back the launch

| | |
|---|---|
| Base MSRP | $5,573.65 (coupe), $5,425.65 (convertible |
| Model Availability | Coupe, Convertible |
| Engines | L88 |
| Features | Exclusive engine, performance package |
| Production Numbers | 216 |

*To make the car eligible for SCCA A-Production and FIA GT events, the L88 had to be a standard factory option, so General Motors quietly offered it to the public. Chevrolet downplayed the L88's estimated 560 hp by officially listing it as 430 hp. (Photo Courtesy Tom Marcucci)*

*The L88 engine evolved from Chevrolet's Mark I line of "W-series" passenger-car engines that started out at 348 ci in 1958. During its Mark IV development, it was redesigned in key areas, and displacement jumped from 409 to 427 ci. (Photo Courtesy Tom Marcucci)*

*Closely related to the L88 package is RPO L89 that added Chevrolet's big-block aluminum heads to the solid lifter 427/435-hp L71. The aluminum heads shaved 75 pounds off the front end. Unlike the L88, you could still order a radio and air-conditioning with the L89 aluminum head option. (Photo Courtesy Tom Marcucci)*

of the shark Corvettes until 1968, and so the 1967 was the swan-song of the midyear Corvette design.

In 1967, Chevrolet offered four different 427 engine combinations, along with the two 327 small-blocks on Corvette's options list. When the production model started in the fall of 1966, the top engine was the L71 427/435 hp, featuring the triangle-shaped air cleaner hiding three 2-barrel Holley carburetors. The mechanical-lifter engine was rated at 435 hp at 5,800 rpm and 460 ft-lbs of torque at 3,600 rpm.

### The L89 Option

Corvette buyers eyeing the L71 427/435 engines could also upgrade to RPO L89, which added aluminum cylinder heads to the L71. The heads provided larger exhaust valves (1.84 inches versus 1.72 inches) and reduced the weight on the front end by 75 pounds. The weight savings were significant, as the engine would now weigh just 40 pounds more than an iron-block 327 V-8. With the larger exhaust, the L89 added about 25 bhp, although General Motors kept 430 hp as the official output. The option was expensive and listed for $398.65. When combined with $437.10 for the L71, the engine ran approximately $805.75, which was a huge investment for the engine at the time. Only 16 L89s were ordered, making it one of the rarest engines ever produced by Chevrolet for the Corvette.

### The Legendary L88 Option

The L89's aluminum cylinder heads were incorporated into what would be the 427's competition-ready package, the L88. The L88 featured 12.5:1 compression, a high-lift cam, a Holley 850 CFM carburetor, and various performance-based integrations, including an open plenum intake manifold and a road draft tube to vent crankcase vapors. A label on the center console served as a reminder that the L88 required a minimum of 103 octane fuel. Additional weight savings came from an aluminum cross-flow radiator instead of the standard copper radiators, and no fan shroud was used.

The L88 also featured its own special stinger hood with an engine air intake bringing in high-pressure air that builds near the bottom of the windshield. Under the hood was an integrated airbox with built-in air filter that completely surrounded the carburetor when closed.

L88s have actually dyno tested at 560 hp, but Chevrolet rated the engine at 430 hp. By understating the horsepower rating to 430, it was hoped that casual buyers would see the L71's 435-hp engine priced at $437.10 compared to the L88's $947.90 and figure they were getting a better deal. And to further

*At the heart of the L88 package was a 427 V-8 similar only in block casting to the 427/425-hp big-block engine first offered in 1966. After two years of development, almost every other component was reconsidered for power and racing endurance. The engines were all built at the Tonawanda, New York, plant and featured the Can Am–spec aluminum heads with 2.19-inch intake and 1.84-inch exhaust valves. (Photo Courtesy Keith Cornett)*

***The last documented L88 produced was a 1969 Fathom Green Coupe built on December 4, 1969. Chevrolet offered the legendary L88 package for three model years, spanning 1967 to 1969 with a total of 216 built. (Photo Courtesy Keith Cornett)***

***The first L88 Corvette to race at the 24 Hours of Le Mans set a GT lap record with an incredible top speed of 171.5 mph down the Mulsanne Straight. The number-9 Corvette was 20 mph faster than the Ferraris next in class. After 13 hours of dominating the GT class, a connecting rod broke and drivers Bob Bondurant and Dick Guldstrand were forced to retire the 1967 Corvette. (Photo Courtesy the Revs Institute, The Eric della Faille Photograph Collection)***

discourage those casual shoppers, both the radio and heaters were deleted from the L88 options list.

Was Chevy lying about the 430 hp from the L88? Not technically. The L88 reached 430 hp at 1,000 rpm less than its peak horsepower achieved at 6,400 rpm. The L71's 435 hp was achieved at its peak performance of 5,600 rpm.

The L88 was more than just an optional engine. As prerequisites for selecting the L88, savvy buyers were required to order the M22 "rock crusher" 4-speed transmission, G80 Positraction, J56 heavy-duty brakes, and the J50 power brake option. Also required were the F41 heavy-duty suspension, K66 transistor ignition, and the C48 header/defroster delete (1967 only), which incidentally offered a credit of $97.85. In late 1969, a heavy-duty dual disc clutch and the turbohydramatic 400 automatic transmission became available.

### *The L88 Goes Racing*

Chevrolet completed the first L88 in January 1967, and with the release coming in the middle of a model year, the casual buyer really had no idea the racing package existed. Total production in 1967 was just 20 cars, and most of them went to well-known race teams with strong connections to Chevrolet.

***Unsponsored and underfunded, this number-89 Corvette L88 raced in the 24 Hours of Daytona by Cliff Gofflob and Jack Blatchford and finished 2nd in class and 11th overall. As the duo did not have a trailer to fit the car, it was driven 1,600 miles to Daytona Beach. Today, this L88 Corvette still retains its Daytona livery, and even the oil stains remain on the side quarter vents. (Photo Courtesy the Revs Institute, The Eric della Faille Photograph Collection)***

The first L88 racer came out of Detroit and Dawson Hanley Chevrolet, which sponsored Tony DeLorenzo Jr., the son of GM's public relations vice president Anthony DeLorenzo. The black 1967 convertible battled in the SCCA Midwest, earning a spot in the SCCA runoffs before being defeated by a Cobra 427.

Don Yenko and Dave Morgan campaigned one of the four L88 Corvettes entered in the 1967 12 Hours of Sebring, where they finished 10th overall and 1st in GT. A great finish considering the car lost its brakes and sat in the sand trap for the final 40 minutes of the race.

The L88 even made it to France for the 24 Hours of Le Mans. The number-9 Corvette from California dealer Dana Chevrolet entered a white/red/blue L88 Coupe with Dick Guldstrand and Bob Bondurant and really made a mark in its first competition abroad. Despite carrying more than 300 pounds over the Ferraris, the Corvette's top speed of 171.5 mph down the Mulsanne Straight was 20 mph faster than previous Corvette entries, and it was 22 mph faster than the fastest Ferrari in GT. A wrist-pin failure in the 1[illegible]th hour ended the L88's chances.

### *Different Body, Same L88 Package*

For 1968, Chevrolet introduced the shark body style that was more aerodynamic than the 1963–1967 midyears, and Duntov stiffened the chassis to pro-

*Despite this being a package for competition, not all L88 owners took their cars to the track. Although the radio was deleted, Chevrolet still offered the L88 owner the ability to add leather seats, headrests, and power windows in addition to items such as a bolt-on hardtop, side exhaust, engine block heater, and tilt-telescopic steering column. (Photo Courtesy Tom Marcucci)*

*Tony DeLorenzo and Dick Lang campaigned the number-14 Owens Corning Corvette to seventh place overall and first in GT +2.0 at the Watkins Glen 6 Hour Race in July 1969. (Photo Courtesy the Revs Institute, The Karl Ludvigsen Photograph Collection)*

vide relief from the previous design's tendency of front-end lift at high speeds. The chassis updates also had the benefit of allowing wider 7-inch wheels with F70x15 tires for stability at high speeds, and lateral acceleration improved to .84 g from the midyear's .75 g. A taller hood included the built-in airbox with cowl induction. Most important, the L88 engines were carried over from 1967 and, with the word now out, Chevrolet quadrupled production to 80 total cars.

Early on, quality and reliability of the 1968 Corvette were real challenges for race teams. Actor James Garner's American International Racing (AIR) had purchased three 1968 L88s and, with Dick Guldstrand's supervision, the cars were prepared and raced at Daytona in 1968. Garner found the cars' unreliability so bad that he sold them after the race and switched to racing Lola T70s in the Can-Am series. Tony DeLorenzo and Jerry Thompson also raced at Daytona and had similar quality issues. Reporting back to Duntov following the race, Chevy engineers quickly addressed the problems. At Sebring in March, three new L88 Corvettes were entered by Sunray DX. Two would retire but a third team with Dave Morgan and Hap Sharp carefully paced their Corvette throughout the race and earned Chevrolet's highest finish at Sebring: 6th overall and 1st in GT!

Corvette engineers worked through the early problems that drivers reported while Chevrolet's new general manager, John DeLorean, addressed the fundamental issues at the assembly plant in St. Louis. Within a year, the plant improved enough to become one of the highest rated in quality within General Motors. For 1969, a total of 116 L88 Corvettes were built.

While the plant addressed the shaking and rattles and other quality issues, Duntov and the Corvette team continued advances with the powertrain and chassis. The major difference for 1969 was that the L88 now had the new open chamber head design that was shared with the ZL1. Drag racers were happy to hear that the automatic transmission was available as well as wider 8-inch wheels. Combined with 4.88:1 gears and the Turbo Hydramatic, a factory stock L88 was capable of running in the mid-11s.

### An Engine Package for the Ages

During the three years of production, Chevrolet built a total of 216 Corvettes with the L88 engine package. Based on their history and provenance as race cars, along with the fact that they were purpose-built with a host of special equipment from the factory, the L88 Corvettes are among the most valuable regular-production Corvettes offered on the market.

With their rarity of only 20 produced (and with just 16 examples still known to exist), the 1967 Corvette L88s are more valuable than the 116 C3 versions from 1968–1969. Setting the world record at auction for a production Corvette was a red 1967 Coupe, which sold for $3.85 million at Barrett-Jackson

*The world record for the highest price at auction for a production Corvette was set in January 2014 at Barrett-Jackson's Scottsdale auction when this red/red 1967 L88 coupe with documentation and a host of desirable options sold for $3.85 million, which includes commissions and fees. The price eclipsed another 1967 L88, which sold in September 2013 for $3.2 million. (Photo Courtesy Barrett-Jackson Auction Co., LLC.)*

in 2014. The C3 L88s still do extremely well, with documented cars fetching on average around $500,000 or more while the more valuable L88s are those that were entered in the major endurance races from Sebring to Le Mans. Those cars can easily sell for more than $1 million.

## 1969 CORVETTE ZL1

Nearly 50 years after its creation, the 1969 Corvette ZL1 has taken on nearly mythic status among collectors and Corvette historians. Perhaps it's because only two were officially produced. Most enthusiasts have never seen one in person, let alone watched one thunder down a quarter-mile drag strip.

As Chevrolet's performance division (led by Duntov) improved upon the Mark IV's 427 cast-iron block engines, it was also pursuing an aluminum-block version of the L88 for racing. The ZL1 would prove to be one of the most

| Base MSRP | $9789.75 (coupe), $9,446.75 (convertible) |
|---|---|
| Model Availability | Coupe, Convertible |
| Engines | ZL1 |
| Features | Exclusive engine, racing package |
| Production Numbers | 2 (confirmed) |

*The ZL1 engine package was released in the middle of the 1969 model year and was slated to replace the legendary L88. The all-aluminum engine was strengthened in key areas and featured stronger connecting rods and open-chamber heads that improved upon the L88 design. It was much lighter as well, weighing about the same as a 350-ci small-block. (Photo Courtesy Keith Cornett)*

*Duntov was asked what kind of person would buy the ZL1, and he responded, "First, they will have a lot of money." Not only was the ZL1 package expensive at more than double the price of the base Corvette, Duntov was also referring to the ZL1 being solely for off-road use at the track; therefore, the buyer would have to have another car to serve as their daily driver. (Photo Courtesy Keith Cornett)*

powerful engines produced in the era, and because it was intended for racing, it was offered as a regular-production option to qualify it for various sanctioning bodies.

Fred Frincke was the expert when it came to forging engines, and the ZL1 started as a block of heat-treated 356 T-6 aluminum alloy. The engines were assembled at New York's Tonawanda engine plant in what was described as a "surgically clean" assembly area under a 100-percent parts inspection policy. Based on the L88 design, the block was changed to account for areas that needed to be thicker to withstand the power and heat that would be generated internally. Additional bolts were used to secure the cylinder heads, and cast-iron sleeves were inserted in each cylinder bore for additional protection. External braces were found at the front of the block where the intake manifolds are bolted down. When completed, the aluminum block engine shaved 100 pounds off the front end of the Corvette.

The ZL1's camshaft was different from the L88's design; it featured higher valve lift and shortened the open period to optimize performance with the aluminum heads. Topping the engine was Holley's 850 double pumper that fed fuel into those huge cylinders. The ZL1 ran at a compression ratio of 12:5:1 and required a minimum of 103 octane "or engine damage may result" as warned by a sticker placed on the center console. When properly set up, the engine was capable of 585 bhp at 6,600 rpm, according to the book *Corvette: America's Star-Spangled Sports Car* by Karl Ludvigsen.

### Pricing and Production

We look back on the ZL1 and wonder why such a complete, factory-built racing engine would only produce two known examples. It simply came down to the price. The ZL1 aluminum block added $4,718.35 for just that RPO; that's four times the price of the L88. Like the L88, the car was equipped with required options that included K66 Transistorized Ignition System, F41 Special Front and Rear Suspension, J56 Heavy-Duty Brakes, and G81 Positraction. When all was said and done, the car would MSRP around $10,773, which was a huge investment at the time when the price of the base 350-ci Stingray Coupe was just $4,781!

Fred Frincke has claimed that 154 ZL1 427s and 549 L88s were built at the Tonawanda powertrain plant outside of Buffalo, New York. Other researchers say the number of ZL1 engines is 184. According to Chevrolet engine researcher Fran Preve, his research of Chevrolet's official "Summary of Engines Shipped" shows 94 ZL1 engines built for Corvettes with 80 manuals and 14 automatics. Another 90 ZL1 engines were built for F-body Camaros through the COPO system.

As mentioned previously, only two are recorded officially for production, and yet there are currently three 1969 Corvettes with a strong case for being a real ZL1. Only one contains the documents going back to its original owner, a manager at the St. Louis Corvette factory. It didn't help that reporting wasn't very detailed at certain points in Corvette history,

*The aluminum ZL1 motor proved to be the era's most powerful engine ever offered in a production automobile and can trace its lineage to the equally legendary L88 RPO. Like the L88, it was also factory rated at 430 hp but in reality the actual output was closer to 585 when properly set up with the racing exhaust manifolds. (Photo Courtesy Steve Burns)*

*When the Corvette ZL1 is at speed, a pocket of high pressure air forms at the base of the windshield. Engineers took advantage of this high-pressure air to use cowl induction, which sucks the cold air in through ducts and feeds it into the carburetor that is enclosed with an integrated air filter when the hood is down. (Photo Courtesy Keith Cornett)*

*Much like the special-edition Corvettes we see today, the ZL1 featured an interior dash plaque to educate the passenger who might not be acquainted with the fact that a 427-ci engine resided under the hood. (Photo Courtesy Steve Burns)*

*John Maher bought this 1969 Corvette ZL-1 to go drag racing. Known at the track as "Winning Automatically," the aluminum race engine was mated to an M40 Turbo 400 automatic transmission. (Photo Courtesy Steve Burns)*

## Central Office Production Orders

One of the major early supporters of the ZL1 was Chevrolet Engineering's performance products manager, Vance Piggins. He decided what could be ordered through the Central Office Production Order system that allowed vehicles to be built with non-standard but approved Chevy RPOs. In 1968, Piggins lobbied for support for an aluminum 427 big-block on behalf of the McLarens SCCA Can-Am Challenge Team. With that engine, the British McLarens and their drivers, Bruce McLaren and co-driver Denny Hulme, dominated SCCA for five years, winning 32 out of 37 races.

But another opportunity came from Chevy dealer Frank Gibb, who made a name selling high-performance Chevrolets. He contacted Piggins and agreed to purchase 50 Camaros equipped with the ZL1. His initial order led to a total of 69 ZL1 Camaros created. Once the first Camaros arrived at Gibbs dealership, he was shocked to learn the MSRP was more than $7,200 and, as a result, he ended up selling only 13 ZL1 Camaros. The others were traded with other dealerships and even some had their engines removed and swapped with other lower-cost engines to enable the sale.

***The first ZL1 engines went to Can-Am racers but Chevy Engineering's Performance Group manager, Vince Piggins, saw potential for the all-aluminum engine in passenger cars. Duntov liked that it dropped significant weight off the front of the car. The RPO was quietly added so that it would be homologated for racing. (Photo Courtesy Keith Cornett)***

***The key to the ZL1 package was its aluminum block mated to the L88/L89 aluminum cylinder heads. Together the package brought the weight of the engine to 25 pounds less than the standard cast-iron 350-ci V-8 engine. (Photo Courtesy Keith Cornett)***

## 1969 ZL1 Press Cars

Every year the long-lead press from auto magazines and enthusiast publications previewed the Chevrolet lineup. The cars could be seen, driven, and, in the Corvette's case, tested. For 1969, Duntov planned a little something extra for the press.

Two 1969 Corvettes with ZL1 V-8s were specially modified for the test: a white coupe that Duntov set up for road racing and an orange coupe set up for drag racing.

Duntov's white coupe weighed 2,909 pounds and featured fender flares with wide Firestone racing tires and a wide-open side exhaust. Equipped with an M22 Rock Crusher 4-speed and set up with 3.07 gears, it ran the quarter mile in 12 seconds at 116 mph.

The orange coupe was even more special. Engineers Tom Langford and Gib Hufstader went to work with Langford and were able to coax 710 hp from the engine, while Hufstader shed weight by removing steel reinforcements and even re-creating the bumpers in fiberglass and then having those chromed. Now weighing in at around 2,800 pounds, the orange coupe was further armed with a high-stall Turbo Hydramatic automatic transmission and a rear differential with 4.88:1 drag racing gears and 9-inch racing slicks.

Nearly 30 journalists had the opportunity to strap into the orange coupe and make the quarter-mile run of their lives. With the automatic transmission, it was just a matter of hitting the gas and hanging on as 11-second quarter-mile passes at 127 miles per hour were easily reached. The best run of the day involved revving to 6,000 rpm and dumping it into gear, launching the car to a time of 10.89 seconds at 130 miles per hour!

***Not too many people have witnessed firsthand the performance capabilities of these cars. Back in the day,* Road & Track *tested the sub-3,000 pound ZL1 with a 0–60 mph run in 4.0 seconds and the quarter mile in 12.1 seconds at 116 mph.* Popular Hot Rodding's *quarter mile was even better with a run of 11.0 seconds at 129.45 mph. (Photo Courtesy Steve Burns)***

and especially in 1969 with the high volume of cars running at the St. Louis plant. There just wasn't enough time. It's been reported that five or six ZL1s were built as test mules, and some others may have been created as brass-hats (one-off productions for executives). One ZL1 engine was even installed in the 1969 Manta Ray concept.

## 1970–1972 ZR1 AND 1971 ZR2 SPECIAL PURPOSE PACKAGES

The 1970 model year marked a turning point in Duntov's autonomy over the Corvette. Chevrolet was losing both market share and revenue, so it turned to former Pontiac general manager John DeLorean to right the ship. DeLorean's policy of deproliferation eliminated costly low-production

| | |
|---|---|
| Base MSRP | $6,190 (1970 ZR1 coupe), $5,817.95 (1970 ZR1 convertible), $7,243 (1971 ZR2 coupe), $7,006 (1971 ZR1 convertible) |
| Model Availability | Coupe, Convertible |
| Engines | LT1, LS6 |
| Features | Special performance package |
| Production Numbers | 65 |

***Duntov saw the potential of building an L88-style special racing package based on the LT1 V-8 which resulted in RPO ZR1, a small-block version of the L88 with the same chassis preparation, heavy-duty brakes, suspension, and cooling. (Photo Courtesy Steve Burns)***

options, including the top engines planned for the Corvette in 1970, the 454-ci LS7 and the LT2, the would-be successors of the 427-ci L88 and ZL1.

In Corvette history, the 1970 LS7 was the engine that never was. The 454-ci V-8 featured the 454 block with aluminum heads and a solid-lifter camshaft. The engine had its specs published in the auto magazines, and Paul Van Valkenburgh drove a 1970 LS7 Corvette from Los Angeles to Detroit and wrote about the car in *Sports Car Graphic* magazine. With specs listed as 460 hp at 5,200 rpm, it also featured the M22 Rock Crusher

***Although the ZR-1 name was first made famous as the C4's King of the Hill run from 1990 to 1995, and again as the C6 Blue Devil from 2009 to 2013, the first use of the ZR1 RPO came back in 1970 as Duntov once again fashioned a factory-prepped race car orderable from your local dealership. (Photo Courtesy Steve Burns)***

and Chevrolet's new twin-disc 10-inch clutch. Valkenburgh said that with a full fuel tank, two passengers, and full kit of luggage, the car could turn a 13.8-second quarter mile at 108 mph. The trick, he said, was trying to keep the tank full, as the LS7 had a voracious appetite for fuel.

Another obstacle for Duntov's team was his former boss, Ed Cole, who had been leading General Motors since 1967. In 1970, Cole first issued a decree that by 1971, all GM vehicles would operate on fuel with an octane level no higher than 91. The move was designed to move the fleet toward the use of lead-free fuels that were needed for the future implementation of catalytic converters. The result was that Corvette engineers had to revert to the compression levels from the mid-1950s to satisfy the requirements; engines such as the L88 and its required 103 octane fuel would not make the cut.

The second change came later in 1970, when all engines were marketed with the net-horsepower number, which took into account power loss from the operation of the engine.

### *The Return of the High-Performance Small-Block*

Since his time at Chevrolet, Duntov had always been known as an ardent supporter of lightweight, high-performance small-block engines. But he also loved horsepower, and if going to the big-block 427s would make the Corvette more competitive against the Shelby Cobras, then "there was no replacement for displacement" as the popular hot-rodder saying goes. But in 1970, Duntov got another opportunity to return to his roots with a new solid-lifter small-block V-8 called the LT1 that was very much like his Duntov cams and fuel-injected V-8s from the late 1950s and early 1960s.

Herb Fishel was the engineer behind the LT1, a new solid-lifter 350-ci V-8. With a generous cam timing, the LT1 used aspects from what was learned with the L88, including larger 2.5-inch exhaust pipes, a larger Holley 850 CFM carburetor, and Delco's transistorized ignition, features that were usually found only on the big-block V-8s.

The LT1 was rated at 370 hp at 6,000 rpm and 380 ft-lbs of torque at 4,000 rpm. The small-block could send the Corvette through the quarter mile in 12.2 seconds at 102 mph.

### *The ZR1 Special Purpose Package*

Whether or not the legend is true that ZR1 stands for "Zora's Racer," Corvette history as written says that Duntov did indeed package the new high-winding solid-lifter LT1 small-block for SCCA B-Production racing. Most know about the ZR1 from the C4 days (1990–1995) and the reintroduction of the nameplate for Chevrolet's first supercharged Corvette in 2009. But RPO ZR1 first made its debut on the books in 1970 as a performance package for the Corvette.

This successor to the L88 Corvette came equipped with the potent 370-hp LT1 small-block, and all the specialty options that were found on the L88s that were retired the previous year. The ZR1's LT1 engine used a different assembly process than the regular-production engines as it was fitted with a lightweight L88-style 10.5-inch flywheel and bellhousing as well as a high-torque starter.

The package included an M22 Rock Crusher 4-speed heavy-duty transmission, J56 heavy-duty brakes with power assist, dual-pin front calipers, semi-metallic brake pads, transistorized ignition, special high-capacity alu-

*Herb Fishel was the engineer tasked with developing the LT1 engine. He tells the story of Duntov continually coming by engineering to see if the LT1 was finished. When that day came, Fishel went looking for Duntov and found him in a meeting. On seeing Fishel, Duntov asked if the LT1 was finished. When Fishel said yes, Duntov immediately walked out of the meeting, saying to Fishel, "Let's go for a drive." (Photo Courtesy the Revs Institute, The Karl Ludvigsen Photograph Collection)*

*The ZR1 Engine Package option was omitted from GM literature until well into the model year run, which started in January 1970. To order one of these cars, you either had to be part of an organized race team or know the right people who could place the order for such a car. (Photo Courtesy ProTeam Corvette Sales)*

*Even though the ZR1 was set up as a racing package with no convenience options, the interiors were still nicely appointed. The ZR1's center gauge cluster is missing a few items, but Chevrolet supplied the cars with special panels that covered the deleted radio and heater/AC controls. (Photo Courtesy ProTeam Corvette Sales)*

*With the pressure on automakers about fuel economy and pollution controls, 1971's ZR2 Special Purpose Package would be Duntov's final hurrah for elevating Corvette performance. When equipped with the 4-speed manual and a 3.36:1 limited-slip differential, the Corvette could rocket from 0–60 mph in 5.3 seconds and could run the quarter mile in 13.8 seconds at 105 mph! (Photo Courtesy ProTeam Corvette Sales)*

*The higher revving solid-lifter LT1 was fitted with equipment previously found on the L88 big-blocks, including larger 2.5-inch exhaust pipes, an aluminum radiator with surge tank and metal fan shroud, a 10.5-inch flywheel, a high-torque starter, and transistorized ignition. (Photo Courtesy ProTeam Corvette Sales)*

minum radiator, and a suspension that included special springs, shocks, and front and rear stabilizer bars. Add-ons included metal fan shrouds and a coolant expansion tank; the latter was found exclusively on ZR1-equipped LT1s.

To discourage street use, the ZR1 wasn't available with any of the creature comforts such as air-conditioning, power windows, power steering, radio, alarm system, rear window defroster, or special trim items such as the P02 wheel covers. The options available were the deluxe interior and the tilt/telescopic steering column.

### Price and Production

Production of the ZR1 was limited to 1970–1972, the same three-year time span of the LT1 engine. The ZR1s of the 1970s were the rarest small-block Corvettes ever produced. During the three-year run, only 53 cars were ordered with RPO ZR1: 25 in 1970, 8 in 1971, and 20 in 1972.

### The 1971 ZR2 Special Purpose Package

With the various corporate edicts in place and the cloud of fuel economy regulations beginning to descend on the automotive industry, the 1972 ZR2 Special Performance Package would be the last of Duntov's special-purpose packages in the Corvette and the last high-performance Corvettes to be built until the ZR1 name was resurrected in 1990.

***The big-block RPO LS6 Chevy V-8 had the same 4.251-inch bore as the 427 it replaced, but the stroke jumped from 3.76 to 4.00 inches. For use with the new fuels, it had a mere 8.5:1 compression ratio, but Duntov compensated for this by using a high-performance cam grind and a single Holley 800-cfm carburetor. The LS6 developed peak power at 5,600 rpm and produced 475 ft-lbs of torque at 4,000 rpm. (Photo Courtesy ProTeam Corvette Sales)***

***The ZR2 Special Racing Package was initially slated for release in 1970 alongside the small-block ZR1, but a four-month strike extended the 1969 model year and disrupted the Corvette team's plan. The ZR2 package was in further peril when the big-block LS7 engine originally slated for the package was canceled. (Photo Courtesy ProTeam Corvette Sales)***

Initially, the top dog engine of the early 1970s was supposed to be the LS7, but that engine was dropped just before 1970s' production was to start, leaving the LS5 with its 454/390-hp engine as the only big-block motor in 1970. That would change again in 1971 with the introduction of the one-year-only LS6, a 454-ci V-8 with aluminum heads and a power rating of 425 hp. Only 188 regular-production Corvettes were built with the LS6, which is less than 1 percent of the 21,801 Corvettes built during the year. The LS6 added $1,221 to the coupe's MSRP of $5,496, a 22-percent increase over the base 1971 Corvette.

The ZR2 special-purpose package was built around the LS6 aluminum-head 454-ci engine and included a heavy-duty, high-capacity aluminum radiator without a shroud, the dual-plate clutch, M22 Rock Crusher heavy-duty 4-speed, J56 dual-pin heavy-duty brakes, F41 heavy-duty suspension with special springs, shock absorbers and front and rear stabilizer bars, and the transistorized ignition. Like the ZR1 and the L88s before it, the car was offered without the ability to add power steering, automatic transmission, radio, and air-conditioning.

In terms of power, the LS6 was second to the L88. As tested at the time by one of the leading automotive magazines, the LS6 was capable of a 0–60 mph time of 5.3 seconds, and the quarter-mile stats were 13.8 seconds at 105 mph.

### 1970–1972 Corvette ZR1 Production

| Year | Coupe | Convertible | Total |
|---|---|---|---|
| 1970 | 17 | 8 | 25 |
| 1971 | 7 | 1 | 8 |
| 1972 | 14 | 6 | 20 |
| **Total:** | **38** | **15** | **53** |

### Pricing and Production

The ZR2 Special Purpose Package was one of the rarest single-year packages assembled for the Corvette. Chevrolet would assemble just 12 examples (10 coupes and 2 convertibles) with the RPO costing $1,747 and a total MSRP starting at $7,243.

### 1971 Corvette ZR2 Production

| Year | Coupe | Convertible | Total |
|---|---|---|---|
| 1971 | 10 | 2 | 12 |

***The 454-ci LS6 was the last of the big-block performance engines produced for the Corvette. Its aluminum heads had an open-chamber design and featured forged internal components, a special camshaft, and a Holley 800 cfm 4-barrel carburetor. (Photo Courtesy ProTeam Corvette Sales)***

## 1980 CORVETTE 305 CALIFORNIA

If any model of Corvette in this book can be debated as to whether it should be considered a special edition, it would be the 1980 Corvette 305 California. The car is heralded as one of *Time* magazine's 50 Worst Cars of All Time, and *Edmunds* called it the worst Corvette ever. It's not a car for collectors, and they can be notoriously hard to sell. Having said that, the 1980 Corvette 305 California fits the description of being a special edition: a one-year-only RPO with a unique engine. Plus the fact it was offered in America's most populous state with sales of 3,221 of the 40,614 Corvettes sold during the model year.

The late 1970s and early 1980s were already feeling the brunt of the corporate decisions made a half-decade earlier to address fuel economy standards. The Corvette wasn't immune to these changes, but 1980 seemed to magnify the difference in the Corvette's performance at the start of the 1980s versus the heady-horsepower days of the early 1970s. Even the Corvette's speedometer was dumbed down to a federally mandated maximum of 85 mph.

Corvette engineers were doing their part to increase the fuel efficiency by effectively reducing the weight of the car by more than 250 pounds through the use of aluminum and plastics. A redesigned exterior featured an integrated front and rear spoiler that helped lower the coefficient of drag (C3) from .503 to .443.

| Base MSRP | $13,090.24 |
|---|---|
| Model Availability | T-Top Coupe |
| Engines | LG4 |
| Features | Exclusive engine, available only in California |
| Production Numbers | 3,221 |

### *California Regulations Render the Corvette Engines Illegal*

In 1980, Corvette offered two V-8 engines with different displacements for the first time since 1974. But that wasn't a good thing in the days of rapidly increasing Corporate Average Fuel Economy (CAFÉ) fuel standards. Chevrolet was already working on the C4, and changes in 1981 would mean just one standard V-8 would be offered. Unable to certify its L48 in 1980 to California's higher emission control standards and with no money available to make a compliant version, Chevrolet was forced to sell the Corvette in California equipped with the LG4 305-ci V-8 found in the Camaro and other Chevrolet passenger cars.

The LG4 305 V-8 was rated at 150 hp and was installed across the Chevrolet product line with appearances in the Camaro, Caprice, Malibu, and even pickups. With the Corvette, engineers were able to raise horsepower to 180, just

*With California taking the lead in reducing automotive pollutions, the state's environmental standards were a real conundrum for Chevrolet. Either offer the 305-ci LG4 engine or not sell the Corvette in America's largest state. Chevrolet chose the engine, and 3,221 were sold. (Photo Courtesy Jeff Romm / Corvette Mike)*

*Adding insult to injury, California buyers could get the 1980 Corvette only with the 305-ci V-8 and an automatic transmission. Corvettes with automatic transmissions were easier to pass emissions, as the manuals released additional exhaust pollution when the clutch was engaged. (Photo Courtesy Jeff Romm / Corvette Mike)*

*Chevrolet's cost-effective 305 engine was developed as an all-purpose economy V-8 during the 1970s that could provide better fuel economy than the 350. It was more powerful than Chevrolet's V-6 and inline-6 engines of the era. The 305 became known as GM's corporate engine during the 1980s with the V-8 offered as standard (or the only V-8 option) on many GM vehicles, including the Camaro, Monte Carlo SS, and C/K-series of trucks. (Photo Courtesy Jeff Romm / Corvette Mike)*

*The 1980 Corvette California is lamented in the hobby due to its smaller 305-ci V-8, which produced 180 hp, 10 less than the 350-ci L48 sold in the other 49 states. But it wasn't the lowest of the C3 era. The 1975 base Corvette engine that offered just 165 hp, the lowest of any Corvette since the 1953–1954 Blue Flame 6-cylinder, was rated at 150 hp. (Photo Courtesy Jeff Romm / Corvette Mike)*

### 1980 Corvette Engine Options

| Name | Capacity | Horsepower | Torque |
|---|---|---|---|
| LG4 | 5.0L | 180 hp at 4,200 rpm | 255 ft-lbs at 2,000 rpm |
| L48 | 5.7L | 190 hp at 4,200 rpm | 280 ft-lbs at 2,000 rpm |
| L82 | 5.7L | 230 hp at 5,200 rpm | 275 ft-lbs at 3,600 rpm |

10 less than the L48 350 V-8. To get the added horsepower, the LG4 used stainless-steel headers and the new closed-loop control system that would become Chevrolet's Computer Command Control (standard on all 1981 Corvettes). It monitored exhaust air-fuel ratios and could adjust up to 10 times per second to create an optimum mixture of fuel through the Rochester Quadrajet carburetor.

The only transmission available for the LG4 305 was Chevrolet's 3-speed automatic. The standard rear axle ratio was 3.55:1; the same as the L82.

## Price and Production

Corvette prices rose significantly for the 1980 model year and, as a result, sales were down from 1979's all-time high of 53,807. MSRP was now $13,140.24, up 28.5 percent from the previous year. Chevrolet sold 40,614 Corvette Coupes for the model year, and of those, a total of 3,221 were equipped with the California 305 package. The one-year California 305 package represents 7.9 percent of total production. The package selection generated a $50 credit.

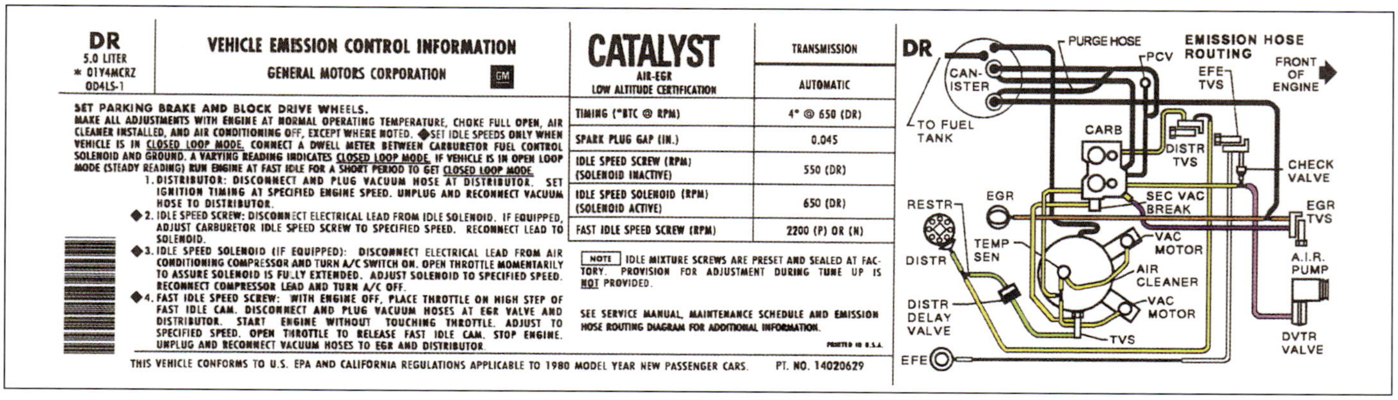


*The LG4 305 and the 350 L48/L82 engines were nearly indistinguishable from each other. However, reading the upper left-hand corner on the air cleaner's smog tag will show either a 5.0L (305) or 5.7 for the 350-ci. (Photo Courtesy Eric Crotty)*

## 1983 CORVETTE

Only two models featured in this book were prototype Corvettes and never offered for sale to the public: the 1963 Corvette Grand Sport racers and the 1983 Corvette. Like the 1963 Grand Sports, the legend of the 1983 Corvette deserves to be told.

The Corvette team started working on the fourth-generation Corvette around 1978, but plans really fell in place once production moved from St. Louis to Bowling Green. Other than the Cross-Fire 350 V-8 that carried over, the 1983 Corvette was completely redesigned and was a showcase of engineering and technology.

The new Corvette was planned to go on sale in October 1982, but quality control issues with an emphasis on making sure the technology was tested thoroughly pushed the introduction to March 1983. Because of the late start in the 1983 model year and the fact that the car met all the 1984 federal emissions and safety standards, Chevrolet President Robert Stempel declared the new Corvette as a 1984 model.

### *The First 1983 Corvettes*

Engineering assembled 18 preproduction prototypes for testing purposes and then 43 pilot line cars followed. The pilot line cars were the first to be built at Bowling Green assembly using production tooling. The pilot line cars were built as non-saleable units, meaning they could not be sold.

| | |
|---|---|
| Base MSRP | Not offered for public sale |
| Model Availability | Coupe |
| Engines | L83 Cross-Fire |
| Features | Only surviving 1983 model |
| Production Numbers | 43 produced, 1 remaining |

***Chevrolet planned to celebrate the 30th anniversary of the Corvette with a redesigned model in 1983. Quality issues and ensuring new technologies worked the way they should have pushed back the introduction to the middle of the 1983 model year. As the new Corvette met all 1984 safety regulations, it was sold as the new 1984 Corvette. (Photo Courtesy Keith Cornett)***

***Dealers began taking orders for the 1984 in January 1984 and the first Corvettes arrived in March. With the extended selling period, the 1984 went go down as the second-highest production of the Corvette with 51,547 total. (Photo Courtesy Keith Cornett)***

The first 33 pilot cars were assembled in the summer of 1982. All would have the RPO MD8 automatic transmissions with the GU2 2.73 axles. None were RPO Z51. An interesting note is that the first VIN was supposed to be painted in RPO 53U Gold Metallic. Records show that it was changed to 70U Spectra Red.

The final 10 pilot cars were built in November 1982. These were also classified as non-saleable units. All these had HE3 3.07 rear axles, and 5 of the 10 were Z51s. Of the 10 cars, 6 were white while the other 4 were silver. These were the cars featured at the long-lead press introduction at Riverside Raceway in Riverside, California, in December 1982.

Multiple accounts say that Bowling Green eventually kept 10 of the cars for production evaluation and testing purposes, and the other 33 were sent to Chevrolet. During their time in Detroit, the cars were put through intense product development and evaluations at the Warren Technical Center and the Milford Proving Grounds, and some were even used for crash testing.

### *How the Only 1983 Corvette Was Saved*

Of the 43 Corvettes produced as pilot-line cars in Bowling Green, only the number 023 Corvette was spared from the crusher. Following its production, the car was sent to Milford for testing, where it was used for shock tuning before it went back to Bowling Green for use as a training car. Because these prototypes were all non-saleable units with 1983 VINs, they eventually served out their purpose and all 43 were ordered to be destroyed.

Typically, the non-saleable cars to be destroyed were loaded on a carrier and sent to Detroit where they have the facilities to do it. However, the decision was made to crush the 1983 Corvettes on-site at the assembly plant. A local company was hired, and a portable crusher was brought to the plant to dispose of 9 of the 10 cars.

The person responsible for making sure the cars were crushed was Ralph Montileone, the operations engineering manager at the plant. Ralph says it came down to a new pair of cowboy boots and inclement weather as to why the car wasn't crushed that day with the others. After looking at the wet parking lot and then down at his new boots, Ralph figured the final car could wait to be crushed the following day. When Ralph showed up the next day, he was surprised to learn that the crusher had already departed the facility.

With the crusher gone, Ralph told his superiors about the missed car and then parked the remaining Corvette out behind the assembly plant until plans could be made to destroy it. The car would sit behind the plant for more than a year, occasionally protected by a tarp.

### *A New Lease on Life*

In June 1984, Paul Schnoes was tasked as general manager of the Bowling Green assembly plant. After a few weeks on the job, he noticed the white Corvette parked in the back and started asking questions about it. Realizing the historical significance of this being the only 1983 model, he promptly had it brought inside the plant and cleaned up. After some time went by, it became common knowledge that the plant had the only remaining 1983 Corvette. Word came down from Detroit that they didn't need the car and allowed the assembly plant to keep it. The car became part of the history of the new Corvette factory.

When the National Corvette Museum was eventually completed in 1994, the car was donated to the facility with General Motors retaining ownership. Today, the world's only 1983 Corvette is the centerpiece of the National Corvette Museum.

*The 1983 Corvette underwent many repaints during its stay at the Bowling Green assembly plant. At one point, the bottom half of the car was painted blue while red stripes flowed from the hood down to the sides of the car. In the background on the right is longtime plant manager Wil Cooksey. (Photo Courtesy the National Corvette Museum)*

*One of the differences between the 1983 Corvette and the regular-production 1984 Corvette is the wheels. Today, the 1983 Corvette wears the prototype wheels that were featured in the original 1983 catalog but never installed on any regular-production Corvette. (Photo Courtesy the National Corvette Museum)*

*The number 023 Corvette was 1 of 11 pilot-line cars to be painted white, and it also featured a blue interior. All 1983 Corvettes had RPO MD8 automatic transmissions. Although never released, the 1983 Corvette is one of only four years of Corvettes that were not built with a manual transmission: 1953, 1954, 1982, and 1983. (Photo Courtesy the National Corvette Museum)*

*Although the National Corvette Museum has displayed the 1983 Corvette since 1994, mechanical issues prevented the car from starting. That changed in 2016 when the museum's new restoration and preservation department fixed the extensive fuel issues plaguing the car after decades of sitting. To celebrate, the world's only 1983 Corvette takes a few laps around the Corvette Museum. (Photo Courtesy the National Corvette Museum)*

CHAPTER 6

# DEALERS, TUNERS, AND THIRD-PARTY SPECIAL EDITIONS

With a rich history of more than 65 years, the Chevrolet Corvette has become an automotive icon. But that doesn't mean the car can't be improved, at least in the minds of those who want to build their own sports car using the Corvette as the starting point. Over the years, many car builders, engine tuners, and even former GM employees have set about to create their own version of the Corvette.

Coach building can be a very expensive business to enter, and the individuals and organizations that have been successful at it have usually found a formula that combines additional performance with unique designs.

It would be impossible to list all of the third-party special-edition Corvettes that have been built over the years. In this final section, we take a look at some of the more prominent dealers, tuners, and third-party special-edition Corvettes that have been offered.

***Unique special editions were built using America's favorite sports car. (Photo Courtesy Chris Chessnoe)***

## Baldwin-Motion

From the early 1960s to the mid-1970s, if you wanted a Corvette that would absolutely kick butt at any drag strip in the country, Joel Rosen at Long Island's Motion Performance was the man to see. The partnership with Baldwin Chevrolet, a small dealer on Long Island that formed Baldwin-Motion, would go on to produce hundreds of high-performance Corvettes, Camaros, and other Chevrolets, as well as a number of personally customized Corvette models.

Joel Rosen was a fan of high performance and racing from his high school days when he hung out with the car guys and learned about modifying engines. After a stint in the US Air Force, when he learned the finer points of engine rebuilding, Rosen returned to Coney Island, working for a shop that specialized in high-performance Chevrolets. After six months, he attempted striking out on his own with a shop in the Catskills. That didn't fare so well, and he closed and returned to Brooklyn, taking over Neclan Service Station. For the next few years, his two-stall garage did all of the general repairs and tune-ups that a neighborhood garage does, but Rosen always had time to work on the fuelies from area Corvette owners.

Rosen bought his first Corvette in 1961, a 1958 fuelie with the Heavy-Duty RPO 684 brakes option, and although it was his daily driver, it was raced it extensively. On his honeymoon, he and his new bride, Judith, drove the Corvette north to the Catskills, which coincidentally, was hosting a sports car hill climb competitions. Rosen entered the event and crashed his Corvette in excess of 100 miles an hour, flipping three times before coming to a stop. Luckily, he suffered only mild injuries, and he and his bride had to take the bus back home.

His next Corvette was a 1962 327/360-hp fuelie finished in Marlboro Maroon. In addition to participating in hill climbs and sports car competition, Rosen finished first in the 1962 Long Island Sports Car Club racing season. In 1963, with his racing bonafides established, he changed the name of Neclan Service Station to Motion Performance. With the change of name, Rosen passed on the grocery getters and other general automotive repairs to focus exclusively on performance. He installed a Clayton chassis dynamometer and became the go-to shop for small-block Chevy performance upgrades as well as dyno-tuning fuel-injected Corvettes.

Rosen sold the 1962 for the first 1963 fuel-injected Sting Ray Coupe in the New York area. Black with a white stripe, the car was affectionately named "Skunk." Both Rosen and his wife would rack up the awards that year with the car. And with his success on the track and his shop's dyno, his business boomed overnight. Three years later, the Rosens relocated to the suburb of Baldwin on Long Island. Motion Performance would set up shop on Sunrise Highway not far from Baldwin Chevrolet.

Chevrolet introduced the 1967 Camaro in the fall of 1966, and it became the genesis for the Baldwin Chevrolet–Motion Performance col-

*The Baldwin-Motion partnership between Baldwin Chevrolet and Motion Performance started as a collaboration to build high-performance Camaros in 1969. Corvettes joined the offerings not too long after. (Photo Courtesy Martyn L. Schorr)*

*Motion's founder, Joel Rosen, was engaged in general automotive repair in the early 1960s at a Shell Station on Long Island. His reputation grew from his own racing efforts, and in 1963 he began building and servicing high-performance cars exclusively through his shop that was renamed Motion Performance. (Photo Courtesy Martyn L. Schorr)*

*Joel's vision for the Phase III GT was to build a high-performance Grand Touring sports car that could compete with Europe's finest. The super-fast Corvette was considered more practical than the standard-production Corvettes as Rosen gave it a larger cargo area to hold enough luggage for extended cruising. (Photo Courtesy Martyn L. Schorr)*

*Baldwin-Motion generally offered two package levels for the Camaros, Corvettes, and other high-performance cars that came through Motion Performance. The SS level would get you 425 hp while the Phase III package offered 500 hp or more. The cars could be ordered through Baldwin Chevrolet or direct from Motion, and GMAC financing was available. (Photo Courtesy Martyn L. Schorr)*

*Martyn Schorr joined Joel Rosen as the adverting and marketing machine behind Baldwin-Motion and Motion Performance. The in-your-face advertising reached the appropriate target audiences in Martyn's* Cars *magazine and other trade publications. Following his stint with Baldwin-Motion, Martyn became the first editor of* Vette *magazine. (Photo Courtesy Martyn L. Schorr)*

laboration. Rosen met with Baldwin's parts manager, John Mahler, and *Cars* magazine editor Martyn Schorr, and the group discussed building a dealer-sponsored Camaro race car to drum up parts sales for the dealership. With the dealer's consent, a base Camaro with a gold exterior was delivered to Motion Performance, where an early L88 crate engine was installed. With a Hurst-shifted 4-speed and heady-duty suspension, the base Camaro suddenly was a fire-breathing race car. Marveling at how simple it was to swap in the 427 crate engine, a plan was hatched for creating and selling private-label Camaros.

***Rosen had seen the Mako Shark II concept car when it was introduced in 1965. In 1972, Rosen set about creating a streetable version of the concept that he would call the Maco Shark. (Photo Courtesy Martyn L. Schorr)***

Rosen saw the SS-427 Camaro program as an opportunity to keep his shop busy and have ready access to Chevrolet's high-performance parts. Baldwin Chevrolet would supply the Camaros (with 396/375-hp engines) as well as the 427-ci replacement engines and factory performance parts. Motion Performance would do all the work in creating the 425- to 500-hp Camaros, delivering them back to Baldwin Chevrolet where the customer would take delivery. Schorr, who would later start *Vette* magazine, served as the public relations point man, handling the advertising and promotion of the Motion-built cars.

From 1967 through 1974, Baldwin-Motion offered its SS (425 hp) or the Phase III (500-plus hp) on hundreds of Camaros, Corvettes, Novas, Chevelles, and even the V-8–powered Vegas. Cars could be ordered at Baldwin Chevrolet, although many buyers placed the order through Motion Performance. The cars were financed by GMAC, and all the work was guaranteed. Not only did each car come with a warranty, the Phase III models included Joel Rosen's performance guarantee to run at least 120 mph in 11.50 seconds or better with an approved driver on a American Hot Rod Association (AHRA) or National Hot Rod Association (NHRA) drag strip. Rosen claims that not one car was ever brought back!

Schorr's bold advertising helped bring in the customers. The ads featured large print and stark black-and-white graphics that advertised "The Quickest and Fastest Supercar! SS-427 Camaro!" Along with a menu of high-performance parts, the ads always included the phrase "Dyno-Tuned and Ready to Wail." From 1968 until 1974, Schorr produced Baldwin-Motion catalogs, and each included ordering information for Baldwin-Motion cars.

The Baldwin-Motion partnership ended as the high-performance era was drawing to a close. Baldwin Chevrolet was sold in 1973 and became Williams Chevrolet and then Lions Chevrolet. The dealership closed its doors for good in the 1980s.

It was in 1974 that the Environmental Protection Agency (EPA) took an interest in aftermarket automotive sales and zeroed in on Motion Performance after one of Schorr's articles, "King Kong Lives on Long Island," featured a 454-ci Super Vega. The EPA presented Rosen with a cease and desist order, halting the building and selling of new cars with powertrains not available from the factory. The Department of Justice order was backed by a fine of $10,000 per emission device removed, which translated to $50,000 in fines for each Super Vega that Rosen had built. Rosen settled with the EPA in 1975, paying a $500 fine and agreeing to honor the terms outlined. Rosen continued to build high-performance Chevrolets, which were invoiced and prominently stated "for export" or "for off-road use only."

The first Baldwin-Motion branded Corvettes arrived in 1968, although sales were limited due to 1968's poor build quality. The SS-427 Corvette was offered for $4,899.95 for a coupe or $5,099.95 for a convertible. The dyno-tuned Corvettes were mostly stock, but an upgrade package was offered that came with Rosen's 160-mph written guarantee. Rosen's Corvette business took off in 1969 with three offerings, the SS-427, the Phase III SS-427, and the new Phase III GT.

## THE BALDWIN-MOTION PHASE III GT

The Phase III GTs were a departure for Motion Performance: They included major enhancements to the body along with the engine. Pricing for the GTs started at $10,500, and additional upgrades were available. Motion built 12 Phase III GTs from 1969 through 1971, and it's been said that no two were alike because they were customer builds and the bodies varied as Chevrolet updated the Stingray in those three years. Except for the first three GTs that retained their pop-up headlights, most of the GT cars featured faired-in front headlights while the round taillights where changed to three horizontal lenses per side. The rear notchback window was removed, and the rear cargo space was greatly enhanced. Rosen customized the cargo area with carpet and speakers and topped it with a large fastback-style window. The Corvette now had room for luggage or golf clubs, like a proper GT sports car.

Rosen's Phase III GT prototype was powered by Motion's blueprinted 500-hp V-8 fitted with headers and factory side exhaust, a Motion Super/Spark CD ignition, and a 1,050-cfm Holley 3-barrel carburetor mounted on an alloy high-rise intake. Later builds could be outfitted with engines ranging from a small-block V-8 to the all-aluminum ZL1 racing engine. Further

***The Phase III GT Corvettes built by Motion evolved as Chevrolet released new engines and body styles. This Phase III GT Corvette featuring a 454-ci V-8 with Motion-branded upgrades produced up to 500 hp. (Photo Courtesy Martyn L. Schorr)***

design cues included a scooped Phase III hood, shark-style functional side vents with flared fender wells, and a Le Mans-style quick-fill gas cap.

The Phase III GT was completed in time for the car to be shown at the 1969 New York International Auto Show, and Rosen was strategically set up next to Lamborghini, which was showing off its new Miura. A visitor to the booth was Corvette chief engineer Zora Arkus-Duntov, and he and Rosen talked all about big-block motors. Duntov encouraged Rosen to build some customer cars with the GT.

| Base MSRP | $10,500 to $16,283 |
|---|---|
| Model Availability | Coupe |
| Engines | 350-ci, 427-ci |
| Features | Blueprinted engine with quarter-mile guarantee, custom body and interior |
| Production Numbers | 12 |

***Rosen's Performance guarantee read: "We think so much of our Phase III Supercars that we guarantee they will turn at least 120 mph in 11.50 seconds or better with an M/P-approved driver on an AHRA- or NHRA-sanctioned drag strip. Phase III Supercars are completely streetable, reliable machines that will run these times off the street." (Photo Courtesy Martyn L. Schorr)***

***Rosen (left) displayed his first Corvette Phase III GT at the New York Auto Show. Corvette chief engineer Zora Arkus-Duntov (right) made a beeline to the Baldwin-Motion display, and these two promoters of Corvette performance were said to have engaged in conversation about the upcoming ZL1 aluminum racing engine. (Photo Courtesy Martyn L. Schorr)***

On June 3, 1971, Rosen made the final Phase III GT delivery to a cardiologist from Savannah, Georgia. Dr. Henry Rollings took delivery of his air-conditioned, 500-plus-hp 1971 Phase III GT from Joel Rosen at Motion Performance in Baldwin, New York. Power was supplied by a blueprinted and balanced 454 LS6 big-block built to LS7 specifications and fitted with a GM high-performance hydraulic cam, open-chamber L88/ZL1 aluminum heads, headers, and a Holley 4-barrel. Backing up the potent Phase III engine: a massaged M40 Turbo Hydramatic, Hone overdrive, and a 4.88 Posi rear.

*Motion Performance built Maco Sharks from 1971 to 1978, but hundreds of Maco body kits were sold into the 1980s. This German-built Maco Shark was spotted by Joel and Martyn during a trip to Holland in 1978 for an SCCI Euro-Meet at the Zandvoort GP track. (Photo Courtesy Martyn L. Schorr)*

## MOTION MACO SHARK CORVETTE

In 1965, Chevrolet introduced the Mako Shark II concept car that greatly influenced the final design of the C3 Corvettes starting in 1968. Rosen had instantly fallen in love with the Mako Shark II and eventually set about re-creating a show car heavily influenced by the original.

Rosen started with designs from John Silva at Silva Auto Engineering, who had prototyped a Mako Shark II–styled body kit. Rosen went to work creating molds while refining the fit and finish. The Silva-designed Shark was not a true Mako Shark replica, although it retained the key design cues that included the domed tilt-front hood, tapered backlight with louvers, and the slanted rear fascia with three horizontal brake lights per side. Motion's Le Man's-style fuel cap was moved off-center and to the left of the tapered rear, and the headlights were relocated to the grille. Rosen called it the Maco Shark to avoid issues with GM's legal department.

| Base MSRP | $17,039.75 |
|---|---|
| Model Availability | Coupe |
| Engines | 350, 427, 454 |
| Features | Custom built to order, blueprinted engine, custom body and interior |
| Production Numbers | 6 |

Motion Performance completed its first Maco in 1971, and the company began marketing and building customer cars in 1972. Although Motion Macos were designed to be driven, more than one was built to be a show car. One example was sold to Anthony Dedentro of New York, whose Maco was built on a 1970 Corvette with a 350-ci V-8 engine and factory air-conditioning. The car featured a special diamond-tufted interior and other custom touches, including bubble-style taillights, and cost $17,039.75, making it one of the most expensive Maco Sharks built and sold by Motion Performance.

*Building the Maco Sharks was labor intensive and expensive. While the model thrived with mail-order body kits available, Motion built very few Maco Sharks in-house. The Maco Sharks that were built by Motion can be identified by their standard collection of Phase III parts. (Photo Courtesy Martyn L. Schorr)*

## MOTION MANTA RAYS

Chevrolet redesigned the Mako Shark II concept in 1969 and reintroduced it as the Manta Ray. Design changes included a longer and more horizontal rear, a buttress-style rear window treatment, and a new front spoiler. Under the hood was an all-aluminum ZL1 racing engine.

As Motion was ending the Phase III GT program, Rosen was influenced once again by the Corvette concept. By combining the Maco Shark and GT styles, Rosen created his own version of the Manta Ray, which integrated Chevrolet's new federally mandated polyurethane bumpers into the design. The Manta Ray received the GT's front faired-in headlights and kept its standard hood instead of the tilt-up Maco hood. The rear was all Maco with the boat-tail backlight with louvers and a large upswept spoiler. Orange paint, side pipes, and turbo-finned wheels completed the Manta Ray design. Under the hood, Rosen upgraded the 1973's 454/275 LS4, beefing it up to the 425-hp specs of the LS6 454-ci V-8 and mating it to a 4-speed manual transmission.

History will record that only three Manta Rays were completed by Motion Performance. Unfortunately, the first was lost in an accident shortly after it was completed. The second Manta Ray was also equipped with a 454 V-8 and 4-speed manual. That car appears to be lost to history, as its whereabouts are unknown to this day. That leaves the final Manta Ray. Red with black trim, the 1973 was originally equipped with a 350 V-8 and mated to an automatic. The car went through a succession of owners, one who added nitrous and drag raced it routinely. It eventually found its way to Missouri, where it was bought by the owner of a body shop, Rayburn Pennington. Believing it was some sort of California custom car, Pennington eventually learned of Motion Performance and met Joel Rosen at Bloomington Gold. Rosen confirmed it as Manta Ray number 3. The car was fully restored back to original Motion specs, and it sold at auction in July 2016 for $100,000.

| | |
|---|---|
| Base MSRP | N/A |
| Model Availability | Coupe |
| Engines | 350, 454 |
| Features | Custom built to order, blueprinted engine, custom body and interior |
| Production Numbers | 3 |

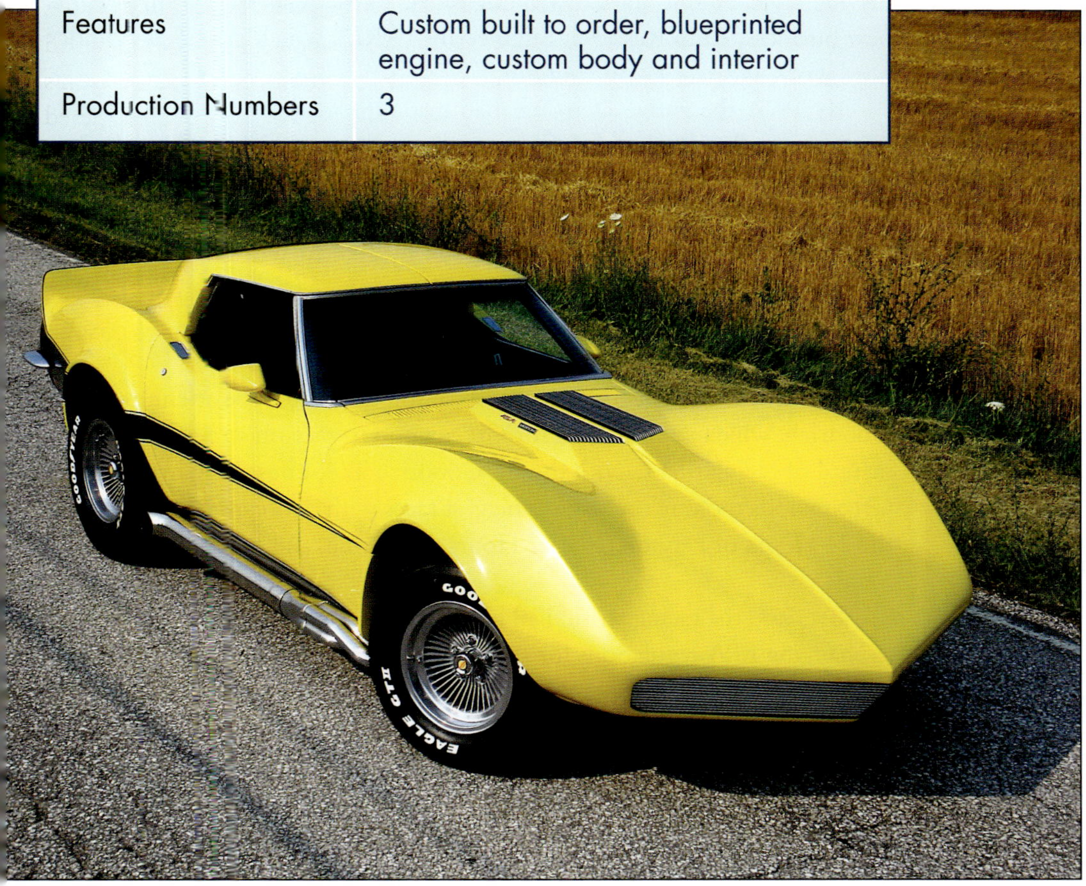

*The 500-hp Motion Moray Eel was a one-off Corvette that featured the front of the Maco Shark (with some changes to the hood) while the rear of the car was outfitted with the Phase III GT design. (Photo Courtesy Martyn L. Schorr)*

## MOTION CAN-AM SPYDER

In the mid-1970s Rosen was looking to build a new kind of car and wanted to build it using the current C3 Stingray body. However, it also had to be a fast car with the kind of performance synonymous with Motion.

In the early 1970s, Zora Arkus-Duntov and Corvette engineer Gib Hufstader assisted in the design of John Greenwood's wide-body C3 Corvette race cars that were campaigned in International Motor Sports Association (IMSA) races. Greenwood's extreme wide-body race cars had the wild looks that intrigued Rosen; the inspiration for the Motion Can-Am Spyder was born.

Rosen debuted the first Can-Am Spyder at the 1977 New York Auto Show. The car sat on 60-series tires on 10-inch wheels that were tucked under the exaggerated rear fenders that grew out of the doors. A functional hatchback was included, and Rosen gave the car six taillights tunneled into the rear while the front pop-up headlights were changed to fixed lights covered with plexiglass. A departure from the original big-block prototype, the production Spyders were all turbocharged small-blocks. Pricing for the Spyders started at $10,000 and three were officially produced.

### *The End of an Era*

Rosen continued designing and building street cars into the late 1980s with the latest models Chevrolet

| | |
|---|---|
| Base MSRP | $10,000 |
| Model Availability | Coupe |
| Engines | 350 |
| Features | Turbocharged small-block, custom exterior |
| Production Numbers | 3 |

***The prototype Can-Am Spyder Corvette was red with white accents and, like all Motion builds, it was built for show and go! Powered by a 466-ci big-block, the silhouette racer design was a show winner and appeared on multiple magazine covers. (Photo Courtesy Martyn L. Schorr)***

***The last Baldwin-Motion car produced was a medium blue 1974 L88 Corvette. After a succession of owners, Rosen was able to buy the car back and restore it. It's currently owned by noted Baldwin-Motion collector Dan McMichael. (Photo Courtesy Martyn L. Schorr)***

offered, including a line of Phase III Camaros and the SS Monte Carlo Aerocoupes. Rosen eventually retired from car building, and he and Judith moved to Florida. Today he runs a successful model building company called MotionModels.com. He lent his name to a new line of 1969 Camaro Supercoupes built with modern high-performance engines in 2005, and he continues to play a part in Baldwin-Motion history by offering to document and authenticate any Motion-branded car.

## Greenwood

One of the great Corvette success stories is that of John Greenwood and the racing legacy that he and his brother Burt left behind on the Corvette world. The son of a GM executive (his dad worked at the tech center), Greenwood was another teen who spent his youth in the 1960s building engines and racing big-block Chevys on Detroit's Woodward Avenue. After progressing through driver's school in 1968, the engineer in him realized that he could set up the suspension and car's geometry to better suit his driving style, and he started winning races. Those wins would support his new business, Auto Research Engineering (ARE), which provided cylinder head work and race engine building.

By 1970, the native Detroiter had made his mark on the racing scene. With his brother Burt and Art Jerome (former crew chief for Tony DeLorenzo), Greenwood dominated the previous year's championships, driving the Owens Corning Corvettes to win the SCCA A-Production Championship with a star-spangled livery designed by Randy Wittine, a designer at Chevrolet. He returned in 1971 and did it again.

### *Greenwood's Star-Spangled Corvettes*

Greenwood's back-to-back championships attracted the attention of BF Goodrich, which struck a deal for Greenwood to race on street-legal radials instead of racing slicks. With the BF Goodrich T/A Lifesaver Corvettes, the Greenwoods took on the world's biggest races with two-car teams entered in the 24 Hours of Daytona, the 12 Hours of Sebring, and the 24 Hours of Le Mans.

By 1974, the racing world had been impacted by the oil embargo as well as changing EPA regulations for street cars. By contrast, the racing sanctioning bodies were allowing more modification to the Corvettes to keep them racing. The GT rules were rather liberal, and teams had wide latitude in the construction of their cars. Pitching in to help was Zora Arkus-Duntov and Corvette designers Jerry Palmer and Randy Wittine, who assisted with the new design. Duntov suggested angling the top surface of the wheel flares to create additional downforce. Burt Greenwood also saw an opening in the rules that would allow wheelwell flares that would be open in the back to vent high pressure air. The Greenwoods introduced their 1974 IMSA race car, an exaggerated wide-body C3 Corvette with serious aerodynamics, at the

***John Greenwood found much success racing the C3 Corvettes, and for the length of his career he drove nothing but Corvettes. Ever. His cars were famously decked out in a red, white, and blue racing theme with stars and stripes. (Photo Courtesy Burt Greenwood)***

***Corvette chief engineer Zora Arkus-Duntov was a big fan of Greenwood, who was as good a mechanic as he was a race car driver. Greenwood used both the L88 and ZL1 racing engines in his race cars as well as offering turbocharged V-8s in his street cars. (Photo Courtesy Burt Greenwood)***

Detroit Auto Show. When you think of the big aerodynamic C3 Corvette race cars from the 1970s, it's the Greenwoods that set the standard.

### *Greenwood Custom Cars Are Born*

Rick Mancuso, a fellow racer and the owner of a Chicago-area car dealership, was instrumental in leading the Greenwoods to produce street versions of the Greenwood race cars. As the Greenwood brothers saw it, offering custom-built Corvettes for the street would help offset the costs of their own racing program. The first series of cars were mostly stylistic, with Greenwood's aerodynamics as the major upgrades. The later series

***Duntov was always happy to help fellow racers and sent Greenwood new heavy-duty parts to try out in exchange for feedback. In case of failure, they were sent back to Chevy engineers for analysis. (Photo Courtesy Burt Greenwood)***

*John Greenwood and his brother were designers and builders of a series of Corvettes bearing their name. The Greenwoods found that they could apply their racing knowledge to street cars and sell them. The proceeds went to supporting their racing efforts throughout the 1970s. (Photo Courtesy the Lingenfelter Collection)*

saw the Greenwoods offering a number of high-performance options as more racing technology found its way to the street cars. From 1975 to 1981, the Greenwood brothers built a total of 43 custom Corvettes.

## THE SEBRING GT

The first series of the Greenwood-produced Corvettes were built between 1975 and 1977 and used donor bodies from those years. The Sebring GT street Corvettes were reminiscent of the Sebring 75 Corvette racers with wide-body doors and rear ends featuring molded spoilers. A vent was integrated into the front fender, but its function was mostly cosmetic. One of the identifying trademarks was the hand-painted "John Greenwood GT" signature across the rear spoiler.

Customers were able to upgrade the standard Corvette's suspension with upgraded shocks, sway bars, and stiffer springs that greatly contributed to improved cornering. The wide-body rear fenders helped cover the 10-inch American Racing Vector wheels with BFGoodrich Radial T/A tires. The 10-spoke wheels were accented with Greenwood GT badged center caps while another Greenwood logo was situated on the B-pillars. The Sebring GT Corvettes were numbered and fitted with a plaque designating the car's serial number.

The GT models were designed in Greenwood's Troy, Michigan, shop in late 1974 and early 1975. The initial parts were made by Diversified Glass Productions and were installed and painted at the Greenwood facility. An

| | |
|---|---|
| Base MSRP | $16,000 to upgrade or $29,000 with new car |
| Model Availability | Coupe, Convertible |
| Engines | 350 |
| Features | Custom exterior, performance suspension, wheels, badging, interior plaque |
| Production Numbers | 32 |

*The Sebring GT was the first Corvette to be customized based on Greenwood's racing experience. The wide-body and the exterior rear vents became signature design cues of the Greenwood Corvettes. (Photo Courtesy Burt Greenwood)*

estimated 32 Sebring GT Corvettes were built at a cost of approximately $16,000, or twice that of the standard production Corvettes. Rick Mancuso, a Chicago auto dealer and racer from Skokie, Illinois, commissioned 15 of the Sebring GT Corvettes to be sold through his dealership.

## THE SPORTWAGON

John Greenwood didn't invent the station wagon Corvette, but many say his design was the most aesthetic and functional of those that came out of the 1970s. Copying a style pioneered from another Detroit customizer named Chuck Miller, the Sportwagon featured a tapered rear roof with Plexiglas side windows and a tempered-glass rear hatch with gas struts. Above the rear hatch was an aerodynamic airfoil that assisted in keeping the rear glass clear. The original Sportwagon built by Greenwood was done with his ex-girlfriend's 1975 Corvette, and to give the cargo area a flat floor, the spare tire was removed and a new fuel cell was dropped in its place. A skinny tire in the cargo area served as the spare. However, most Sportwagons continued to use the stock fuel cell.

From the original Sportwagon, molds were made (unfortunately, the quantities are unknown today) by Diversified Glass and later Ed Brown and his son, who worked with Greenwood in Michigan and then in Florida after the Greenwoods moved to Altamonte Springs. The Greenwoods had briefly worked with American Custom Industries (ACI), which manufactured parts at its Toledo, Ohio, plant, but the relationship soured quickly and the Greenwood brothers ended the relationship with ACI and Bob Schuller under less-than-cordial terms.

| | |
|---|---|
| Base MSRP | Not offered for public sale |
| Model Availability | Coupe |
| Engines | L48, L82 |
| Features | Custom wagon conversion |
| Production Numbers | 1 |

*The 1973 12 Hours of Sebring was nearly canceled after the track lost its FIA accreditation. IMSA stepped in, and Greenwood helped finance the track to keep the gates open. His Corvette liveries at Sebring in 1975 and 1976 reflected his commitment to keeping Sebring going. (Photo Courtesy the Revs Institute, The Karl Ludvigsen Photograph Collection)*

| | |
|---|---|
| Base MSRP | N/A |
| Model Availability | Coupe |
| Engines | L48 Turbo |
| Features | Custom exterior, turbocharged V-8, performance suspensions, wheels, badging, interior plaque |
| Production Numbers | 3 |

*Greenwood began turbocharging Corvettes with the addition of the Turbo GT models in 1977. Three 1978 Turbo GTs were completed. (Photo Courtesy Burt Greenwood)*

***Greenwood's Turbo GT used the base L48 engine for its lower compression, and he fabricated a crude water-injection system out of the windshield wiper fluid reservoir. The Air Research Turbo featured a blow-through design that required a pressurized Holley carburetor sealed under a cover. (Photo Courtesy Burt Greenwood)***

## THE TURBO GT

The Turbo GT Corvettes from Greenwood grew out of the Sebring GT project with the creation of a fastback coupe concept with aggressive aerodynamics. The prototype was built from a 1976 Corvette, and its wide-body characteristics appeared more integrated into the Corvette's body than the Sebring GT's. The car was mocked up as a turbo and sent out to the SEMA show, where it was shown to rave reviews, and advance orders were received. However, production was delayed because fulfilling the orders for the Sebring GT was the greatest priority.

Production for the Turbo GT cars began in 1977 and three were built from donor 1978 Corvette models. With Chevrolet's new fastback design, the rear design process was made easier. The rear wing was made wider to fit flush with the wide-body fenders, and its upturned trailing edge better managed the airflow over the rear of the car. On the front fenders, the quarter panel featured a vent with five vertical gills. The hood featured one NACA duct on the right side for additional cooling of the engine compartment.

The engine chosen for the project was Chevrolet's base L48 engine, and it was used for its lower compression levels (8.5:1) over the L82 due to high boost pressures causing detonation issues. A water-injection system using the windshield washer reservoir created a primitive intercooler system. The Air Research Turbo was customized from a blow-through design with the turbo blowing directly into the top of the pressurized Holley 650-cfm carburetor, which was sealed with a cast aluminum cover.

Like all Greenwood cars, the suspension was upgraded to Greenwood's specifications and included Koni coil-over shocks and thick anti-sway bars, and the rear suspension was Bob Riley's "Unequal Length A-Arm" used by the 1977 tube chassis race car with upper and lower A-arms that helped to virtually eliminate squatting and diving under heavy acceleration and hard braking.

The three Turbo GT Corvettes were identified by their center console badge featuring the year and build sequence for each of the cars.

## THE DAYTONA TURBO

The most radical of Greenwood's creations was a result of IMSA's vague rules regarding the size and shape of the fenders and spoilers. Greenwood exploited this to create an aerodynamic shark where every inch of the body was designed for either engine/brake cooling, reducing drag, or creating

| Base MSRP | $37,000 |
|---|---|
| Model Availability | Coupe |
| Engines | L48 Turbo |
| Features | Radical custom body, turbocharged engine, wheels, badging, interior plaque |
| Production Numbers | 5 |

***The first Daytona Turbo was a prototype built on a 1980 Corvette for a team that ran the car with a ZL1 aluminum racing engine. The response resulted in the production of four other Daytonas. Sadly, the whereabouts of that Daytona prototype is unknown to this day. (Photo Courtesy Keith Cornett)***

downforce. The Greenwood Daytona Turbo's most notable design feature was the elongated rear with the large molded spoiler. The fenders were pushed out farther from the body, and the C3's Coke-bottle design was effectively straightened via a large side rocker panel connecting the front to the rear. The front quarter panels were vented on top as was the hood, which contained two air intake ducts toward the front. Vents located near the base of the windshield took advantage of the high-air-pressure area to help dissipate heat from the engine compartment.

Officially, five Daytona Turbos were constructed by Greenwood. The prototype was built in 1980; four others were built in 1981. Depending on the options, the Daytona was priced anywhere from $37,000 to $53,000! Eckler's Industries also began producing body kits and assembled a few complete cars, but the exact count is unknown. The Daytona Turbos were all upgraded with Bilstein gas shocks, heavier sway bars, and a tweaked steering box. Three-piece BBS wheels sized 8 inches in front and 10 inches in the rear were included along with the race-proven Kevlar brake-cooling fans. Three of the Daytonas came with the standard rear suspension, and two were upgraded to Greenwood's rear suspension with coil-overs. Four of the five were specially modified automatic transmissions; however, the first production Daytona was equipped with a 4-speed transmission.

One change from the GT Turbos was that the system was switched to a Turbo International draw-through system, so the previous blow-through system's pressured cap on the carburetor was replaced with an aftermarket air cleaner.

Identification of the Daytona is possible due to the dedicated following the cars have. However, the Daytonas were first constructed without one of Greenwood's plaques ready from the beginning. Three of the Daytona's were sold through Rick Mancuso's Lake Forest Sports Cars dealership, and Mancuso added his own plaques and numbered them (out of sequence) as L.F.S.C. number 001 to number 003. The other two Greenwoods sold directly and received their own plaques.

## THE GTO

The GTO was the final turnkey C3 Corvette offered by Greenwood. The GTO was similar to the Daytona, but it was more refined due to design changes based on updated IMSA rules as well as experience gained from racing the Daytona in IMSA competition. IMSA's rulebook on the spoiler design was no longer vague, and the Daytona's long tail was now outlawed. Greenwood was forced to update the spoiler design, making it much closer to that found on the production car. The spoiler was larger, but its design more closely resembled the stock spoiler on the 1982 Corvettes. The GTO required a high-profile hood to fit the big-block V-8 with Greenwood's crossram fuel-injection system. The hood's design was reminiscent of the 1965–1966 big-block hoods and featured working vents on each side of the power bulge to draw out hot air.

Just two Greenwood GTOs were constructed. The first was built on a 1981 Corvette and is black with a saddle interior. The second GTO was black with a red interior and holds the distinction of being one of only two Greenwood turbocharged cars with a 4-speed manual transmission. The other is the National Corvette Museum's 1981 number 001 Daytona Turbo. It's possible that more than two Greenwood GTOs exist, but records were lost when its Florida warehouse flooded after a hurricane.

### *Greenwood C4 Body Kits*

With the introduction of the 1984 Corvette, the car that John and Burt Greenwood had come to know so well had been completely redesigned. One of the first packages they offered for the C4 was the ability to turn the 1984 Corvette into a fully functional convertible. Greenwood was also looking at different powerplants for the C4 and already decided that there was no replacement for displacement. Greenwood planned packages around a

| Base MSRP | N/A |
|---|---|
| Model Availability | Coupe |
| Engines | L82 Turbo |
| Features | Custom body, performance suspension, wheels, badging, interior plaque |
| Production Numbers | 2 |

***Greenwood's GTO was raced in IMSA by T&R Racing as the number-13 Corvette. As IMSA changed the rules regarding the spoiler size, T&R Racing changed from the Daytona to the more aerodynamic GTO body and broke several track records with speeds in excess of 200 mph. (Photo Courtesy Burt Greenwood)***

***Greenwood found the C4 Corvette generation difficult to work with and the quality not up to his standards. Greenwood would mostly be known for the various aerodynamic kits offered directly and through resellers, such as Eckler's Industries. (Photo Courtesy Burt Greenwood)***

350 supercharged engine, a 383 stoker, or the big 572-hp big-block. However, as quality conscious as John and Burt were, re-engineering the C4 was proving to come at too high a cost; from there they moved to providing C4 Corvettes with better aerodynamics with an add-on Greenwood ground effects kit.

Greenwood's aerodynamics kits proved very popular on C4 Corvettes, and pretty soon Greenwood would make a version for the C5 Corvette. The kits included a front spoiler, lower side skirts, and a lower rear fascia. A small rear wing spoiler was also part of the various kits. Thirty years after their introduction, Greenwood's C4 aero kits are still being manufactured and sold through dealers across the country.

John Greenwood passed away on July 7, 2015, at age 71 after a battle with cancer. His legacy and commitment to Corvette will live on through the cars built by him and his brother Burt. The Greenwood legacy and the brothers' lifetime commitment to building and racing Corvettes was cemented when both John and Burt Greenwood were inducted into the National Corvette Museum's Corvette Hall of Fame in 2018.

## Callaway Cars

Following the introduction of the C4 Corvette in 1984 and the L98 engine in 1985, Chevrolet continued to look at new ways to increase the performance of its engines. Turbocharging was one of the solutions, although at the time most turbochargers were found on the smaller imported engines. Chevy engineers had been testing a variety of single and twin-turbocharged engines since the 1970s, and even a V-6 turbo was reviewed and then discarded as being wrong for Corvette's image. But then a 1985 Callaway turbocharged Alfa Romeo GTV6 showed up in Corvette Engineering's war room, a place where competitor cars were benchmarked against the Corvette. It turned out that the Callaway version of the 2.5L turbocharged V-6 was faster than the V-8-powered 1985 Corvette and was reliable to boot. Soon after, Corvette chief engineer Dave McLellan placed a called to Reeves Callaway about turbocharging the Corvette.

***Reeves Callaway of Callaway Cars has been building his own vision of high-performance and exotic sports cars using the Corvette as his canvas for more than 30 years. (Photo Courtesy the Lingenfelter Collection)***

McLellan had already started on the LT5 engine project. The naturally aspirated four-valve dual overhead cam engine was then being developed by Lotus Engineering, a firm owned by General Motors at the time. However, developing new engines from the ground up takes time, and while the project would eventually yield the 375-hp LT5 for the Corvette ZR-1, it wouldn't hit the streets until 1989 as a 1990 model. During the development phase of the LT5, McLellan's team met with Reeves Callaway at his shop in Old Lyme, Connecticut.

### *Enter Reeves Callaway*

Reeves Callaway had ambitions as a race-car driver and was modestly successful, winning the Formula Vee Series before ending up as an instructor at the Bob Bondurant School. BMW had used Bondurant's School for its dealers to test drive the BMW 320i Coupe. When the program ended, Callaway borrowed one of the used BMWs and took it back home to Connecticut, where he set about engineering an increase in horsepower with a fabricated turbo unit.

Thanks to an article by *Car and Driver* magazine's Don Sherman, the word on Callaway's aftermarket turbos for BMW got out, and soon Reeves and a group of friends were building and selling the units as fast as they could. That work led to Alfa Romeo contracting Callaway to provide the Twin Turbo GTV6. While enthusiasts loved the additional horsepower the Twin Turbo GTV6 provided, Alfa Romeo's corporate leaders pulled out of the US market in 1986, ending the program before it ever got going.

To say that the call from Chevrolet came at an opportune time would be an understatement for both parties. The LT5 project was underway, but it still wasn't known whether it would turn out as an engineering exercise or reach production. For Callaway, the loss of the Alfa Romeo project had dashed his hopes of working with an automotive manufacturer for selling his modified cars.

### RPO B2K Is Born

In the fall of 1985, Chevrolet shipped one of its prototype twin-turbo V-8s to Callaway, who went to work on it with the ultimate goal of producing an engine that would offer 400 hp, 0–60 mph in 5 seconds, and a top speed of 170 mph. The main concerns were the packaging of the twin turbos, intercoolers, and associated plumbing of a turbocharged engine as well as the reliability that a corporation like General Motors would require. Reeves and his engineers made it all work, producing an engine that in 1987, its initial year of production, developed 345 hp and 465 ft-lbs of torque. Chevrolet officially assigned RPO B2K to the twin-turbo Corvette.

Callaway became the first vendor in GM's history to be offered its own RPO despite the fact that RPO B2K wasn't a factory-installed option. Dealers and their customers ordered the Corvette and the twin-turbo option at participating Chevrolet dealers. The stock-engine Corvettes were assembled at the Bowling Green assembly plant and the completed Corvettes were drop-shipped to Callaway's facility in Connecticut, where they were modified with the twin-turbo option. Following its transformation, the Corvette was then shipped back to the participating dealer for customer delivery.

## 1987–1991 C4 CALLAWAY B2K

The 1987–1991 Callaway B2K Corvettes were powered by a 5.7L TPI V-8 with twin turbochargers and dual intercoolers. Air to the turbos was fed through two NACA ducts integrated into the Corvette's hood on 1987 models. The 1988–1990 B2K-equipped Corvettes had flat hoods with intercooling ducts underneath, and 1991 B2K Corvettes had a unique set of inlets on top of the factory hood. The two turbochargers sat low in the engine and were packaged with one on each side of the oil pan. Air was fed through a special airbox and then routed through the center frame rail crossmember. The turbochargers compressed the air, feeding the twin intercoolers prior to being fed into the intake manifold. All of the Callaway twin turbos featured an auxiliary fuel-injection system called the micro-fueler assembly, which contained two additional Bosch fuel injectors at the front of the intake that fed additional fuel into the system while under boost. In 1988 and 1989, the twin-turbo option would add another 142 hp over the stock L98's 240 hp to get 382 hp and 565 ft-lbs of torque, climbing to 390 hp in 1990, and in its final year of 1991, 403 hp and 575 ft-lbs of torque.

All Callaway B2Ks had their own badging and branding throughout the car that included Callaway-designed emblems and other special touches. The integrated boost gauge on the dash was added as well as decals for fuel requirements.

The Callaways could be ordered in both coupe and convertible configurations under RPO B2K, with SEO Z5G in 1988–1991 adding specific equipment, including J55 heavy-duty brakes, long air dam, power-steering cooler, and sport mufflers. Many performance options, such as the FX3 suspension, were also available. In fact, most regular Corvette options were available to Callaway buyers.

Over the five years of production, the Callaway B2K options continued to evolve. In 1987, optional 16-inch cast Dymag magnesium wheels were

| Base MSRP | $19,995 to $33,000 (plus C4 Donor) |
|---|---|
| Model Availability | Coupe, Convertible |
| Engines | L98 Twin-Turbo |
| Features | Custom twin-turbo, badging, wheels, embroidery |
| Production Numbers | 510 |

***Chevrolet initially approved the RPO B2K and believed it would result in just 25 Corvettes going through the Callaway transformation. In the end, a total of 510 were produced. (Photo Courtesy Chris Chessnoe)***

*One of the most famous Callaways ever produced is the 1988 Sledgehammer. The car achieved a top speed of 254.76 mph in October 1988 at the 7.5-mile oval track at the Transportation Research Center (TRC) in Ohio. More remarkable is the fact that the car was driven from Connecticut to Ohio and then back again following the test. (Photo Courtesy Chris Chessnoe)*

offered by Callaway. Later the wheels were increased to a 17-inch diameter, and in 1988 they became standard equipment, the same year the RPO price increased to $25,895. Also in 1988, buyers could select the 4-speed automatic transmission; that option would be available through 1989.

### *The Quest for Speed*

As Callaway's engineers continued to improve performance, eventually hitting the original target of 400-plus hp, Reeves was also attacking top speed records in magazine shoot-out tests in specially modified Callaway Corvettes. At the Gathering of Eagles, hosted by *Car and Driver* magazine, Callaway achieved speeds of 233.1 mph in the 1987 Callaway Top Gun Corvette and was crowned winner of the event. Callaway planned on returning the next year with what would be known as the Callaway Sledgehammer. To achieve those higher speeds, Reeves turned to designer Paul Deutschman to create a new aerodynamic rebodied Callaway C4 that would be stable up to 250 mph. The resulting design was called the aerobody, and it was offered as an option midway through 1989. The aerobody Callaway Corvettes are very distinguishable for their low aerodynamic profile and additional openings in the front fascia for increasing airflow.

The final hurrah for the Callaway B2K Corvette program was Callaway's Speedster model, which was introduced at the 1991 L.A. Auto Show. With a further modified L-98 equipped with Callaway's two turbochargers, it was capable of 450 hp and 600 ft-lbs of torque. Only 10 were produced at a price of $250,000.

The B2K option was a risky move for Chevrolet. In 1987, when it was first offered, the option cost $19,995 plus the $27,999 MSRP for the car, making the total price nearly $48,000. And it only went up from there, selling for $28,895 for the next three years (1988–1990) and by its final year of production in 1991, $33,000.

Chevrolet estimated that it could sell 25 twin-turbo Corvettes in a year, based on the high price. But those estimates proved to be way off. Callaway produced 188 B2K Corvettes in their inaugural year and a total of 510 cars over the five years the B2K option was offered. The collaboration with Callaway proved to Chevrolet that its customers were willing to pay for performance and were more than willing to shell out $50,000 for the prestige of owning the highest performing Corvettes offered. The success of the Callaway twin-turbo Corvette paved the way for the Corvette ZR-1.

## 1992–1996 CALLAWAY SUPERNATURAL CORVETTE

In 1992, Chevrolet introduced the second-generation small-block V-8 called the LT1. Considering that it required a complete reworking of the B2K option, Callaway decided to go a different direction by generating additional power through increased displacement, natural aspiration, and finesse. The Callaway SuperNatural could be ordered as an LT1 car or LT5 car. Callaway designated the LT1 as the CL1 while the LT5 was the CR1. Buyers had a host of options to choose from, including the aerobody, special exterior colors, full-leather interiors, wheels, brakes, and exhaust packages.

As Callaway's knowledge of working with the new engines grew, so did the performance characteristics of its engines. Introduced in 1992 as a SuperNatural 400, designating 400 hp, the second-generation small-block V-8 evolved each year with the 425-, 435-, 440-, and finally the 450-hp models for LT1-based cars and the 475- or 490-hp models offered for the LT5 models.

A total of 17 ZR-1 SuperNatural CR1s were built between 1992 and 1995, making these cars very rare. Even rarer were the three LT-5s that were turbocharged. Two Super Speedsters and one coupe were built, each with their own special options.

| Base MSRP | $33,000 (ZR-1) |
|---|---|
| Model Availability | Coupe, Convertible, ZR-1 |
| Engines | LT1, LT4, LT5 |
| Features | Custom engine, Callaway aerobody, custom suspension, wheels, badging |
| Production Numbers | 17 |

| Base MSRP | $200,000 |
|---|---|
| Model Availability | Coupe |
| Engines | LS1 |
| Features | Custom wide body and interior, Le Mans-spec engine, badging |
| Production Numbers | 25 |

**_Callaway's C12 project was the platform that Callaway used when he took the cars racing at Le Mans in 2001 and 2002. The cars were 2 meters wide to take advantage of the regulations. Callaway would take pole position for the 2001 24 Hours of Le Mans in their C12 race car. (Photo Courtesy of the Lingenfelter Collection)_**

| Base MSRP | $225,000 (coupe), $235,000 (convertible), $350,000 (speedster) |
|---|---|
| Model Availability | Coupe, Convertible, Speedster |
| Engines | LS3 |
| Features | Supercharged V-8, custom exterior and interior, suspension, brakes, badging, interior plaque |
| Production Numbers | 15 (11 Coupe, 3 Cabrio, 1 Speedster) |

**_Callaway's Speedster designs shocked and amazed the automotive world. On the company's 20th anniversary on August 18, 2007, the 700-hp Callaway C16 made its debut at the Pebble Beach Concours d'Elegance. (Photo Courtesy the Lingenfelter Collection)_**

## 1997–2001 CALLAWAY C12

Originally designed to race at Le Mans (and win the GT2 class), the C12 built upon the 1997–2004 Corvette and was a combined effort between Callaway Cars in the United States and Callaway's Germany division, Callaway Competition. Many believed the C12 referred to cylinders, but it actually referred to Callaway's sequential project order with this being the 12th project. The C12s were equipped with a coil-over suspension featuring its own unique control arm forgings and tuned, adjustable dampers. A new body designed by Paul Deutschman was approximately 2 meters wide to take advantage of Le Mans dimensional regulations. The C12 road cars were powered by the SuperNatural engine package, which was now being offered on the next-generation small-block V-8 from Chevy dubbed the LS-Series.

Only 25 Callaway C12 road cars were built. When new, they retailed for approximately $200,000 and are sought by collectors worldwide.

Callaway's C12.R race car took pole position at Le Mans in 2001, beating Porsche, Ferrari, and other world-class marques in the GT2 class.

## 2005–2013 CALLAWAY C16

Callaway announced the next model in its continued evolution with the Chevrolet Corvette. With the 6.0L LS2 V-8 now powering the Corvette, Callaway shifted focus once again and turned to supercharging for increasing performance. With a roots-type Eaton/Magnuson supercharger onboard, the modified Callaway powerplant boasted 616 hp and 582 ft-lbs of torque. Reeves also went to work on the suspension with the lessons learned from his GT2 race cars, using the Eibach coil-overs, forged aluminum control arms, and lateral composite leaf springs. Once again, Dymag-forged magnesium wheels with carbon fiber rims in 19/20-inch configurations were sourced and wrapped with Yokohama AdvanSport 285/30ZR19 (front) and 325/25ZR20 (rear) tires.

The coupe was introduced first with an announcement on November 30, 2006, and was followed soon by the C16 convertible that made its debut at the New York International Auto Show in April 2007. Paul Deutschman, who continued the look of Callaway's evolution by redesigning all the body panels from the Corvette, drew both.

*Callaway's supercharge-enhanced Corvette Z06 now had 757 hp and 777 ft-lbs torque. The latest Callaway ran 0–60 in 2.8 seconds and the quarter mile in 10.5 seconds at a trap speed of 131 miles per hour. (Photo Courtesy Chris Chessnoe)*

The 616-hp Callaway was capable of 0–60 in 3.5 seconds and the quarter mile in 11.2 seconds. The convertible was estimated to have a top cruising speed of more than 200 mph. More important, for more mundane drives around town, the Callaway performed equally well with a fuel rating of 18 city/28 highway. The Callaway C16 was emission compliant worldwide and was backed with a 5-year/100,000-mile powertrain warranty.

Callaway C16s were all built to order. The C16 cockpits were retooled in German leather and Alacantara. Callaway fixed-shell racing seats were fitted, and owners could choose between a series of harness styles while retaining power adjustability and heating elements. Interior enhancements placed the Callaway badge on the door sills, the passenger dash, and the steering wheel.

Celebrating its 20th anniversary and 30th as a company, Callaway announced the C16 Speedster as the flagship model, joining the C16 Coupe and C16 Cabrio. This supercharged and intercooled 700-hp Callaway C16 Speedster debuted at the Pebble Beach Concours d'Elegance on August 18, 2007.

## 2005–2013 CALLAWAY C17

As the Corvette continued its maturation into the sixth-generation models, so did Callaway's business model. Callaway Corvettes were sold through select Chevrolet dealerships, and the C6 Corvettes were converted by Callaway's expert crafters who continued to push the boundaries of performance. By supercharging, Callaway could extract more power with improved durability, easier maintenance, emission compliancy, and instant power. Callaway's supercharged engines were launched with the LS2 6.0L, producing 560 hp and then were increased to 580 hp with the introduction of the LS3 in 2008. For the LS3, Callaway also offered an optional Magnuson TVS2300 supercharger that resulted in 606 hp. The Z06-based 7L Callaway Supercharged Corvette was capable of 652 hp.

## CALLAWAY SC606

Branded as the SC606 (with "SC" standing for supercharged), Callaway made 606 hp with an Eaton TVS2300 roots-type supercharger installed on top of the LS3. Fed 7.0 psi of boosted air, the 606-hp powerplant made 553 ft-lbs of torque. The Callaway SC606s were distinguished by the carbon fiber hood bulge along with Callaway badging and forged nine-spoke alloy wheels from OZ. While most opted for just the engine package, perhaps along with the Double-D stainless-steel exhaust system, Callaway offered a number of optional packages designed to make the most of your experience, including suspension, brakes, and wheels.

Callaway buyers had an ample menu of upgrades to select from:

- Adjustable Eiback coil-overs and new front and rear anti-roll bars: $5,760
- StopTech brake package added bigger rotors and calipers: $9,820
- Wheels and tires package featured OZ wheels with Michelin PS2s: $4,950

| Base MSRP | $21,395 plus C6 Corvette |
|---|---|
| Model Availability | Coupe, Convertible, Grand Sport |
| Engines | LS3 |
| Features | Supercharged engine, custom badging, interior plaque |
| Production Numbers | Undisclosed |

*Callaway's SC606 featured a supercharger on top of the C6 Corvette's LS3, which improved horsepower from 430 to 606 in 2010. This Callaway SC606 Grand Sport has crisscrossed the United States as Callaway representatives drive to various Callaway dealers and Corvette events. The Grand Sport has racked up an impressive total of 172,000 miles without any mechanical issues. (Photo Courtesy Chris Chessnoe)*

- Interior Alcantara leather steering wheel: $3,590
- Recaro race seats: $8,970

## CALLAWAY 25TH ANNIVERSARY B2K GRAND SPORT

In early 2012, Callaway announced the building of a special run of 25 Corvette Grand Sports for the 25th anniversary of RPO B2K, the first turbocharged Corvettes offered by the factory. Although today's RPO B2K has traded in the turbos for a supercharger, the end result was equally impressive.

The 25 B2K Anniversary Corvettes were all built the week of April 2, 2012. The 26th unit, a pilot car that was number 00, was on display during the National Corvette Museum's Bash event later in the month.

The RPO B2K Anniversary Corvettes were all Cyber Gray Grand Sports made up of both coupes and convertibles. With the exception of two 3LT-equipped models, the Callaway B2Ks were mostly 4LT interior trim and were offered in both 6-speed and automatics. The interior featured Ebony-colored seats with a Callaway steering wheel, door sills, and floor mats. Three B2Ks were built with the 3LT equipment group, and one had an override for black headlights.

Each of the Callaway B2K Corvettes received the trademark Callaway hood along with exposed carbon fiber on the rear spoiler and splitters. The RPO B2K Corvette features an LS3 with a Callaway SC620 supercharger, capable of 620 hp. That's nearly the same power as the 638-hp Corvette ZR1!

With a Grand Sport convertible in 4LT trim level, MSRP for these Corvettes was $124,050.

| Base MSRP | $52,980 plus 2012 Corvette Grand Sport |
| --- | --- |
| Model Availability | Grand Sport |
| Engines | LS3 |
| Features | Supercharged engine, custom badging, interior plaque |
| Production Numbers | 25 |

*Callaway returned to its roots in 2012 and created a limited-edition run of Grand Sport Corvettes called the 25th Anniversary B2K Editions. It's the special edition to celebrate a special edition, and 25 Anniversary B2Ks were sold at an MSRP of $124,050. (Photo Courtesy Leonard Wiggins)*

## 2014–PRESENT CALLAWAY C20

If you've got it, flaunt it! That could be the motto for Callaway's third-generation supercharger system that was officially unveiled at the National Corvette Museum's Bash event in April 2014 on the Callaway SC627 Stingray. One year later, it was joined by the Callaway SC757 Z06. Similar to previous Callaway models, the number following the "SC" was the official horsepower rating.

Callaway's new supercharger system used an Eaton 2300-cc TVS four-lobe high helix rotor pack for its reliability and thermal efficiency. The

| Base MSRP | $17,995 (SC627), $18, 495 (SC757) (plus C7 Donor) |
| --- | --- |
| Model Availability | Coupe, Convertible, Grand Sport, Z06 |
| Engines | LT1, LT4 |
| Features | Supercharged engine, custom hood, badging, interior plaque |
| Production Numbers | Undisclosed |

*Callaway's Eaton 2300-cc TVS Supercharger system and unique triple-element intercoolers take more air than the stock unit, plus the system is inherently cooler from air passing over the top of the supercharger unit, which sticks through the hood in true shaker fashion. (Photo Courtesy Keith Cornett)*

patented design featured triple-element intercoolers that allowed much cooler air temperatures than previous designs. But the most striking feature was that the top of the supercharger protruded through the hood much like the shaker designs from the muscle-car era. This setup allowed air passing over the hood to cool the supercharger even more, allowing more heat transfer capability which leads to increased power.

Under the hood, the black supercharger was surrounded by a carbon fiber engine cover that hid two of the intercoolers mounted on each side. The engine cover was inscribed with SC627 or SC757, depending on the model (Stingray/Grand Sport or Z06). Another nice touch was a Callaway Engineering plaque with a VIN that goes to the authenticity of the vehicle.

Callaway did very little mixing up of the already comfortable cockpit of the C7 Corvettes. Instead were the kind of enhancements you would expect in a specially produced car. Along with Callaway floor mats and sill plates, the interior dash plaque read "Callaway Supercharged."

Several options were available, including the stainless-steel Double D exhaust system handcrafted by Callaway, a short-throw shifter for the manual 7-speed transmission, and a custom-fitted indoor car cover with embroidered logo. A Callaway key fob was also part of the $16,995 package.

The Z06 version, Callaway's SC757, was armed with a 32-percent-larger-displacement supercharger over the stock Chevrolet model (2300 cc versus 1740 cc), and produced 757 hp and 777 ft-lbs of torque. That power translated to 0–60 mph in 2.8 seconds and a quarter-mile time of 10.5 seconds. In 2016, a Callaway SC757 Z06 Coupe ran 202 mph at the Mojave Magnum, a 1.5-mile top-speed event.

| Base MSRP | $14,990 |
|---|---|
| Model Availability | Coupe, Convertible, Grand Sport, Z06 |
| Engines | N/A |
| Features | Rear hatch assembly, carbon fiber |
| Production Numbers | Undisclosed |

***The Callaway AeroWagen started as a concept drawing from longtime design collaborator Paul Deutschman. Once the shooting brake design was shown to the public, Callaway judged the response as favorable and put the AeroWagen hatch into production. The first AeroWagen was shown publicly in early 2017.***

## C7 CALLAWAY AEROWAGEN

Callaway Cars officially unveiled the long-awaited shooting brake version of Callaway's C7 models known as the Callaway AeroWagen. The unveiling took place during the National Corvette Museum's annual Bash event in April 2017.

The AeroWagen hatch assembly was a part-for-part replacement of the original C7 Corvette's hatch and used all the original hardware and latching mechanisms. The AeroWagen could be fitted to any of the standard-production Corvettes as well as all Callaway models. Nothing was modified, so owners can always revert back to the original hatch. The cost of the AeroWagen hatch was $14,990 and included the Callaway AeroSpoiler.

The AeroWagen component changed the profile of the Corvette, and while it did add some additional cargo room in the rear, the gains were negligible. Callaway said the AeroWagen hatch did help with aerodynamic airflow over the rear of the coupe, but again, those gains were also said to be negligible.

During the unveiling event at the NCM, Reeves Callaway said the AeroWagen represented a slightly different direction for the company from generations past. Callaway had previously offered fully rebodied Callaway Corvettes, such as the C12 and C16, but for the C7 generation, customization of the body was limited to specific projects, such as the AeroWagen.

## Lingenfelter Performance Engineering

*Car and Driver* magazine once referred to John Lingenfelter as "the most prolific purveyor of horsepower they had ever seen." John's goal was to be the fastest of all time. In turn, he would put the knowledge he learned from the track into the cars and trucks of customers who flocked to his Decatur, Indiana, shop as he helped fulfill the dreams of others who wanted to go fast as well.

Lingenfelter grew up in East Freedom, Pennsylvania, and his father was a mechanic who imparted his automotive acumen on his son at an early age. After high school, Lingenfelter attended Penn State University, where he studied mechanical engineering. Following graduation, he took a job in the engine lab with International Harvester in Fort Wayne, Indiana.

It was during this time that Lingenfelter began racing seriously, and he won his first NHRA title in 1972 racing a Super Stock 1969 Camaro. Having fully caught the racing bug, he left International Harvester in 1974 to race full-time. Over his illustrious racing career, Lingenfelter earned a total of 13 NHRA titles including 3 Super Stock titles, 9 Competition Eliminator titles, and 1 in Pro Stock Truck.

*The Lingenfelter C6 25th Anniversary Commemorative Edition offered an astounding 750 hp from its 427-ci twin turbo engine. That's 350 hp more than the brand-new C6 Corvette Z51 Coupe. (Photo Courtesy the Lingenfelter Collection)*

*When it came to building Corvettes for customers, John believed that the car should be dependable enough to be used as a daily driver. His twin-turbo packages earned much praise from customers for their power and reliability. (Photo Courtesy the Lingenfelter Collection)*

### *Horsepower with No Compromises*

Building and racing Chevy small-blocks came naturally to Lingenfelter, and soon he was building the engines for other racers as well. In 1984, Lingenfelter broke into the mail-order business by offering a 383-ci small-block under the Lingenfelter Performance Engineering name, and sales were better than anyone expected. That same year, Chevrolet offered the tuned-port injection as part of the 1985 Corvette; soon after, Lingenfelter Performance Engineering was offering engine packages ranging in sizes from the 383 to 406 and then 461. To build those larger engines, Lingenfelter redesigned the intake manifold runners and plenum from the Corvette's TPI system while maintaining drivability and legal emissions. Along the way, his knowledge of working with the Corvette's electronic fuel injection cemented his reputation as an EFI specialist.

One of the hallmarks of a Lingenfelter-enhanced Corvette was that his customized cars could be used as everyday drivers. "Horsepower with no compromises" was the mantra and his goal of going faster meant building a 200-mph car that also had air-conditioning and all the comforts you would expect.

### *The Callaway Sledgehammer*

Lingenfelter caught the attention of Reeves Callaway, who was working on the 1988 Callaway Sledgehammer. Callaway theorized that with the right engine and aerodynamics, he could rocket a Corvette to 250 mph. The kicker was that the car had to maintain its drivability and driver comforts such as air-conditioning and windshield wipers. Lingenfelter's answer was a twin-turbo 900-hp 355-ci small-block. Joining a group of Callaway engineers, Lingenfelter drove the car from Callaway's headquarters in Connecticut to Ohio, and from there he drove the silver Sledgehammer to a recorded top speed of 254.76 mph.

The experience with the Sledgehammer led Lingenfelter to build another twin-turbo small-block, this time making 1,400 hp. The engine was dropped into a 1989 Firebird Trans Am that he took to the Bonneville Salt Flats. Although his goal was 300 mph, he fell just short with a run at 298 mph. After a few more top-speed events, including the Silver State Classic (a top-speed event on open roads), Lingenfelter began racing sport compacts and, in 2002, set the record pass of 6 seconds in a 4-cylinder Cavalier.

After the C5 Corvettes arrived in 1997, Lingenfelter began offering twin-turbo packages for the new Corvette, and that's when Lingenfelter Performance Engineering really took off. The packages were very well received, and soon Lingenfelter was offering performance upgrades on not just Corvettes but across a number of Chevy cars and trucks.

### *Tragedy at Pomona*

Competing in his 6-second Ecotec Cavalier in October 2002 at the

*John's handiwork was all over one of the fastest Corvette engines ever produced. In 1988, Lingenfelter drove the Callaway Sledgehammer to 254.76 mph. The four-bolt main NASCAR-spec bowtie engine was rated at 898 hp and 772 ft-lbs of torque. (Photo Courtesy Keith Cornett)*

*The 2016 Lingenfelter Signature Edition number 001 was created to help a charity fundraiser, and the car was shown at major events across the country before a winner was selected. The LPE-enchanced Corvette Z06 came with 800 hp and 800 ft-lbs of torque. (Photo Courtesy Keith Cornett)*

| Base MSRP | $86,995 plus C6 Donor |
|---|---|
| Model Availability | Coupe, Convertible |
| Engines | Lingenfelter 427 |
| Features | Custom body, turbocharged engine, badging |
| Production Numbers | 10 |

Mazda NHRA Sport Compact World Finals at Pomona Raceway, John Lingenfelter was involved in a high-speed crash during his semifinal race against R. J. Simrock. Lingenfelter's Cavalier crossed the centerline and smashed into the opposite lane's guardwall, riding the top of the wall into the top-end sand trap. Lingenfelter was reported to be unconscious after the accident and was airlifted to Pomona Valley Hospital, where he underwent surgery in the following days. His injuries were said to be a broken neck, broken ribs, collapsed lung, and a concussion. Seemingly on the mend he succumbed to complications from subsequent surgeries, passing away unexpectedly on December 25, 2003, at the age of 58.

The staff of Lingenfelter was devastated by the news about their fallen leader, but the team united and worked as hard as they could to keep his vision alive. But after several years of Lingenfelter's absence, and with the

*Lingenfelter detailed the cockpit with the craftsmanship of interior specialist John Caravaggio, who provided his signature Connolly leather-wrapped steering wheel, shift boot, and specially created Commemorative Edition seats with embossed headrests. A plaque with John Lingenfelter's signature resided on the console. (Photo Courtesy the Lingenfelter Collection)*

*At the time of the car's release, Lingenfelter proclaimed performance stats of 0–60 mph at 3.9 seconds, along with a 0–100 mph sprint that took just 7.3 seconds. In the quarter mile, the twin turbo ran 11.6 seconds at 136 mph. (Photo Courtesy the Lingenfelter Collection)*

*The 25th Anniversary Commemorative Edition were Lingenfelter-branded 756 series wheels from HRE. The 19-inch forged three-piece aluminum wheels were fitted with Michelin Pilot Sport tires. A Lingenfelter mini tub kit allowed the rear wheels to be fitted with 345/30/ZR19 tires. (Photo Courtesy the Lingenfelter Collection)*

US economy on the verge of falling into the worst recession since the Great Depression, the company needed a new leader to carry on. Luckily, they didn't have to go outside the family tree. Lingenfelter's second cousin Ken stepped in to lead Lingenfelter Performance Engineering to new heights.

### *A New Leader for Lingenfelter Performance Engineering*

Ken Lingenfelter was the son of a GM employee whose family had moved to the Blue Oval's company town of Dearborn, Michigan, by way of Euclid, Ohio. His father had worked on the assembly line building Oldsmobiles, and Ken's first exposure to racing was behind the wheel of his first car, a 1967 Oldsmobile 442 that he raced against his classmates' Mustang GTs.

Ken Lingenfelter worked a variety of typical jobs while in high school, including as a busboy and then cook at a Howard Johnsons. He took his first real job at the age of 17, working at a real estate title company. Business was very good, so instead of attending college, Ken opened his own title insurance company in 1974 at the age of 22. It grew from two employees to more than 1,000 employees by the turn of the century. Lingenfelter's Metropolitan Title Co. was one of the largest title service companies in the country, with annual revenue of $150 million and mortgage products and services offered in 10 states.

In 2003, Ken sold Metropolitan Title Co., but he would stay on as the company's leader for another five years. It was during this time that John suffered the crash at Pomona and passed away. Four years later in 2007, Ken purchased Lingenfelter Performance Engineering and embarked on his second career in the automotive industry. Since Ken took over the company, he has helped guide Lingenfelter Performance Engineering back to its rightful place as one of the leaders in the aftermarket tuning and performance segment.

## 25TH LINGENFELTER 427 CORVETTE COMMEMORATIVE EDITION

In early 2005, Lingenfelter Performance Engineering announced it would celebrate its 25th anniversary with a run of specially produced C6 Corvettes equipped with LPE's 427-ci twin-turbo engines. The special anniversary edition for Lingenfelter would be offered on a new base C6 Corvette with 25 examples planned.

The package boasted a 750-hp 427-ci engine based on Corvette Racing's C5-R engine. Lingenfelter's own GEN-2 twin intercoolers/twin-turbo package was included. Further enhancements featured the Lingenfelter C6 Corvette exhaust system from Corsa Performance, a heavy-duty dual disk clutch assembly, and Brembo two-piece rotors and four-piston calipers with the Lingenfelter logo.

Lingenfelter also upgraded the aerodynamics of the 25th Commemorative Edition with its signature hood, front spoiler, and side skirts. The one-piece rear fascia had the Lingenfelter logo embossed above the license plate screws.

***Lingenfelter Chevrolet Corvette C6 Commemorative Edition is powered by a 427-ci intercooled twin-turbo engine. Lingenfelter combines the ultimate thrill of wide-open throttle acceleration with a Z51-based hard cornering capability and exceptional braking performance. (Photo Courtesy the Lingenfelter Collection)***

Inside the anniversary edition, the Lingenfelter featured a custom interior with Caravaggio Connolly leather seats, steering wheel, shift knob, and boot. The seats showed off an embossed Lingenfelter logo, and an interior dash plaque had the build number. A Lingenfelter certificate of authenticity and a 3-year/36,000-mile warranty were included.

To order one of the 25 Commemorative Editions, the entire package was specified, and a new donor C6 had to be ordered specifically for the conversion. The Corvettes were shipped to Lingenfelter's shop in Decatur, Illinois, where they underwent the transformation.

***The Commemorative Edition was enhanced with an aggressive-looking body kit. Finding its way onto the Corvette was the Lingenfelter hood, front spoiler, side skirts, and a unique one-piece rear fascia with "Lingenfelter" embossed in the center of the panel. (Photo Courtesy the Lingenfelter Collection)***

## Commemorative Editions by Color

| Year | Quantity | Colors |
|---|---|---|
| 2005 | 2 | All Red |
| 2006 | 6 | 4 Red, 2 Yellow |
| 2007 | 0 | 0 |
| 2008 | 2 | 1 Red, 1 Yellow |

***Price and Production***

The 25th Commemorative Edition package was priced at $86,995 and, with the cost of the donor C6 Z51, the final price was just under $140,000. Lingenfelter completed the first 25 planned cars in September 2005 and production ended with a 2008 model completed in October 2008. The final production tallied 10 Commemorative Editions built between 2005 and 2008.

Records show that eight Lingenfelter CEs were delivered domestically and two were exported to the Middle East. A 2005 red coupe went to the United Arab Emirates and a 2006 yellow convertible was sold to a buyer in Bahrain.

## 2016/2017 LINGENFELTER SIGNATURE SERIES

For the past few years, Lingenfelter Performance Engineering has partnered with the Corvette Dream Giveaway, which raises funds for the charity New Beginnings Children's Home. The Corvette Dream Giveaway offers one lucky winner the opportunity to win two Corvettes: a classic model and a new high-performance Z06 offered with Lingenfelter Performance upgrades.

For 2016, the bar was raised as Lingenfelter offered the new 2016 Lingenfelter Signature Edition Corvette Z06 Convertible, the first in a series of ultra-high-performance Corvettes from Lingenfelter Performance Engineering. The stats were impressive too: 800 hp and 800 ft-lbs of torque, the supercharged Corvette Z06 boasts a 0–60 mph time of under 3 seconds.

*The Lingenfelter Signature Edition Corvette for 2016 featured a black exterior with red accents painted on the hood and side vents. Ken Lingenfelter personally signed the dash. (Photo Courtesy Keith Cornett)*

## The Lingenfelter Collection

Ken Lingenfelter's success in business prior to taking over Lingenfelter Performance Engineering offered him the opportunity to indulge his love of automobiles by creating one of the top car collections in the world. The 150-plus cars on display in the Lingenfelter Collection are housed in a rather nondescript 40,000-square-foot warehouse in Brighton, Michigan.

The Lingenfelter Collection is divided into three main sections and it's advertised as 40 percent Corvettes, 30 percent muscle cars, and 30 percent exotics . . . 100-percent Lingenfelter!

The first section is dedicated to exotics, which includes the $2 million Bugatti Veyron and several Ferraris: a Ferrari LaFerrari, an Enzo, F40, a 288 GTO, 559 GTO, and a Ferrari FF. Other exotics include a Lamborghini Reventon, a Ford GT, and a Shelby Series 1. The second section of the collection is made up of American performance and includes a wide selection of muscle cars, such as Firebirds, Camaros, Novas, and Mustangs. He even has the twin to his first car, the 1967 Oldsmobile 442. The final section is made up of Corvettes and includes a 1953 Supercharged Corvette, a 1954 Inca Silver Styling Corvette, and the 1954 Duntov Mule along with modern Corvettes from Lingenfelter, Callaway, Greenwood, and Guldstrand.

The collection isn't open to the public, but Ken does open the doors many times during the year, hosting everything from charity galas and Corvette clubs to Saturday morning cars and coffee events.

*One of most important Corvettes in the Lingenfelter Collection is the 1953 Duntov Mule. The first Corvette to be fitted with a V-8 engine, Corvette chief engineer Zora Arkus-Duntov used the engineering test vehicle for speed testing prior to making a record speed run at Daytona Beach. (Photo credit: Lingenfelter Collection)*

*The Lingenfelter Collection houses an impressive collection of cars. An estimated 30 percent are exotics, including a Bugatti Veyron and group of various Ferraris led by a Ferrari LaFerrari. (Photo Courtesy the Lingenfelter Collection)*

The Z06 is optioned with the Z07 Performance Package, carbon fiber aerodynamics, and Competition Sport Seats. The Lingenfelter Signature Edition also featured unique black and red exterior styling and came with a serialized dash plaque and exterior badging. Ken personally signed the dash.

Lingenfelter and the Corvette Dream Garage returned for 2017, and that year they offered a new 2017 Lingenfelter Signature Edition Corvette Z06 Convertible, this time in red with black trim.

## 1980 Duntov Turbo

Like many of the legendary people who worked for General Motors and were associated with the Corvette, the car's first and only chief engineer, Zora Arkus-Duntov, marked 65 years of age in 1975 and was forced to retire from the position.

During his final years at General Motors, the automotive landscape changed drastically. The focus on horsepower and performance had been replaced with fuel economy and limiting emissions. Duntov always thought the Corvette should be the tip of GM's technological sword and the car should serve as a showcase of emerging technologies. Late in his career, he was all-in on wanting to build a mid-engine Corvette, but every prototype or concept design was rebuffed by GM management.

With a ton of knowledge and engineering experience that went back decades, Duntov wasn't ready to be out of the game, and so he turned to consulting as a way to continue his contributions to the automotive world. One of the companies Duntov chose to associate with was American Custom Industries (ACI) based in Sylvania, Ohio.

ACI was a manufacturer of Corvette parts and body panels and had previously worked with John Greenwood to manufacture and build Greenwood's custom Corvette bodies. ACI's owner, Bob Schuller, was looking for its next project, and to entice the former Corvette chief engineer, ACI offered to refurbish Duntov's personal 1974 Corvette Convertible in exchange for speaking at ACI's annual open house event. Duntov was impressed with the work and, after some discussions, signed on to consult with ACI on a special new project envisioned by ACI's owner.

***No factory Corvette convertibles had been produced since 1975, and by the 1980s people were becoming nostalgic for a drop-top Corvette. The Duntov Turbo Convertibles were transformed by ACI utilizing the same engineering tricks the St. Louis factory used to strengthen the convertible's frame to prevent body roll and flexing. (Photo Courtesy Mecum Auctions)***

### A Turbocharged Corvette

Like the mid-engine program that went nowhere at General Motors, another of Duntov's performance enhancements for the Corvette was also rejected. Duntov had wanted to explore turbocharging as a way to enhance the declining performance of Chevrolet's small-block V-8s. Chevrolet engineers had already been working with turbocharging Corvettes, but Chevrolet's bean counters insisted that turbocharging would be unprofitable, and that was that.

| | |
|---|---|
| Base MSRP | $30,000 |
| Model Availability | Coupe, Convertible |
| Engines | L48 Turbo |
| Features | Custom body, turbocharged engine, badging |
| Production Numbers | 86 |

***The American Custom Industries (ACI) partnership with retired Corvette Chief Engineer Zora Arkus-Duntov seemed to be a match made in heaven. ACI would have Duntov's name promoting its custom Corvette convertibles while Duntov would have the opportunity to showcase his engineering skills with a turbocharged Corvette. (Photo Courtesy Mecum Auctions)***

***ACI found that it could combine several stock body panels into one larger panel, which eliminated the bonding seams and offered a better fit and finish with fewer individual parts than stock Corvettes coming out of the St. Louis factory. (Photo Courtesy Mecum Auctions)***

When ACI approached Duntov about building a Duntov signature edition with ACI's body parts, he was adamant that the car be turbocharged to increase performance. Schuller realized that Duntov had made his reputation with performance and was happy to let him have his turbo to seal the deal.

### *The Duntov Turbo Corvette*

The initial plan called for building 200 Duntov Turbo Corvettes. Available as either a coupe or a convertible, the donor Corvettes were enhanced with ACIs fiberglass body panels that were based on the Greenwood Corvettes but were more refined. The makeover added wider front end fenders and doors that increased the width of the Duntov Turbo Corvettes by 6 inches over the stock St. Louis Corvettes. Other body changes included ditching the standard pop-up headlights for a pair of single fixed lights while the hood featured vents to help remove the heat from the engine compartment. All Duntov Turbos were to be all white with red interiors and were numbered based on the build sequence.

Under the hood, a Turbo International unit with 7 pounds of boost added an additional 70 hp to Chevy's 350-ci V-8. The suspension was beefed up with Bilstein shocks, and Goodyear's best performing street tire at the time, the Goodyear Wingfoot, was fitted to custom Weld aluminum wheels with P255/60s in the front and P265/60s in the rear.

One of the great design features of the ACI Duntov Turbo was the return of a convertible Corvette model. Chevrolet had stopped manufacturing an open air Corvette in 1975 due to declining sales, and ACI's convertible model helped fill that niche. ACI spent considerable time making sure the new convertible top assemblies were integrated with the Corvette's existing body.

***Turbocharging the C3 Corvette was difficult due to space limitations as well as the amount of heat the turbo unit generated. Running changes to address the heat included adding vents to the hood directly over the top of the turbo unity. (Photo Courtesy Mecum Auctions)***

***The Duntov Turbo was Duntov's chance to show the bean counters at General Motors how wrong they were about offering a turbocharged Corvette for sale. It turns out that they were right, and only an estimated 86 Duntov Turbos were built during its run from 1979 to 1981. (Photo Courtesy Mecum Auctions)***

### *Turbocharged Corvette Brings the Heat*

The most challenging aspect of the Duntov Turbo was the turbo itself, and Duntov was operating for the first time outside of GM's considerable resources. The two main issues were fitting the Turbo International unit into the Corvette's already crowded engine compartment and then dealing with the intense heat that was generated by the unit.

The turbo unit's heat was so intense that it was melting hoses in the engine compartment. To help dissipate the heat, the stock Corvette hood was exchanged for a custom ACI hood that featured louvers directly over the turbo unit. All the hoses, fuel, and oil lines were converted to Aeroquip braided versions, which also added additional costs to the project.

With the development costs starting to spiral out of control, Schuller went back to Duntov and discussed dropping the turbo option. Duntov made it clear that the turbo was his sole reason for being involved in the product and that without the turbo, ACI would not be allowed to use the Duntov name on the car.

### Minimal Performance Gains

The Duntov Turbo's performance gains were nearly insignificant over stock Corvettes. Whereas a stock Corvette could run the quarter mile in 15.9 seconds and featured a 0–60 mph time of 7.6 seconds, the Duntov Turbo shaved 0.4 seconds off the quarter mile for 15.5 seconds and the 0–60 mph time was just 0.1 seconds faster at 7.5 seconds. The Duntov Turbo's top speed was 125 mph.

### Price and Production

With the base MSRP of the 1980 Corvette just above $13,000, the addition of the Duntov Turbo increased the starting price to more than $30,000. Production of the Duntov Turbo started in 1979 and ran through 1981. Official records of the ACI Duntov Turbos are incomplete, as many were lost when ACI moved locations. It's believed that 86 Corvettes received the Duntov Turbo conversion with 27 ACI/Duntov Turbos sold as new offerings and customer conversions making up the rest.

One of the interesting side notes about the Duntov Turbo is that 201 were actually planned with the extra car to be given to Duntov once production surpassed 100. Because that never happened, he did not get the only car that bears his name.

***Because the Duntov Turbo would serve as a showcase of ACI's ability to customize the C3 Corvette, upgrades to the Corvette also found their way to the C3 Corvette's cockpit. Changes included a center console and dash gauge cluster surrounded with wood trim. (Photo Courtesy Mecum Auctions)***

## Dick Guldstrand GS80/GS90

Dick Guldstrand, also known as "Goldy" and "Mr. Corvette," was one of the more unique characters in Corvette's long history of interesting characters. Working with Duntov on the Grand Sport was his only official stint at General Motors, but his contributions to the Corvette over the years were immeasurable. In 1999, Guldstrand celebrated his induction into the National Corvette Museum's Corvette Hall of Fame.

In his early days, Guldstrand's parents wanted him to be a lawyer, but after serving in the army, he went to school for electrical engineering and started a career working in the growing aerospace industry. But it was race cars that would eventually win the battle for his attention, and he never looked back.

### Early Racing Days

A famous alumni of California's dirt tracks in the 1950s, Guldstrand's racing exploits earned him a sponsorship from the dealership H. E. Baher Chevrolet and a fuel-injected Corvette Sting Ray Z06. From 1963 to 1965, he won three consecutive SCCA Pacific Coast Championships, and in 1964 he was named the California Sports Car Club Driver of the Year.

In 1966, Dick received a request from Roger Penske to set up a 1966 Corvette with a pre-production L88 engine and codrive in the 1966 24 Hours of Daytona. Dick picked up the car at the St. Louis assembly plant and made the drive back to Penske's shop in Philadelphia. The 800-mile drive was made even more interesting considering the 1966 Corvette was a heater-delete, and so Guldstrand bundled up in a moving blanket for the entire drive. Guldstrand won the GT class at the Daytona 24 Hour race in both 1966 and 1967.

***Dick Guldstrand was one of those instrumental figures in the hobby who was involved from the beginning. His career culminated in the creation of "Dick's car: the GS90." (Photo Courtesy Ed Baumgarten / ©Mid America Motorworks)***

***Like the 1963 Corvette Grand Sports that added an additional brake taillight to each corner for increased visibility, Guldstrand's GS90 took that design and functionality even further, creating two six packs of brake lights integrated into the rear bumper. (Photo Courtesy Ed Baumgarten / ©Mid America Motorworks)***

He piloted one of the Corvette Grand Sports at the 12 Hours of Sebring for Roger Penske.

In 1967, he joined Bob Bondurant to race a 1967 L88 Corvette at the 24 Hours of Le Mans. In France, Guldstrand made another epic drive after the team forgot to bring a trailer to transport the race car to Le Mans. Guldstrand had to drive the very loud L88 Corvette more than 100 miles through the French countryside. As word got out, large crowds started gathering in the small towns along the way as people turned out to see the American sports car. During the race, the L88 set a GT track record for 171.5 mph on the Mulsanne Straight. After 13 hours, the L88 threw a rod and was out of the race.

### *Mr. Corvette*

In between his racing stints, Guldstrand also worked as an adviser on a number of Hollywood movies including 1967's *Grand Prix* as well as working with Elvis on three different movies, *Viva Las Vegas*, *Speedway*, and *Spinout*.

In 1968, he opened Guldstrand Engineering in Culver City, California, and was instrumental in a number of racing programs, including James Garner's American International Racing team that ran three identical 1968 L88 Corvettes.

In 1985, Guldstrand returned to the track in a C4 Corvette, and that experience led to him offering his first series of specially tuned Corvettes for resale. Dick named his special hot-rod Corvette the GS-80 after the famous Grand Sports but with 80 symbolizing the latest decade.

## 1986–1988 GULDSTRAND GS80 CORVETTES

Dick partnered with Jim Jones and Traco Engineering, another Culver City, California, firm that had been building high-performance racing engines since the 1960s. The Grand Sport 80 offered the stock L98 engine bored to 372-ci (and later 383-ci) with a forged crank and modified aluminum heads among the upgrades. The small-block V-8s made around 375 hp. Guldstrand made a number of suspension upgrades, which lowered the car, and added sway bars, Bilstein shocks, the Z51 rear spring, and special toe-in and caster kits. The changes made the C4 capable of nearly 1 g lateral acceleration on the skid pad. The interior came equipped with racing seats, a five-point safety harness, and a removable 2-inch roll bar as well as a shift light, an oil temperature gauge, and a tachometer.

The GS80s cost an additional $15,000 plus the cost of a base Corvette. Guldstrand built an estimated 36 GS80s, which included just three convertibles.

The Guldstrand GS80s could hold their own on the track, but other than a lower stance, black wheels, and a "Grand Sport 80" emblem on the fenders, the car looked like a Corvette. It would be his next iteration of his vision, the Grand Sport 90, that would allow him to fulfill his dream of offering his own custom car.

| | |
|---|---|
| Base MSRP | $15,000 plus C4 Donor |
| Model Availability | Coupe, Convertible |
| Engines | L98 |
| Features | Custom engines, performance suspensions, racing safety equipment |
| Production Numbers | 36 |

***This black Guldstrand GS80 was originally built for drummer Alex Van Halen and was also featured as a test car in* Road & Track *magazine. The autocross-ready Corvette retailed for an additional $[illegible]5,500 over the price of a base 1988 Corvette. (Photo Courtesy Keith Cornett)***

## 1994–1995 GULDSTRAND GS90 CORVETTES

The story goes that Guldstrand approached General Motors and pitched the idea of building a restyled performance-enhanced version of the ZR-1, much in the same way that Callaway was working with Chevrolet. Guldstrand reportedly asked for 15 ZR-1s and a few million dollars for development. Instead he was given "one car and a blessing."

Undeterred, Guldstrand went to work with a redesigned body by Steve Winter that harkens back to the Grand Sports of the 1960s along with some design cues from the 1963 Ferrari GTO. While every exterior surface except for the windshield and side windows was swapped out, the interior was mostly left alone with just the addition of an interior dash plaque.

Guldstrand threw every trick he knew at the suspension, and D. K. Motorsports enhanced the engine from the standard 405 hp to 475 hp. The GS90 received better tires and new wheels from OZ.

The Guldstrand GS90, known among friends as "Dick's car," made its official debut at the 1994 Los Angeles Auto Show. Guldstrand finally had a car he could call his own. His plan called for building a whole line of GS90s in various configurations, including coupe, convertible, and speedster editions. But the high cost of the cars, $134,000 on top of the ZR-1s MSRP of $68,000, made the Guldstrand GS90s retail for more than $200,000. The deal with Chevrolet never materialized, and only six Guldstrand GS90s were produced.

### *2003 Guldstrand Signature Edition 50th Anniversary Corvette*

By the time the 50th anniversary of the Chevrolet Corvette came around, Chevrolet's version came in an exclusive Anniversary Red exterior with Shale interior. There would be no performance upgrades as well as no exclusivity. Chevrolet built 11,632 Anniversary Editions.

Guldstrand thought the 50th Anniversary should be a truly important sports car, and so he had one last go at remaking Corvettes the way he thought they should be. His Guldstrand 50 is about both flash and performance.

Starting with a 2003 Corvette Z06, the engines were sent to Katech Engineering, the shop that built Corvette Racing's engines in the C5-R. The result was a 7.0L small-block stroked to 427-ci with a conservative horsepower rating of 500 hp and 520 ft-lbs of torque. Flowmaster exhaust provided the soundtrack to the 427's rumble. The free-flow exhaust flowed from a pair of mirrored-D tailpipes. The Z06's suspension was left relatively untouched, although Guldstrand would lower it by 1 inch and add his signature front and rear stabilizer bars. Michelin Pilot Sport tires were mounted to 18/19-inch Fiske wheels also finished in gold.

The exterior was penned by former Corvette designer John Schinella and features DuPont's Anniversary Gold exterior with Colbalt Blue side coves and rear bottom fascia. Matching gold aerodynamic panels were added to the front and sides of the car, toned down versions of those found on the C5-R. The power-dome hood over the 7L 427 V-8 added an attractive set of vents in the middle. European-style taillights offered a slightly different perspective on the rear end.

Inside the Anniversary Z06, gold sport seats had Cobalt Blue side bolsters in suede, and a Dick Guldstrand signature was embossed on the headrests. The Colbalt Blue suede found its way to the center console lid, and the boots of the emergency brake and shifter.

The Guldstrand Signature Edition 50th Anniversary Corvette was $49,300 plus the cost of the 2003 C5 Z06 with a starting MSRP of $51,155.

Dick Guldstrand passed away at the age of 87 on September 7, 2015. He was a true Corvette legend and his influence on the brand is both understated and underappreciated. At least in these special editions, his legend will live on.

| | |
|---|---|
| Base MSRP | $134,000 plus ZR-1 Donor |
| Model Availability | ZR-1 |
| Engines | LT5 |
| Features | Custom exterior and interior, performance suspension, interior plaque |
| Production Numbers | 6 |

***One of Dick's well-known sayings went like this: "We learned very quickly how to make a small fortune building special cars, you start with a very large fortune and build a few special cars and then you end up with a very small fortune." (Photo Courtesy Ed Baumgarten / ©Mid America Motorworks)***

*Dick Guldstrand's third and final act would the 2003 Guldstrand Signature Edition 50th Anniversary Corvette powered by a 7.0L 427-ci V8 capable of 500 hp! (Photo Courtesy Keith Cornett)*

*One of the signature design cues for the Guldstrand GS90 was the white mustache graphic that lines up and continues with the full white body stripe that flows over the car. It's a look that has been featured on the original Grand Sports along with the proposed design for the 1996 Grand Sport model. (Photo Courtesy Ed Baumgarten / ©Mid America Motorworks).*

| Base MSRP | $29,000 plus C5 coupe or convertible |
|---|---|
| Model Availability | Coupe, Convertible, Speedster |
| Engines | LS1 |
| Features | Custom body kit |
| Production Numbers | 27 |

*The Avelate had a much more aggressive look than the standard C5 Corvette and it's toothy front grille is reminiscent of the chrome grilles found on the early C1 Corvettes. Round fog lamps were integrated into the grille that is more pointed than the original C5's look. (Photo Courtesy Keith Cornett)*

## 2001–2003 Avelate Corvette

As each new generation of Corvette takes its place on the world stage, there are always those who prefer the designs of previous models. We've seen over the years as some even take that dream further by trying to re-create the car with a modern retro look. For many of those designers and builders, the Corvette is the perfect canvas for those dreams.

And why not? By the time the fifth-generation Corvette came in 1997, the Corvette offered genuine performance at a traditionally lower cost than its contemporaries. The new LS series of engines were compact and provided the heart for a very robust powertrain starting with the LS1's 345 hp and 350 ft-lbs of torque. Chevy reintroduced the Z06 in 2001 with the LS6 making 385 hp. In 2002, the Z06 gained an additional 20 horses for a high of 405 hp, where it would remain through the end of the series in 2004. Coachbuilders could select a Corvette as their project knowing that the performance aspects were already addressed, and that allowed designers to focus on the outward appearance they wanted their car to project.

One such dream team was made up of Dean Arnold and Don Johnson. Dean, or "Dino," was a well-known hot rod customizer in the Pacific Northwest, while Johnson had spent 15 years on the design staff at General Motors from 1969 to 1984 and worked on both the Camaro and the Corvette.

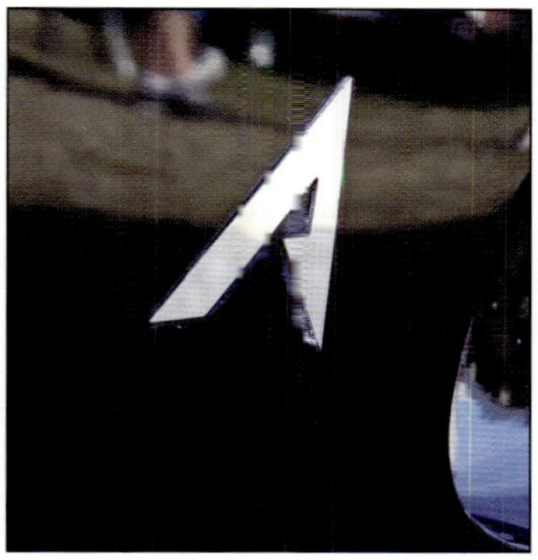

***Duntov detested the 1963's rear window design because he believed it hampered the driver's visibility. Since then, history has been much kinder and the 1963 split window has become one of the most iconic features of the midyear Corvette. The Avelate offered a split-window option but the split was much narrower on the C5 Corvette's rear. (Photo Courtesy Keith Cornett)***

### A Modern Stingray Is Born

Johnson showed Dino some of his personal sketches with many elements coming from the 1963–1967 Corvettes. He believed the current designs coming out of Detroit were bland and that they had lost the hand-sculpted look from the days when Bill Mitchell headed the Styling Department. Dino saw the potential of a modern Stingray Corvette design, and together they decided to build a new Corvette for sale to the public. Their collaboration resulted in the C5-based Avelate, which means, "to achieve the highest quality."

Johnson's designs ended up incorporating more than just elements from the C2 into the Avelate. He also used side coves from 1956–1962, front and rear fenders sharpened like the midyears', and a new hood reminiscent of the early C3s that featured a power bulge that ran down the center. Even the front grille could be loosely tied to the C1.

The one design cue that needed no introduction was found only on the coupe versions. Similar to the famous rear window found only on the 1963 Corvettes, the Avelate Coupes had a similar yet smaller divider running down the middle of the rear hatch, which created a split-window effect.

### The Avelate Corvette

The first Avelate was a Speedster model that made its debut at the Seattle Roadster Show in March 2000. Comments from those who saw the car as well as those who owned it were that they were impressed with the build quality of the car. Although some enthusiasts considered messing with the stock design as it came out of Bowling Green as sacrilegious, others liked getting off the beaten path, and the Corvette Avelate's aggressive yet familiar design did offer just that.

Production of the Avelate Corvette began in 2001 at Arnold's 5,000-square-foot facility in Tacoma, Washington. Customers had their donor cars delivered to the shop, and then the conversion began.

All the Corvette's panels except the lower valence were replaced, and only the mirrors and door handles from the stock Corvettes remained. Production was planned around three models: the split-window coupe, a convertible, and a speedster model with 10 inches chopped off the windshield.

***Dean Arnold and Don Johnson collaborated on the Avelate project from 2001 to 2004. The term* Avelate *means "to achieve the highest quality." Avelate Corvettes featured a large A on the front quarter panels as its branding logo. (Photo Courtesy Keith Cornett)***

### Pricing and Production

The Avelate conversions started at $29,000 above the cost of the C5 donor car and additional upgrades totalling another $20,000 were offered to enhance the performance with a supercharger install along with custom wheels and Brembo brakes. Interiors featured new seat covers in custom colors along with interior badging proclaiming it the Avelate.

Avelate had deals with two Chevrolet dealers to deliver the new cars, and they aggressively pursued getting the car into movies, television shows, and magazines, which would make up for their lack of a true marketing budget. However, a search of the Internet Movie Cars Database website shows 0 listings specifically for the Avelate Corvette.

The company had aspirations to build up to 100 Avelate Corvettes per year, but only 27 were completed between 2001 and 2003. With the economy cooling following the terror attacks on September 11, 2001, the company never realized its goals. As cash flow became tighter, Avelate was approached by an entrepreneur named John Rothman to design and build another custom-designed sports car based on the Corvette. In less than a year, the partnership soured, and Rothman filed a lawsuit against the company. As a result of the suit, Avelate Automotive closed its doors and filed for bankruptcy in 2004.

But that didn't stop Dino and Johnson. Born from the ashes of Avelate Automotive was a new corporate entity called Avelate Coachworks LLC, which concentrated on selling its body panels and split window kits for C5 coupes and convertibles.

Out of the total of 27 Avelate Corvettes produced, 11 were the split windows, 15 were convertibles, and 1 was a speedster.

## AVELATE FIFTY-THREE

Avelate released a new model in 2003, arriving just in time to take advantage of Chevrolet's 50th Anniversary Edition. The Fifty-Three is not a retro recreation but an original automotive artwork design based on how Avelate believed the model would have evolved had it been able to retain the subtle design cues of the first-year model. Offered just like the original with a Polo White exterior and a Sportsmen Red leather interior, the front grille featuring chrome teeth was once again the most obvious clue, but other features were the large exposed headlights, rounded corners, and a rounded trunk with round taillights mounted into the corners.

Avelate planned to manufacture just 100 total of the 53 tribute cars with production divided between 50 coupes and 50 convertibles. In the end only 2 were produced.

## Shinoda/Mears Special Edition

As an automotive designer who worked for both General Motors and Ford in the 1960s, Larry Shinoda is known for designing both the 1963 Corvette Sting Ray and 1969 Ford Mustang Boss 302, two of America's most iconic sport and muscle cars. With those designs on his resume, he opened his own design consultancy where he dabbled in all types of automotive projects.

In the late 1980s, Shinoda was working with a Detroit engineering company that wanted to break into the groups that General Motors used for its projects. Shinoda suggested doing a body kit for the current C4 Corvette to help get the attention of General Motors so that they might be considered for future products. Larry sketched the designs and actually pitched the idea to GM's vice president of design, Chuck Jordan, and John Cafaro, Corvette's chief designer, but the plans just didn't go anywhere.

*Other than custom floor mats with the Rick Mears logo and a Shinoda Design badge, the interiors of the Rick Mears Corvette were standard to the donor car that was used. (Photo Courtesy the Lingenfelter Collection)*

| Base MSRP | $5,200 plus installation |
|---|---|
| Model Availability | Coupe, Convertible, ZR-1 |
| Engines | L98, LT1, LT5 |
| Features | Custom body kit |
| Production Numbers | 11 |

*Former Corvette designer Larry Shinoda drew up the initial plans for his C4 body kit as a design exercise. It came to life after a chance encounter with Indy Car champion Rick Mears, who expressed interest in owning the Corvette after seeing the drawings. After agreeing to attach his name, the Shinoda-designed Rick Mears Corvette was born. (Photo Courtesy the Lingenfelter Collection)*

### *The Rick Mears Corvette*

In April 1989, Shinoda was in Long Beach for the Long Beach Grand Prix and met up with a friend named Jim Williams, whose company sponsored one of Roger Penske's race cars. Williams owned Golden State Foods and supplied food to McDonald's restaurants. Shinoda had previously told Williams about his Corvette designs, and he brought them to Long Beach at Williams's request.

While showing the Corvette body kit plans to Williams, three-time IndyCar driver Rick Mears (he won his 4th Indy 500 in 1991) just happened to be in the same motor home. After seeing the plans, he told Shinoda that he would like to have one of those Corvettes. Williams asked Mears if he would be interested in lending his name to the project. Mears agreed on the spot, and the Rick Mears Corvette was born.

The Rick Mears Corvette made its official debut at the 1990 Los Angeles Auto Show. The new body kit generated quite a bit of interest, and eventually led to a total of 11 Rick Mears Corvettes that were completed.

*Although it was recommended the kit be professionally installed, it was designed to be installed with common tools. Fasteners were included with the package, and with the kit using the stock mount points, little drilling was required. The estimated install time was 25 hours. (Photo Courtesy Mecum Auctions)*

### *Wind Tunnel Tested Design*

Back in Detroit, one of the Rick Mears Corvette body kits was tested by General Motors in its wind tunnel and it was found that the aerodynamics were better than the regular-production Corvette. Shinoda's Corvette had a drag coefficient of .30 vs .34 for the regular C4 Corvette. Shinoda claims much of his work was done on intuition and that he softened the original, enhanced it, and then added a "little bit of Coke bottle." When designing the kit, Shinoda also gave it a number of personal touches, including the stinger-style rear-end treatment as well as removing the "rub strips" that General Motors used to hide the body seams.

### *The Marlboro Racing ZR-1*

One of Penske Racing's sponsors was Marlboro, and Rick Mears drove the red/white number-3 Marlboro IndyCar. Shinoda had designed a version of the Rick Mears Corvette body kit to fit the new 1990 Corvette ZR-1, which had a wider body than the regular Corvette. The ZR-1 body used different mounting locations than the standard Corvettes, and Shinoda said it was a challenge because they had to design a new rocker and gill panel as even the wheelwells were a different size.

The Rick Mears ZR-1 was built by Penske Racing and was dressed in the Marlboro Racing Teams' Indy 500 Hot Licks Red exterior with white accents on the hood and sides, and featured Boyd Coddington chrome wheels. On the quarter panels were two badges, the Rick Mears signature badge and under it the Marlboro Racing logo. The Marlboro Corvette (or Rick Mears 1 as it is also referred to) was then given away as part of a Marlboro sweepstakes.

The unique Corvette surfaced again in January 2008, when it was sold during the Barrett-Jackson Collector Car Auction in Scottsdale, Arizona, for $58,300 The car resides today in the Lingenfelter Collection in suburban Detroit.

### *Pricing and Production*

The Rick Mears Corvette body kit consisted of 11 separate unpainted body panels constructed from reaction-injection-molded polyurethane. Also included were front fog lights, black stainless-steel exhaust tips, and floor mats with the Rick Mears logo. The kit was installed by removing the

*The body kits were initially developed for the standard C4 Corvette Coupe and Convertible. However, Shinoda did design a Rick Mears kit for the wider Corvette ZR-1. On that kit (shown) Shinoda embossed the ZR-1 logo into the front and rear panels. (Photo Courtesy the Lingenfelter Collection)*

*While the standard Corvettes appeared to have a large integrated light housing the fog lights and turn signals under one lens, Shinoda used two individual lamps on each front corner. The C4's pop-up headlights provided illumination at night. (Photo Courtesy the Lingenfelter Collection)*

*The Rick Mears Corvette consisted of a kit that replaced all the lower panels to give it its unique look. In keeping with the exact dimensions, Shinoda created a natural rocker panel along the side, which he said helps the air reattach to the car along the sides as opposed to the stock Corvette's body where the air "boils" off the side. (Photo Courtesy the Lingenfelter Collection)*

Corvette's stock lower panels and adding the new Rick Mears panels. The kit was available for 1984 to 1991 Corvette coupes and convertibles at a cost of $5,200 plus $3,000 for installation.

## AAT 1953 Commemorative Edition

As Chevrolet was closing in on its 50th anniversary year in 2003, the milestone would have some Corvette enthusiasts wishing for the old days, when classic Corvette styling and performance ruled the boulevard. There's nothing like driving classic Corvette, but what if you wanted the best of both worlds? Corvette's iconic design and the performance and dependability of the modern Corvette? Luckily, there was a series of Corvette special editions that offered exactly that.

One of the most unique and easily identifiable Corvette special editions built outside of General Motors was the 1953 Commemorative Edition from Advanced Automotive Technologies (AAT). With a custom front and rear body reminiscent of the original 1953, the 1953 Commemorative Edition is the perfect blend of the modern C5 Corvette chassis and interior melded with the classic looks of the early Corvettes.

The idea originated from a vehicle-design and prototype firm called Magna Steyr, which created the concept in the early 2000s as a proposed design for Chevrolet's 50th Anniversary Corvette. Magna's design chief, Bill Miller, designed the concept using the C5's standard body mounts

## Corvette Designer Larry Shinoda

Larry Shinoda was born on March 25, 1930, in Los Angeles, California. Like typical So-Cal boys, he loved cars and loved to draw pictures of them. As a teen, he enjoyed hot-rodding and street racing, and his pursuits of all things automotive eventually led him to Art Center College of Design. College wasn't for him, though, and labeled as a malcontent, he was kicked out of art school. One of his teachers invited him to present some of his designs to Ford, and he was hired a few months later. Larry spent a year at Ford, and then worked for nine months at Packard before landing a design job at General Motors.

There is a famous story about how Shinoda got put on the Corvette design team: One night when Shinoda was driving home from work, none other than GM's Bill Mitchell pulled up next to Larry's T-Bird at a stoplight. When the light turned green, Mitchell took off in his supercharged Pontiac, but Shinoda's Thunderbird was modded with a Stroppe race-prepped Ford stock car engine, and he easily outran GM's design chief. A few days later, Mitchell tracked down the white Thunderbird at the Chevy Design Studio and asked Shinoda to pull it into the garage. When Mitchell saw the car was equipped with a full roll cage, two 4-barrel carburetors, headers, and heavy-duty shocks, he "just about had a heart attack." It was said that Mitchell recognized Shinoda as a die-hard racer, and he was immediately switched to the Corvette program.

As part of the Corvette program, Shinoda worked on refining several concepts, including one that became the 1963 Corvette Sting Ray Split-Window Coupe. Larry also penned both Mako Shark concepts, the rear-engine XP-819 concept and the engineering test vehicles known as CERV I and CERV II. Shinoda left General Motors in 1968, hired away by former GM executive Bunkie Knudsen. His first design at Ford was a high-performance version of the Mustang that he called "Boss," a tribute to Knudsen. Following his short stint at Ford, Shinoda opened his own design studio where he consulted with various automakers. As a freelancer, he helped design the Jeep ZJ for American Motors Corp. The Jeep eventually became the Grand Cherokee. Larry returned to Corvette designing in the early 1990s with Indy 500 winner Rick Mears to produce the Shinoda Mears Corvette.

Larry passed away in late 1997 at the age of 67, but his contributions to two American automotive icons, the Chevrolet Corvette and Ford Mustang, will forever live on. In 1998, Larry Shinoda was posthumously inducted into the Corvette Hall of Fame at the National Corvette Museum.

*Larry Shinoda was a talented designer who helped create many of the Corvette concepts, including the Mako Shark. Shinoda refined the early Stingray Racer design into the 1963 Corvette Sting Ray. Leaving Chevy for Ford in 1968, he designed the Ford Mustang Boss 302. He returned to his roots in the late 1980s with the Shinoda Rick Mears Corvette. (Courtesy the Revs Institute, The Karl Ludvigsen Photograph Collection)*

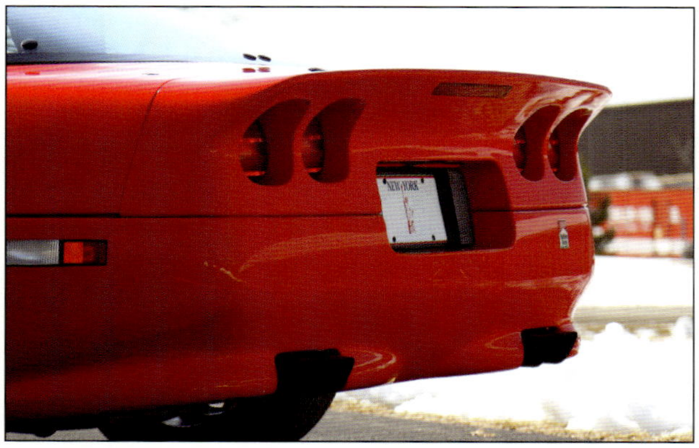

*One of the design cues for the Rick Mears Corvette that Shinoda said he particularly liked was the stinger-style rear-end treatment. The 5 inches of rear spoiler allowed the air to flow cleanly off the rear deck, which has an added benefit of generating additional downforce. The curved rear spoiler also created a unique lighting effect at night. (Photo Courtesy the Lingenfelter Collection)*

*Capitalizing on the Corvette's 50th anniversary, the 1953 Commemorative Edition from Advanced Automotive Technologies (AAT) created the best of both worlds: the iconic styling of the first Corvette with the late-model performance and safety of the C5 Corvette. (Photo Courtesy Maureen Waller)*

| | |
|---|---|
| Base MSRP | $32,500 plus C5 Convertible or Z06 |
| Model Availability | Convertible, FRC, Z06 |
| Engines | LS1, LS6 |
| Features | Custom exterior, interior plaque |
| Production Numbers | 214 |

to fit the new body panels. They then turned to Advanced Automotive Technologies and Steve Pasteiner, a former Buick and Chevrolet designer whose Rochester Hills, Michigan, shop would build the show car concept. The retro Corvette was very well received but, as we all know, Chevrolet went the more conservative route by offering their own 50th Anniversary Edition on the standard coupe and convertibles with special Anniversary Red paint, Shale interior, and special badges as in previous anniversary models.

The 1953 Commemorative's design was just too good to let die as a concept. Recognizing the potential of the retro-concept as well as perfect timing with the coming of Corvette's 50th anniversary, Pasteiner bought the design rights to the 1953 Commemorative Edition and Advanced Automotive Technologies began building and selling its own cars.

### Building the 1953 Commemorative Edition

To start the conversion process, customers provided their own C5 Convertible or Z06 (hardtop) model as the donor car. The standard C5 Coupe with its hatchback was not suitable for the 1953 Commemorative Edition conversion. The donor vehicle was stripped of its fenders, decklid, and hood along with front and rear bumper covers. Other than a small recess cut into the rear trunk, no structural modifications were needed, and all safety requirements stayed in place.

### Pricing and Production

AAT manufactures its own custom panels, and the conversions took about eight weeks to perform at a cost starting at $32,500. Although white was the most popular color, AAT painted a number of CE Corvettes in both traditional and nontraditional colors.

*The 1953 Commemoratives required either a convertible or Z06 donor Corvette for the conversion. The hardtop Z06 gives the special edition a unique silhouette. (Photo Courtesy Mecum Auctions)*

*Although a Z06-equipped 1953 Commemorative Edition Corvette may look similar to the first-year Corvette, there's a vast difference in performance between 1953's original 150-hp Corvette equipped with a 2-speed automatic and the 2003 Corvette Z06 that has 405 hp and a 6-speed manual transmission. (Photo Courtesy Mecum Auctions)*

*The new body used existing body mounts and the turnaround time for conversion was a quick two months by custom car building standards. (Photo Courtesy Maureen Waller)*

***The 1953 Corvette was available only in Polo White with a Sportsman Red interior and a black convertible top, and that same color combination was available as part of the 53 Commemorative Edition. However, it could be customized and painted any color to suit the owner's vision. (Photo Courtesy Mecum Auctions)***

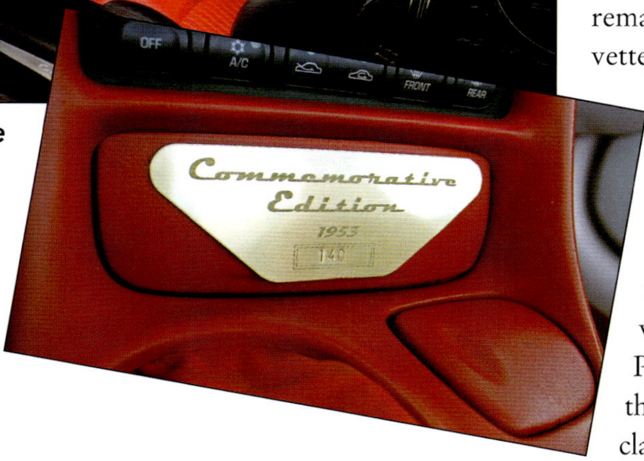


***Donor Corvettes could have their interiors upgraded during the build or left completely stock like this two-tone black and red interior found exclusively on the Z06. (Photo Courtesy Mecum Auctions)***

***Go to any of the major Corvette shows and you'll be certain to spot a 1953 Commemorative Edition. AAT created one of the most successful coach-built Corvettes with a total of 214 Commemorative Editions now on the road. Each one received a plaque with its build number. The series has been concluded. (Photo Courtesy Mecum Auctions)***

***One of the really nice retro touches offered by AAT for the 1953 Commemorative Editions was the custom fuel-rail covers that harken back to the days of Corvette-scripted finned-valve covers. (Photo Courtesy Mecum Auctions)***

A total of 214 1953 Commemorative Editions were built since production first started in 2001. The program for the car has concluded, and no further Commemorative Editions will be built.

## 1954 COMMEMORATIVE SPORT WAGON

As a follow-up to the well-received 1953 CE Convertibles, the CE Wagon edition allowed AAT to reintroduce the retro design of the 1954 Motorama Nomad show car to customers who own a C5 Coupe with the hatchback.

Once again, the C5 donor car was transformed, using the stock mounts while leaving the rear hatch fully functional with all the factory components remaining. The Sport Wagon package was $49,500 plus the Donor C5 Corvette. AAT constructed a total of 14 Sport Wagons.

## Pratt & Miller Corvette C6RS

One of the prominent names to enter the Corvette tuning scene in the mid-2000s was Pratt & Miller, the Michigan-based engineering and fabricator firm responsible for building and managing the factory Corvette Racing Team. Since the race team's inception in the late 1990s, it was Pratt & Miller that created the successful C5-R and C6.R Corvette race cars that earned multiple American Le Mans Series Championships and multiple class wins at the 24 Hours of Le Mans. If any tuning firm knows a thing or two about making Corvettes go faster, it was Gary Pratt and Jerry Miller.

Chevrolet asked Pratt & Miller for help in creating some accessories for the C6 Corvettes and that dive into making the street cars better formed the genesis to building an ultimate Corvette street car heavily influenced by the factory racing program. No special-edition Corvette is a better example of

Because only the C5 Corvette Convertible or Z06 (or FRC) could be used as a donor for the 1953 Commemorative Edition, AAT designed and constructed a retro Nomad version using the C5 Corvette Coupe. AAT owner Steve Pasteiner uses this C5 Corvette Sport Wagon as his daily driver. (Photo Courtesy Steve Pasteiner)

| Base MSRP | $49,500 plus C5 Corvette Coupe |
|---|---|
| Model Availability | Coupe |
| Engines | LS1 |
| Features | Custom exterior, interior plaque |
| Production Numbers | 14 |

The Pratt & Miller Corvette C6RS is not a race car for the road. It's a luxurious road car with a race car's soul. From the team that has won with the Chevrolet Corvette at the world's biggest sports car races, you would expect nothing less. (Photo Courtesy the Lingenfelter Collection)

transferring technology from track to street than the Chevrolet Corvette C6RS.

GT sports car racers in general were very closely related to the street cars they represented on the track; however, those cars were optimized for the track. They tended to be lighter and more aerodynamic, and they had the ability to handle the stresses of racing flat out for hours at a time. Pratt & Miller applied these same concepts to its C6RS. Each component of the Corvette was reviewed and optimized for strength and durability as well as providing better aerodynamics.

### Pratt & Miller Corvette C6RS

The C6RS was conceived, developed, and launched over 2007 and 2008, and the supercar arrived about a year before General Motors introduced the 638-hp supercharged ZR1. Pratt & Miller used the C6 Z06 as its donor vehicle because it was already the lightest of the C6 Corvette models. It featured the 505-hp 7.0L LS7 V-8, which is required for the conversion, and the car has a number of aerodynamic properties including the front air intake and rear brake ducts that form the starting point for the C6RS.

Pratt & Miller started with basics first by lightening the car through the use of carbon fiber materials. Other than the roof, rear deck, and door skins, every other body panel on the Corvette was replaced with lightweight carbon fiber panels designed by the firm. Many of these panels carried design cues from the race cars. The C6RS featured a front fascia with larger air inlets as well as a waterfall-style hood and louvered front fenders designed to extract the hot air from the engine compartment and brakes.

Aerodynamics also played a crucial role in race-car development, and the C6RS benefited from the times that the C6.R race car was tested in GM's wind tunnel. Carbon fiber aerodynamics surrounded the car with a 1.5-inch front chin spoiler, side rocker panels, full-width rear-lip spoiler, and a wide air diffuser on the rear. The rear fenders widened the body by an additional 1.5 inches and allowed the use of wider rear tires.

### Powered by Katech Performance

To power the C6RS, Pratt & Miller turned to its familiar partners at Katech Performance who built the engines for Corvette Racing's C5-R and C6.R racers. The challenge thrown down by Pratt & Miller specified the engine had to be a lightweight aluminum block that utilized the factory exhaust manifolds and catalytic converters. Katech stroked the 7.0L LS7 to 8.2 liters for a compression ratio of 11:1 and many of the stock LS7 parts were swapped for higher-strength components, but the high-flow factory LS7 heads were retained. An aluminum dual-fan radiator from Dewitt helped keep the motor cool while Corsa developed a custom-tuned cat-back exhaust system. Pratt & Miller also utilized 80 pounds of Dynamat heat and sound deadener so the driver could enjoy the sounds of the 500-ci engine without baking from the heat produced in the Corvette's transmis-

| Base MSRP | $187,500 to $300,000 |
|---|---|
| Model Availability | Coupe, Convertible |
| Engines | Katech 8.2L |
| Features | Full carbon fiber body, aerodynamics, lowering system, custom interior, interior plaque |
| Production Numbers | 7 |

*In 2008, the American Le Mans Series (ALMS) featured the Pratt & Miller C6RS as part of their Vitesse sports car fleet that provided shuttles for track officials and gave hot laps to fans and media between racing events. (Photo Courtesy Keith Cornett)*

*"Our goal was to create a Corvette supercar that delivers an extremely high level of performance with extraordinary comfort and reliability," said Gary Pratt, co-owner of Pratt & Miller Engineering. "The Corvette C6RS was inspired by our Corvette race program, but it's not a race car for the street. You can take the Corvette C6RS on a 300-mile road trip, or drive it to a track day and run fast laps." (Photo Courtesy the Lingenfelter Collection)*

sion tunnel.

The Katech-built 8.2L motor delivered 600 hp and 600 ft-lbs of torque to the C6RS. Not only was the engine powerful, but it looked great too with its large carbon fiber air intake and badged Katech Performance valve covers and LS7 intake manifold painted to match the C6RS interior accent colors.

All that power was transmitted to the huge Michelin Pilot Sport Corsa tires. The Michelins were 295/30/18 in the front and 345/30/19 in the rear. The black chrome wheels were 11 inches in the front and 13.6 inches wide in the rear and featured the center lock nuts you would expect to see on a race car. The C6RS brakes were upgraded with Brembo six-piston monoblock front calipers and four-piston monoblock rear calipers with an integrated parking brake.

Pratt & Miller lowered the suspension 1.5 inches with specially tuned dampers and a composite rear-spring rear suspension. To protect all those carbon fiber aerodynamic pieces, an ArvinMeritor Dynamic Hight Control System used electronically controlled air shocks to provide the driver the ability to change the ride height on the C6RS with three settings: Park, Drive, and Entry.

Whether your outlook about the purpose of the C6RS was that is was more track or more street, the bespoken interior of the C6RS offered the best of both worlds. Pratt & Miller designed their own custom high-lateral race seats for the C6RS that featured larger side bolsters trimmed in suede. Customers could choose between a five-point harness or use the standard lap restraints. All around the cabin was a custom hand-stitched interior. The D-style steering wheel had a stitched leather overlay while the wheel itself was a combination of leather and suede. The Dynamat sound insulation material created a quiet interior while still allowing the driver to sample the sounds from the naturally aspirated V-8.

### Pricing and Production

Pricing for the C6RS was significant with the cost of the build coming in at $187,500, and that did not include a donor C6 Z06. Buyers could opt

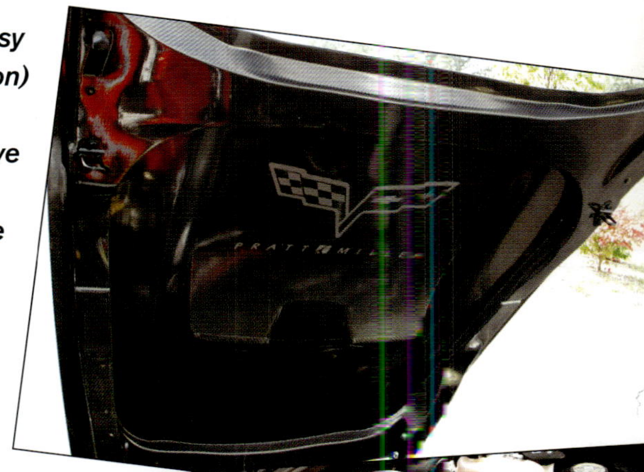

*The C6RS made extensive use of carbon fiber and every panel including the hood was made out of the lightweight material. The carbon fiber hood appeared on the C6RS three years before Chevrolet offered the comparable B92 carbon fiber hood that appeared on the Carbon Edition Z06 in 2011. (Photo Courtesy the Lingenfelter Collection)*

*Pratt & Miller sourced the engines for the C6RS from the same firm that provides the race engines in the GT1 C6.Rs. Katech Performance Engineering created a naturally aspirated 500-ci 8.2L engine capable of producing 600 hp and 600 ft-lbs of torque. (Photo Courtesy the Lingenfelter Collection)*

*Just like the Corvette race car, the Pratt & Miller C6RS was equipped with center locking forged wheels from BBS. The rims are sized 18x11 inches and 19x13.6 inches in the rear and are wrapped with the 295/345 Michelins. (Photo Courtesy the Lingenfelter Collection)*

for additional upgrades, which could push a total investment in the C6RS to nearly $300,000. Pratt & Miller initially planned to build up to 25 of the Corvette C6RSs but in the end just 7 were constructed. Although the C6RS's stiff pricing and an uncertain economy impacted sales, it was the arrival of the 2009 Corvette ZR1 and its 638-hp supercharged LS9 that was one-third the cost of a C6RS that most likely limited sales the most.

*The leather-wrapped interiors used premium materials and included custom leather racing seats designed in-house by Pratt & Miller. The seats featured aggressive bolstering on each side and could be equipped with a five-point safety harness. (Photo Courtesy the Lingenfelter Collection)*

*The first Pratt & Miller C6RS went to Jay Leno, former host of the* Tonight Show *and the owner of a major car collection. Jay wanted to show that high-performance cars and alternative-fuel technology are not diametrically opposed concepts. His C6RS is powered by a Katech 8.2-liter V-8 capable of running on E85 ethanol. (Photo Courtesy the Lingenfelter Collection)*

## Hennessey Performance Engineering

John Hennessey is another tuner/builder to make his mark on the Corvette hobby with his company Hennessey Performance Engineering. Hennessey rose to fame by competing in various high-speed automotive events in 1991 with a modified Mitsubishi 3000GT VR-4, which he called the VR-200.

*Owned by a Vietnam veteran, this custom-wrapped Corvette Z06 was brought to Hennessey Performance for a HP1000 upgrade. The owner describes the car as a rolling memorial and tribute to his fellow Marines who gave their lives during the Vietnam War. (Photo Courtesy Hennessey Performance)*

*The Corvettes that go through Hennessey Performance to receive most of their modifications under the hood. Exterior changes included badging advertising the package (HPE850), as well as this Hennessey script that replaces the factory Corvette badge. (Photo Courtesy Hennessey Performance)*

In May 1991, Hennessey drove from Houston, Texas, to Ely, Nevada, to compete in the Nevada Open Road Challenge in May 1991. With no experience in open road racing, he finished in 4th place with an average 164 mph on the 90-mile course. In July (again driving from Texas to Colorado), he fulfilled a lifelong dream when he competed in Colorado's Pikes Peak International Hill Climb, finishing in 10th place. The following month, he competed at the Bonneville Salt Flats, setting the record in the F-Production/Supercharged class with an average of 176 mph on the two-way course.

Hennessey's first win catapulted him to fame in November 1991. Nevada's Silver State Classic allowed participants to drive flat out on a closed public road. During the race, Hennessey's 450-hp 3000GT was flying across the desert when he came across a group of turkey vultures dining in the middle of the road. One of the giant birds hit the headlight assembly, caving it in. Despite this, Hennessey won the Unlimited Class with an average speed of 166.3 mph on the 91-mile course.

The VR-200 became the first package offered by what was then called Hennessey Motorsports. Hennessey would also offer parts on other turbo cars including the Toyota Supra and Mazda RX7. The Dodge Viper made its debut in 1992, and Hennessey's name would soon become synonymous with tuning the V10 Vipers.

After building a number of cars with various horsepower upgrades using the "Venom" moniker, Hennessey joined the 200-mph club in 1997 in a Viper GTS 650R with a speed of 203 mph at the Honda Proving Grounds' high-speed oval test track. The following year, he debuted the Venom 800

***The HPE1000 would bring supercar-like performance to the Corvette Z06. With 1,008 hp and 823 ft-lbs of torque at the ready, the car goes 0–60 mph in 2.5 seconds, runs a quarter-mile in 9.7 seconds at 147 mph, and will top out at more than 220 mph. (Photo Courtesy Hennessey Performance)***

package, the first twin-turbo V10 package that would propel the Viper to 197 mph in the standing mile, as well as a 0–60 mph time of 2.9 seconds and the quarter mile in 9.9 seconds.

During the next 10 years, Hennessey's business grew from 5 employees to 30. He acquired the Lonestar Motorsports Complex just west of Houston. The IHRA-sanctioned track featured an eighth-mile dragstrip that would eventually be lengthened to a quarter mile. Next door, a new 30,000-square-foot facility for Hennessey Performance Motorsports was constructed. It also became the home of a new venture called Tuner School, where budding mechanics could learn the ropes about modifying and tuning vehicles.

Hennessey will be the first to admit they were known as the Viper Guys, and he doesn't shy away from the description. In the mid-2000s, the company began branching out with projects that included a 234-mph twin-turbo Ford GT and a supercar based on a Lotus Elise that would eventually become known as the Venom GT. With the introduction and much fanfare for the C6 Corvette ZR1, Hennessey would add GM's performance cars to its lineup with tuning packages available for the Corvette, Cadillac CTS-V, and the fifth-generation Camaro.

### *Hennessey Tunes the Corvette*

Hennessey's first major project for the Corvette ZR1 came in 2009 with Hennessey's ZR700 package. To achieve the target of 700 hp from the stock 638, the package used a new supercharger pulley to increase boost while air flow was improved with a K&N intake, stainless steel headers, and high-flow catalytic converters. The new configuration was reprogrammed in the engine management system.

The ZR750 was even more powerful and provided 755 hp and 728 ft-lbs of torque. Hennessey claimed performance times of 0–60 mph in just 2.8 seconds, a quarter-mile ET of 10.3 seconds at 139 mph, and a top speed in excess of 224 mph.

The 2014 Corvette Stingray hadn't even started production when Hennessey Performance announced multiple upgrade packages would be available. They included naturally aspirated upgrades, supercharger-based packages, and several twin-turbo packages.

Hennessey's offering for the LT1-equipped Stingray and Grand Sport grew from four to seven different packages, ranging from the naturally aspirated HPE500 that offers 500 hp to the supercharged HPE1000 that makes 1,008 bhp and 918 ft-lbs of torque.

As Chevrolet brought out the higher performance models in the Corvette Z06 and the 2019 ZR1, Hennessey had multiple upgrade packages ready to go. For the Z06 package, Hennessey added the HPE750, HPE850, and HPE1000 packages. When the 2019 ZR1 debuted in late 2017, Hennessey's top package would take the stock 755-hp ZR1 to 1,200 hp.

## Hennessey Corvette Stingray First to 200 MPH

The Corvette Stingray was capable of reaching 180 mph from the factory, but this 2014 Arctic White Corvette Stingray with Hennessey's HPE600 became the first Stingray to break the 200 mph barrier.

With the HPE600 package, the naturally aspirated LT1 received a horsepower boost to 600 hp with a Nitrous Express 100-hp system and the additions of long-tube headers, ported factory cylinder heads, high-flow cats, as well as an HPE camshaft and engine tune.

The 200 mph run was done under cooperation of the Texas Department of Transportation, which monitored the Stingray to confirm a newly completed toll road's automated sensors could pick up a car traveling well over the speed limit. John Hennessey was behind the wheel as the HPE 600 Stingray reached 200.6 mph, verified by a VBox data acquisition system and police radar.

***After John Hennessey broke the 200-mph mark in the Corvette Stingray on a closed toll road in Texas, he remarked, "The Corvette was very stable and easy to drive at 200 mph." (Photo Courtesy Hennessey Performance)***